Sociology in Times of Glocalization

By Christian Karner

ANTHEM PRESS

Anthem Press
An imprint of Wimbledon Publishing Company
www.anthempress.com

This edition first published in UK and USA 2023
by ANTHEM PRESS
75–76 Blackfriars Road, London SE1 8HA, UK
or PO Box 9779, London SW19 7ZG, UK
and
244 Madison Ave #116, New York, NY 10016, USA

British Library Cataloguing-in-Publication Data
A catalogue record for this book is available from the British Library.

Library of Congress Cataloging-in-Publication Data
A catalog record for this book has been requested.

ISBN-13: 978-1-78527-4-121 (Hbk)
ISBN-10: 1-78527-4-120 (Hbk)

This title is also available as an e-book.

CONTENTS

ACKNOWLEDGMENTS

Unlike for previous books, the prehistory for this one is difficult to trace. It is, in many respects, the joint outcome of several previous research projects or at least tangentially related to them. It bears the imprint of many influences, not all of which are immediately apparent. In part, this book constitutes my attempt to reflect on the world in the early twenty-first century *and* on what, over a twenty-year period, teaching and doing sociology at this particular historical juncture have taught me. Given the complex and multiple contexts to this book, listing all those who have helped me along the way is no easy task. I shall therefore confine myself to thanking those whose influence has been the most direct and enduring.

For years in a previous job at the University of Nottingham, I co-taught a postgraduate module on "globalization, identity and citizenship." It was in the course of some thought-provoking discussions with some excellent students from around the world that I first began to think about writing a book on how glocalization challenges sociology and how the discipline in turn has responded or might need to respond. Those seminar discussions in Nottingham, which took place between 2007 and 2014, were wonderful examples of research and teaching enriching one another and of *the sociological imagination*, in C. Wright Mills' conceptualization, being put to work collectively. I would therefore like to thank successive cohorts of MA students at the University of Nottingham for their willingness to share, debate, and reflect on "the glocal" in their individual and in our shared lives. Over the years, and across universities, colleagues past and present have supported me and my work through their own research, their time, and friendship. I would particularly like to thank the late Alan Aldridge, Meryl Aldridge, Edwin Bacon, Esther Bott, Rachela Colosi, Yuliya Hilevych, Sam Hillyard, Ute Hirsekorn, Rico Isaacs, the late Christopher Johnson, Julia O'Connell Davidson, Sam Okyere, Alison Pilnick, Abigail Powell, Davide Pero, Nick Stevenson, Gary Saunders, Anna Tarrant, Amal Treacher Kabesh, Simone Varriale, and Elisabetta Zontini. A particular debt of gratitude is owed to John Holmwood for his generosity and support at crucial moments, and to David Parker; David and I conducted research together for a decade, resulting in a body of work that continues to shape how I think about urban sociology. Parts of Chapters 5 and 6 of this book build on this enriching period of collaborative work. Similarly, other parts of Chapter 6 also build on a previous project with my close friend Marek Kazmierczak, whose support and energy have been a wonderful gift. Importantly, the ongoing motivation provided by the following friends further afield has been humbling and is greatly appreciated: Giorgos Bithymitris, Douglas Davies, Seth Kunin, Zinovia Lialiouti, José Lopez, David Luft, Laura Morowitz, Frédéric Moulène, Despina Papadimitriou, and Bernhard Weicht. My work on this book also benefited from a concurrently unfolding collaboration on a separate project with Dirk Hofäcker, as well as from research stays at Panteion University in Athens and at the Center Austria at the University of New Orleans. In the latter setting, I would particularly like to thank Günter Bischof and Marc Landry for their hospitality and support. Many thanks are also due to Megan Greiving and her team at Anthem Press as well as to Srinivasan Parthiban for their support and expert guidance at different stages in this book's production process.

Parts of what follows contain moments of autobiographical writing and reflection. It is therefore only fitting to conclude my acknowledgments of gratitude by mentioning those closest to me, who inspire and move me on a daily basis. They include my close friends Tarig Hilal, Steven Purdie, and Ines Zollner-Schwetz, my uncle Wolfgang Karner, as well as my cousin Sandra Schnabl; most of all, my in-laws Dimitris Lekkas, Aggeliki Vasili, Nikoletta, and Stavrina Lekka, my parents Christa and Peter Karner, and my wife, Chrysanthi Lekka. Each of them, in different places and ways, lives—though not necessarily by choice—the kinds of "glocalized lives" that lie at the heart of this book. Most importantly, each of them lives their glocalized life with dignity, respect, responsibility, care, and love for others. It seems clear to me that those are the very (and only) qualities that can get us through the many crises that define these times of glocalization.

INTRODUCTION: *GLOCALIZATION* AND ITS EPISTEMOLOGICAL CHALLENGES

Setting the *Glocal* Scene

Recent decades have seen much talk about globalization. Yet, the term is often treated with little definitional care. What is more, there appears to have been a significant recent shift in the connotations intended by many of those who speak about "globalization." Until not long ago commonly used as a neutral or in some cases celebratory shorthand for a growing degree of interdependency and interconnectedness spanning national and other boundaries, globalization has of late acquired more negative connotations to many. For instance, in his 2018 speech to the UN General Assembly then-US president Donald Trump set up a dichotomy between "patriots" and "globalists," unambiguously siding with the former and finding deep fault with the latter. Almost instantly UK Brexiteer Nigel Farage tweeted his support for Donald Trump's speech and with it, one assumes, for the ideological binary it had contained (Euronews, September 25, 2018). In further illustration of how ideas today spread with a previously unknown speed and geographical reach, it did not take long for this juxtaposition of "patriots" to (negatively evaluated) "globalists" to also feature in statements made by Hungarian nationalists and Italian EU sceptics. Reflecting the circulation of figures of speech, the worldviews and political blueprints they contain and help articulate, this was merely one instance, albeit a particularly high-profile one, of some of the phenomena that define our era. These phenomena include our technological ability to share but also contest ideas instantaneously and across vast stretches of space. The issue at hand extends further to a paradox, namely the fact that some of the very illustrations of our global interconnectedness, ideational and technological, simultaneously contain a strong critique of such interconnectedness. The politicians just mentioned thus self-consciously also addressed transnational, if not even global audiences, and they did so by employing the very technological means that partly define our global era, only to advocate a return to something "smaller." It is safe to conclude that to each of the politicians in question this "smaller" domain is that of the nation-state, which—in such statements—is shorn of all the historical guilt, or even of awareness or any memory of the many atrocities committed in the name of "nations" over the last 200 years. Concurrently, the "patriots" Trump, Farage, and their many re-tweeters had in mind were presented as being allegedly under threat by the forces of globalization, against which—so the ideological "logic" continued—"patriots" were portrayed as fighting a righteous "battle." Written into the deep structure of nationalism (e.g., Hutchinson 1987; Karner 2020a) is a view of history that combines all of this and more: a glorified view of the national past (i.e., Trump also claimed in the same speech, in historiographically at best hugely selective and highly problematic ways, that only "sovereign and independent nations are the vehicles for freedom and democracy"); strong and negative views of the present (i.e., in the cases at hand, all purported ills are attributed, at least implicitly, to "the globalists"); and promises of an imminent political turn-around, a national revival that will variously "make America great again," "win control back," close borders, or undo decades of European power sharing and integration.

This book is about paradoxes of this kind, and much more. This is a book about contemporary globalization and the many counterreactions against it. But it is also a book about what all this means for sociology as a scientific discipline focused on social relationships, political structures, group definitions, and the historical shifts that impact on them all. Like any science, sociology operates with a particular methodological repertoire, with a series of assumptions and procedures for collecting and analyzing data. Yet, there are also some sociological particularities, some of which the discipline in turn shares partly with some of its closer "cousins" across the social sciences and humanities, while others appear to be particularly pronounced within sociology. Methodologically speaking, or delving yet deeper into the realm of epistemology (which pertains to foundational questions about the premises, on the basis of which claims to knowledge are made and defended), sociology is an internally highly heterogeneous discipline. Running through it is a bifurcation that too often unhelpfully separates two distinct types of sociologists and sociologies. The first, quantitative sociology, is grounded in the *positivist* tradition and its postulate of regularities and patterns underpinning social life. Quantitative sociologists seek to discover such regularities through statistical analyses of numerical data arrived at through large-scale surveys or (quasi-) experimental methods. One of the intentions and applications of this sub-disciplinary tradition is to discover correlations between independent and dependent variables: for example, between various demographic and social characteristics on one hand, and ideas, dispositions or behavioral patterns on the other.

Needless to stress that globalization and its counterreactions offer a wealth of questions and fields of applications to quantitative sociology (e.g., Tausch 2007; Burstein and Vogel 2010).

The second subdiscipline, meanwhile, grounded in a *humanistic* or *interpretative* tradition, works with different assumptions and addresses very different kinds of questions. Social life is here viewed through a prism that looks for its symbolic dimensions and contextual specificities (instead of attempting to discover underlying and generalizable regularities). Sociologists working within this second tradition, whose methodology and epistemology are known as *qualitative*, look for very different phenomena in the settings they seek to understand. Qualitative sociologists are driven by the quest to capture people's ideas, values and experiences, their perceptions and interpretations of their place in the world and history, their understandings of "right" and "wrong" and what those are themselves believed to be based upon. In short, qualitative sociologists—along with many of their colleagues in social anthropology, cultural studies, and various branches of history and the humanities at large—try to capture and understand the *symbolic universes* and *meanings* a particular group of people or individual find themselves a part of, in a particular part of the world and at a given point in history. This last sentence contains, as we shall discover, the seeds of the challenges addressed in the present book. Anchored in sociology's qualitative tradition, it is from within it that I seek to trace some of the implications of globalization for sociology. More narrowly, this book attempts to sketch how long-distance interconnections impact both people's symbolic universes and patterns of meaning *and* (qualitative) sociologists, ethnographers and others trying to understand such (local) life-worlds.

Anticipating a little more of what follows, I argue across the ensuing chapters that contemporary globalization presents a number of profound social and scientific challenges. Globalization affects many of the people sociologists study, which in turn creates novel circumstances and conditions for sociologists as scientists of the social. We will explore just how far-reaching those changes have been, both in sociopolitical and in social scientific domains. With regard to the latter, it can indeed be argued that globalization presents some forms of sociology with a crisis. At the same time, I will demonstrate that subbranches of the discipline have responded with impressive methodological and conceptual reflexivity and innovation. In a further step, one which will only be touched upon and anticipated here, the question will arise as to whether qualitative sociology—in partly reconfiguring itself in and for our age of global interconnectedness—may be able to help address some of the social and political dilemmas and challenges brought about by contemporary globalization and the counterreactions against it.

From Sociology's Purported "Decomposition"
to Its Possible Renaissance

In the early 1990s, the late American political sociologist Irving Horowitz postulated that sociology was faced with a potential "decomposition" largely of its own making. Horowitz detected the roots for this in another bifurcation, this one primarily political rather than methodological, which had also run through sociology since its early days. To paraphrase Horowitz, we ought to begin by remembering two of the discipline's founding-fathers' contrasting positions on how, or if at all, sociology was to interface with political struggles. For Karl Marx, and those later generations of social scientists who have seen themselves as grounded—at least in part—in the Marxist tradition, the question had a clear answer: the point to philosophy, and by extension to sociology, was to do more than merely describe and explain social realities; the ultimate purpose was taken to be to change those social realities and particularly the inequalities written into them. Max Weber, by contrast, advocated a different relationship between social research and the worlds it strives to illuminate.[1] In his famous and complex essay on *Objectivity in social science*, Max Weber (1988 [1904]) argued that the sociologist's aim was to contextualize, understand and trace the consequences of social actors' ideas, beliefs and values. One could not, however, "legislate" over such ideas and values, let alone impose one's own. Weber's argument has been read as a call to separate (social) science from value-judgments (Dahrendorf 1973: 92). To Horowitz, the issue Weber highlighted had, by the 1990s, returned to haunt sociology. According to Horowitz, much of the discipline had continued to try to "legislate," however implicitly, over widely held values and beliefs. More accurately, Horowitz encouraged a reexamination of how many sociologists argued politically. Too often, so Horowitz implied, political positions were presupposed by sociological research. This not only ran the danger of "turning" potential students "off," it also threatened to compromise scientific objectivity and could even border on the circular: rather than making political recommendations on the basis of new findings, which is of course a legitimate and laudable ambition for social research, too many sociologists, Horowitz suggested, were or were at least widely perceived to be constrained by their own ideological "beliefs." *A priori* political positions, so the charge, too often impacted the collection and analysis of new data (Horowitz 1993: 12–23).

The problem Horowitz postulated pertained to the question as to where, if at all, sociological research ought to interface with or inform political blueprints and decisions. Horowitz's own answer was clear, namely that political recommendations could emerge at the end, but not be presupposed at the outset, of the research process. To the present author, these critical questions should at least be borne in mind more than three decades on. This is particularly so as others have taken the opposite viewpoint to Horowitz, arguing instead that sociology today is facing an "identity crisis" because it has allegedly lost sight of its original aspiration, namely to "make good on the eighteenth-century Enlightenment promise of creating [...] a world in which humans exercise dominion over nature without exercising dominion over each other" (Fuller 2006: 1). I return to this contested and challenging question as to sociology's normative and political orientations at various points in the discussions to follow. However, this is not the only profound challenge now facing sociology and its relationship with the social worlds that constitute its objects of research and analysis. A second set of challenges goes beyond the political to affect the epistemological bases of sociological research. This epistemological challenge lies at the heart of this book.

To understand this epistemological challenge, some definitional work on globalization, its constitutive features and counterreactions to it is required. For this, we also need to bear in mind that as a concept, "globalization" has had its share of vocal critics. Some of those have suggested that globalization is "in danger of becoming [...] the cliché of our times," or "the big idea" that purports to include too much to explain anything at all (Held et al. quoted in Pries 2005: 168). Such concerns need to be taken seriously. In this book, we discover that the term globalization often serves as shorthand with which politicians, so-called ordinary citizens, opinion makers and some academics refer to a range of recent changes, shifts and dislocations, all of which implicate—or are seen as implicating—outside forces and dynamics with palpable and far-reaching local consequences. What is more, we will see that such larger, outside forces and *flows* manifest across a range of economic, social, political, and cultural domains. Globalization, whatever else the term is assumed to describe, is multidimensional and involves changes that originate, or are perceived as originating, elsewhere (i.e., outside the boundaries of the nation-state) and that impact locally.

As my starting point I propose a return to Arjun Appadurai's (1990) influential take on globalization and the conflicts it spurs. According to Appadurai, globalization in the contemporary era comprises a number of "global flows": namely those of people (*ethnoscapes*), money (*financescapes*), technologies (*technoscapes*), ideas and ideologies[2] (*ideoscapes*), and mediated information (*mediascapes*). Further, Appadurai was among the first to note that the constant traffic of people, money, technology, ideas and mediated information across national boundaries and vast distances had not resulted in cultural standardization. As such, he levelled a powerful (if implicit) criticism against the then standard assumption, which appeared to receive powerful backing form prominent sociologist George Ritzer's work on

The McDonaldization of Society (1993), that globalization was tantamount to cultural homogenization. On the contrary, far from these global flows levelling and erasing local particularities, Appadurai (1990: 295–308) observed that what we were witnessing was a disconcerting, not only potentially violent process of the "forces of sameness and difference cannibalizing" one another. Put more simply, globalization is not making the world more equal, despite our growing interconnectedness, neither economically (Milanovic 2016) nor culturally. Instead, globalization results in locally experienced conflicts between moves toward some homogenization and at times powerful counterreactions that insist on and celebrate particularism and difference.

Similar insights and elaborations on the complicated consequences of interconnectedness were soon to follow. Arguably most influential was Roland Robertson's (1995: 30) concept of *glocalization* that centered on "the reconstruction" of "home, community and locality" under new conditions: "the local" was thereby recognized as "an aspect of globalization," namely through the "simultaneity and [mutual] interpenetration" of the two geographical scales, the distant and the close-by. The perhaps inescapable local impact of globalization is here acknowledged, but the shape that impact takes is contingent on local factors and actions. Building on Robertson, amongst others, German sociologist Ulrich Beck (2000: 46) would in due course speak of a "local-global nexus." This provides the ideal point of departure for the following discussions. Synthesizing the different conceptual strands just mentioned, the *local-global nexus* can be defined as comprising the constant in- and out-flow of financial resources, people, information, representations and various other social and cultural *things*. These multiple flows not only happen in both directions, but localities and local actors are here acknowledged as active participants in—rather than merely passive recipients of—transnational flows. Such a nexus can also take multiple forms; cultural homogenization may indeed be prominent, or conversely, in other settings, a local reassertion of particularism and concurrent re-entrenchment of locally meaningful boundaries vis-à-vis global influences may dominate; or, perhaps most commonly, these two tendencies may sit alongside one another, in different forms and appropriations. We will discover different shapes, forms and nuances of such *nexi* in the chapters to follow. What is more, thirty years after its original formulation, Appadurai's definition needs some revision and extension. In our now full-blown digital *information age* (Castells 1996), *technoscapes* and *ideoscapes* take yet other and more various forms than they did in 1990. To state the obvious, the Internet and social media have had an enormous accelerating and multiplying effect on the global flows of technologies and ideas. As we shall also discover in the following chapters, there are yet other, additional (social and cultural) *things*—foremost amongst them natural resources, commodities and other material objects, signs and entire sign systems—that constitute further "global cultural flows."

Two important questions arise at this point. First, attentive readers may already query how novel this social condition of people living in *local-global nexi* actually is. Second, we have now reached the point in the argument where I need to specify quite why any of this might constitute a challenge for sociology. At closer inspection, we shall see that the two questions are not unrelated. As for the first question, it is vital for us not to succumb to a widespread form of historical myopia, or even amnesia, that is arguably typical of our (postmodern) era (Jameson 1991). Transregional, even global interconnectedness is anything but new (e.g., Martell 2017: 32–55). At the same time, the myopia implicit in much talk about globalization, which assumes the latter to be historically novel, is not surprising. "We" are taught history through a lens that centers on particular, clearly delineated collectives, such as "civilizations," ethnic or religious groups, and—most consequentially—nation-states. However, contact (ranging from trade and intermarriage on one end of the spectrum, to warfare and attempted destruction of others on the other) and various exchanges, interdependencies, the diffusion of ideas and technologies—in short interconnectedness—has also been part of the human condition, in all its diversities, for millennia. Cities and city states, markets, trade routes, the spread of knowledge, the rise of world religions, highly exploitative economic and political relations (e.g., from slavery to imperialism and colonialism) are all examples of long-distance, sometimes global interconnections that defined previous historical eras. One of the most impressive works of social science of recent decades, David Graeber's magnum opus on the history of *Debt* (2012), shows precisely this. Graeber maps alternating "cycles" onto what historians term the *longue durée*. In the "axial age" (800 BC–AD 600), Graeber shows, economic systems were based on coinage, exchange, and simultaneously defined by war and slavery; this was followed by the Middle Ages, when "virtual credit money returned [...] and slavery largely disappeared" (Graeber 2012: 297), which of course did not mean the end of long-distance connections. The next shift Graeber traces led to the "age of the great capitalist empires" and "exploration," it saw a return from "credit economies" to "gold and silver [...] vast empires and professional armies, massive predatory warfare [...] [and] chattel slavery" (Graeber 2012: 308). What is significant for our purposes is not only Graeber's impressively long historical lens, but his demonstration that long-distance economic connections have taken different, often highly exploitative and violent forms, and that political systems of economic production and exchange have also been subject to profound, cyclical shifts. Put more simply, globalization has a long history[3]; it has taken different forms at different times; and some of its manifestations have included entanglements with some of history's darkest chapters.

Having thus dispelled the common and ultimately untenable proposition that in talking about globalization we are describing something purportedly entirely new, we next need to ponder what may then distinguish our current form of globalization from previous ones. One of the most compelling answers to this question has centered on the frequency, speed and ease, with which long distances are now being "breached," crossed, or spanned. One formulation of this has been David Harvey's concept of "time-space compressions" (1989), enabled by developments such as our era's information and communication technologies. Thanks to those, communication across vast geographical distances is now indeed instantaneous and global. It is not the existence of "global cultural flows" (in Appadurai's terminology), then, nor the counterreactions and political confrontations triggered by them, that are novel about our current form of globalization. What is distinctive is their reach, their speed, and the extent of their impact on local life-worlds.

It is here that the second question, which was already anticipated above and will accompany us throughout this book, acquires particular salience. This central question asks how well-equipped sociology, particularly in its qualitative form, is to capture and make sense of the multiple, global cultural flows that, while anything but new, now move faster, more frequently (and some of them more easily), and reach further and deeper than arguably ever before. This will require engagement with a range of recent sociological studies of today's global flows and local appropriations of, and responses to, them. Yet more fundamentally, this also necessitates reflexivity on some of the epistemological premises underpinning such sociological work. In other words, this book is an attempt to reexamine—in light of the workings of *glocalization* today—some of the often implicit but foundational assumptions underpinning qualitative sociological research and its claims to knowledge of the social world. In parts of the following chapters, we will (re-)turn to several such premises. Two sets of such assumptions will be particularly prominent and therefore warrant some preliminary comments already at this stage. The first of these assumptions shares conceptual space with conventional approaches, which have already been mentioned, to studying and teaching history. Sociology, too, often works with the (implicit) presupposition that its focus has obvious and clear external boundaries. This is, for example, implicit in the methodological principle of sampling: that is, of selecting a subset of individuals, case studies, scenarios, etc. deemed to be representative of a larger population or phenomenon. Closer to the qualitative and ethnographic end of the methodological spectrum, meanwhile, the idea of studying a very particular context or setting also presupposes clear boundaries that delineate a coherent focal point for sociological investigation. And written into many studies based on qualitative interviews or focus groups is the idea, whether or not stated explicitly, that the views, feelings or experiences captured are more than mere snapshots taken at a particular time, in specific circumstances; the implicit assumption often, though by no means always, made in such research is that the positions captured possess at least a certain durability and say something more or less characteristic at least about the particular people being interviewed. However, what happens when our "global cultural flows" are taken more seriously, in their impacts on places, people, their experiences, but also on the research process? In an era of systemic, global interconnectedness and flows that cut across boundaries, of what exactly—or of which population—can a sample of research participants be considered to be representative? Does it still make sense to study localities, or to focus on specific settings more or less independently of their much wider contexts, when their presumed external boundaries are constantly crossed, or "breached," by multiple flows from elsewhere and to elsewhere? And if we now live in complicated "local-global nexi" (and perhaps in several all at the same time), what impact do their constitutive flows have on experiences, views, values and shared meanings? How enduring or stable can such social and cultural phenomena still be presumed to be?

The second set of assumptions requiring renewed disciplinary reflection acquires particular significance in light of the very plausible postulate that a world of ever more systemic, faster, wider and more frequent interconnectedness is also a world of growing complexity (e.g., Urry 2000: 121). One of the core insights to emerge from this book will be a (re)statement of modesty: global interconnections implicating the financial, the technological, the semiotic, the geopolitical, the ideological and much more confront us with complications, entanglements and complexities that transcend not only the (or this) individual social scientist's powers of understanding and analysis. This much is hardly surprising. What is more perturbing, however, is the fact that this seemingly obvious and certainly necessary admission flies in the face of a subtle but important assumption underpinning much, though again by no means all, qualitative sociological research. The assumption in question manifests in approaches to qualitative interviewing that take it as given that research participants, straightforwardly, have and will share the answers to our research questions. What, however, if this cannot or should not be taken as given? What if our scientific answers to our scientific questions demand much more of an acknowledgement of our (interconnected) world's complexities and the many ways in which those far transcend any one person's comprehension? In other words, might we need to acknowledge that much qualitative interviewing has expected far too much, or the wrong thing, of research participants? Les Back (2007: 9–12) puts it most clearly, when he critically revisits the frequently made assumption that "people are experts in their own lives." Back encourages us to reexamine this assumption. Such rethinking, as parts of this book will argue, is both necessary and has far-reaching implications for (qualitative) sociology.

To anticipate a little more of the discussions to follow, I shall argue that the challenges and questions contemporary glocalization generates present opportunities for sociology's disciplinary renewal rather than cause for despair. What is more, I shall also show that there are clear signs of sociologists and other social scientists already rising very productively to the challenges at hand. At the same time, recent and ongoing social transformations also, inadvertently, make a strong case for a critical reexamination of some of the epistemological, methodological and political premises underpinning much contemporary, qualitative sociology. Such reexamination, I shall suggest, promises not only to further sharpen our sociological lenses, but might enable us to contribute with greater confidence and authority to some of today's enormously important public debates and processes of decision-making. What follows, then, is a "journey" through recent sociological research, conceptual and thematic discussions pertaining to globalization and its counterreactions, and wider theoretical and epistemological questions.

Outline of a Series of Challenges

Well-read sociologists might detect an intertextual allusion in the subheading to this section, namely to one of sociology's true (modern) classics—Pierre Bourdieu's *Outline of a Theory of Practice*. In this, one of his earliest books, Bourdieu formulated and illustrated some of his most enduring concepts. Those included that of the *habitus*—or the "generating structures" that bear the imprint of people's structural and cultural subject positions and, by enabling "improvisation," also facilitate their ongoing reproduction in novel circumstances; of *doxa* (or uninterrogated cultural "common-sense"), and the effects of "objective crisis" on it (Bourdieu 1977: 167–171). For present purposes, the allusion to Bourdieu's early masterpiece contained in the subheading above is premised on formal rather than substantive similarities. One of the particularities of *Outline of a Theory of Practice* are its alternating registers, or Bourdieu's recurring movements between detailed ethnographic data and reflections on his work in Kabylia, on one hand, and theoretical abstraction, definitional work and the formulation of key concepts on the other.

Although my empirical and conceptual concerns differ from Bourdieu's, the chapters in this book reveal a similar movement back and forth between their two constitutive, argumentative strands. In my case, those comprise, first, (existing) empirical insights into multiple global flows and the ambivalent local reactions to them; and, second, the epistemological challenges and questions posed by such "local-global nexi." Another way of putting this is to describe this book as an attempt to build on Thomas H. Eriksen's (2015: 371–390) argument that globalization entails the "disembedding" of capital and "cultural phenomena" from space, which is then being countered by "localizing strategies" for "reembedding." This book probes deeper and asks: what, in sociological terms, do we already know about such *dis-* and *re-embedding* of capital and culture in our current epoch? What do we still need to find out? And, arguably most fundamentally, what can we know about such phenomena, what are the (perhaps changing) parameters, promises and limitations of sociological knowledge, or claims to knowledge, under such conditions?

Overall, this book makes a case for reinvigorating the *sociological imagination*, which was seminally defined by C. Wright Mills (2000 [1959]) as the ability to recognize that the purportedly private contains widely unrecognized but distinctly "public issues"; and to relate biographical, often seemingly individualized experiences to their much deeper historical and much wider structural conditions of possibility. In essence, the sociological imagination demands thorough contextualization, the *conditio sine qua non* for all social science. Against the historical backdrop provided by contemporary globalization— which, as we will see, needs to be comprehended as "both a process and [emerging] structure[s]" (Lemert 2015: 95)—such contextualization and, through it, the application of the sociological imagination are faced with distinctive challenges: namely how to record, capture and make sense of emerging structures and of processes that, by definition, span geographical distances in multiple and complex ways whilst transforming people's life-worlds. Put more simply, contemporary globalizing forces present sociology with novel methodological and epistemological issues. It is the task of this book to outline those issues and to assess how successful sociology has been at confronting them. As we shall discover, it is no easy task to specify methods that enable the sociological imagination to work under the particular conditions we face today. Some long-established methodologies, assumptions and approaches are indeed in need of being rethought and refined. However, the promise this task holds is very considerable. Sociology, and the particular form of contextualization and vantage points it can enable, have arguably never been as urgently needed as they are today. Its insights are precisely what is missing from much public debate. There is urgent work to be done, and much excellent work is already being done. What follows is one sociologist's attempt to distil both, the particular challenges at hand, and examples of how some contemporary sociologies are beginning to meet them.

A preliminary question remains: Why should, or why does, the phenomenon of multiple, constant flows across long distances (and the ensuing interconnections and interdependencies) create a challenge for sociology in the first place? And might this question about the workings of a particular social science under specific historical and structural circumstances be related to the broader question as to why the same circumstances are also widely perceived as challenging by many of the people sociologists study? To get a handle on this, we may turn to Marc Augé's (2008: 11–19) understanding of ethnography as entailing the "cobbl[ing] together [of] a significant universe" and the "interpret[ation of] the interpretation others make." The first of these points echoes seminal definitions of culture, that is, the central unit of analysis for many an anthropologist and qualitative sociologist, as "systems of symbols" and hence meanings (e.g., Geertz 1973: 250, 52) that can only be understood in their generative contexts. The second point relates to what is known as the "double hermeneutic" (e.g., Giddens 1984), which describes the analysis of qualitative data as a "second order interpretation" focused on local, research participants' "first order interpretation" (i.e., their *culture*) (Geertz 1973: 15). Put differently, qualitative analysis involves a secondary layer or step of the social scientist's meta-interpretations being added to the (preexisting) interpretations of social realities recorded by and among research participants; in other words, qualitative social scientists make sense of how the people they study experience and make sense of their life-worlds. As we shall see in due course, one difficult question arising here pertains to the relationship and potential differences between research participants' primary and the sociologist's secondary interpretations. More immediately relevant, however, are Augé elaborations on what exactly ethnographers study:

> The property of symbolic universes is that they constitute a means of recognition, rather than knowledge, for those who have inherited them: closed universes where everything is a sign; collections of codes to which only some hold the key but whose existence everyone accepts; totalities which are partially fictional but effective [...] One of the major concerns of ethnology has been to delineate signifying spaces in the world [...] universes of meaning, of which the individuals and groups inside them are just an expression, defining themselves in terms of the same criteria, the same values and the same interpretation procedure. (Augé 2008: 27)

The question as to what happens when such *universes of meaning* turn out to have highly porous external boundaries lies at the heart of the present book. Arguably a hallmark of our times, the constant flow of signs, commodities, people, finances, technologies, information, waste and more breaches the boundaries of such purportedly "closed universes" of locally meaningful signs, codes, values and interpretations. If we take globalization as a phenomenon seriously, as I suggest we must, then this appears to have far-reaching implications on how any qualitatively oriented social science needs to define and conceptualize its units of analyses: as open rather closed, as emerging and changing fragments rather than "totalities," as blurry phenomena, the "inside" and "outside" of which may be much harder to differentiate than in the just-quoted account. At the same time, there is no doubt that many people perceive and think of "their cultures" in terms that closely resemble Augé's depiction. Some of the contexts we will encounter in this book also raise the interesting follow-on question, which pushes in a political rather than a methodological direction: is part of the widespread unease with globalization evident today perhaps due to this contradiction between many people's lived experiences of constant cross-border flows and their arguably nostalgically distorting images of locally, allegedly formerly shared understandings, values and codes? If so, what are the implications of this for a sociology of glocalization?

Weaving Existing Threads Further

The criticism that the foci and approaches informing *some* sociological work are too narrow and hence out of step with the ever-widening scale of structures of translocal or transnational interconnectedness is certainly not new. It is a criticism commonly associated with the notion of a "methodological nationalism" (Wimmer and Glick-Schiller 2002): this describes the misleading, interrelated assumptions that, first, social life is reducible to publics and life-worlds provided by nation-states; and, second, that purportedly "national societies" thus constitute the only viable units of social scientific analysis. Put more simply, if ours is indeed an era of globalization, then a sociology focused on the nation-state "container" (Beck 2000), or yet more narrowly on isolated localities, is in danger of missing some of today's defining characteristics. This is not to say that globalization cannot be accessed and understood from the vantage points of particular localities or nation-states. On the contrary, parts of what follows will show that localities and nation-states continue to be vital starting points and points of reference for sociology. However, the latter must go further, we need to be able to recognize, document and analyze how the local and the national are being profoundly reconfigured today. In other words, and to distil the central questions asked in this book, what are the epistemological implications (for sociology) of living in a world of multiple flows and hugely complex interconnections? How can any of these flows and interconnections be known, captured and made sense of?

How do we know what we (think we) know about social life under the particular structural and historical conditions of the present? To address these questions, globalization and glocalization need to be broken down into at least some of their constitutive units, flows, interconnections and the various (counter-) reactions to them.

However, before delving into these challenging questions, further definitional ground needs to be cleared and established conceptual terrain be resketched. As has already been hinted, as a phenomenon—or as an ontological entity, so-to-speak—"globalization" has had its sceptics. According to some of them, there is a danger of inflationary usage of the term at the expense of analytical insight (Held et al. quoted in Pries 2005: 168). Others have suggested that for the notion of "globalization" to generate discernible analytical dividends it needs to be shown to go beyond some of its conceptual "cousins," which include "internationalization, liberalization and universalization" (Scholte quoted in Martell 2017: 7, 8). Despite undeniable overlaps, these latter dimensions differ from my preferred conceptualization. As has been argued, I subsume under globalization multiple global flows, which—though not new—today show wider reach, command greater geographical and social space, occur with greater frequency, and certainly move at increased pace when compared to previous eras. What is more, the derived concept of *glocalization* has pushed the debate in further, important directions by showing that globalization unfolds, by definition, in relation to other geographical scales that include the national, the regional and the local. Consequently, the global is rethought through its complex and contingent impacts on local life-worlds and the variable responses to multiple and multidirectional flows.

Alongside skeptical voices, other commentators have insisted that, notwithstanding the many existing frameworks and competing understandings of what exactly it entails, globalization is "one of the most important concepts of the beginning of the twenty-first century" and lies "at the heart of a renewal of the intellectual background of the social sciences" (Le Coze 2017: 60). Already at the turn of the millennium, John Urry had formulated the argument yet more forcefully, suggesting that new social realities in fact demanded sociology's reorientation: our epoch's "diverse mobilities" and "global 'networks and flows'" had, so Urry, begun to "transform the historic subject matter of sociology" by "undermin[ing] endogenous social structures" that had previously been presumed to "possess the powers to reproduce themselves"; an emerging, "post-societal phase," so the argument continued, necessitated "new rules of sociological method," while the notion of a geographically delineated society would henceforth primarily be invoked by often reactionary "'national' forces seeking to moderate, control and regulate" the "networks and flows criss-crossing their porous borders." (Urry 2000: 1) The argument that changing social realities demand of sociologists that they adjust their methodological approaches also featured in Charles Lemert's subsequent observation. For him, our novel "global realities" throw "social structures of all kinds" into sharp relief; they call for "global methods" that are necessarily different from those that worked reasonably well when social things were more simply "protected by the nation-states;" and such methods adjusted to the "global things" of our age require, in part, a *"getting close at a distance"* (Lemert 2005: 187). Significant parts of this book trace which global methods are already on offer, how they are being applied, and what they are capable of showing. As we will see, "getting close at a distance" is indeed part of what is required. But there are other novel strategies on offer, too, some of which have been pioneered as "travelling methods" (Knowles 2014), or as a "thinking with all our senses" that can sharpen our "attention to the hidden life of objects and places" (Back 2007: 8, 9).

The sociological significance of the global-local nexus, then, includes the fact that it confronts us anew with questions about social reality and its building blocks (i.e., *ontology*), about the philosophical premises underpinning our knowledge-claims about those (new) social realities (i.e., *epistemology*), and about suitable *methods* for capturing them. The observation that we are now having to rethink both *how* we research and *what* we research is not new, but these questions are in urgent need of further discussion and reflection. Already in the early years of the new millennium Ludger Pries observed that the widening of the "spatial scope of human action" pans out in highly asymmetrical ways; whilst its various impacts are indeed global, our era's new opportunities often exacerbate preexisting segmentations and hierarchies further, by being "enjoyed by only one-tenth of the world's population." Alongside, today's structural shifts also exercise a "deep influence" on "the units of observation and analysis in the social sciences" insofar as "societal practices, symbol systems and artefacts that form sociology's field of study are shifting in their spatial reach" (Pries 2005: 167, 168). Ulrich Beck and Edgar Grande have also called for "research units *beyond* methodological nationalism": those need to be attuned to today's particularities by simultaneously being "free[d] from the 'container' of the nation-state, while refusing to take refuge in abstract concepts of 'world society'" (Beck and Grande 2010: 426). What follows then, are thematic and methodological snapshots and discussions of how qualitative sociology has already responded to the challenges of glocalization and its always context-specific particularities and tensions; and suggestions of what still needs to be done, how else the sociological imagination may be put to productive use in relation to some of the most pressing concerns of the twenty-first century.

To anticipate more of the ensuing discussions, I will argue that an epistemologically convincing, qualitative sociology of glocalization must include the following: an expanded methodological arsenal and a sharpening of our senses to the many ways in which global flows impact and reshape the local. Hence, what is required are new ways of looking, listening, smelling, tasting and empathizing; a revisiting of previous research sites and localities that have been tangibly altered by recent social changes; as well as new vantage points and the willingness to explore social domains, both long-established and newly emerging, in which the dynamics of globalization play out. More specifically, each of the chapters focuses on a particular "flow and scape," whereby Appadurai's understanding of globalization is simultaneously reappropriated and expanded. Chapter 1 begins our journey with an exploration of how globalization manifests, often very uncomfortably for many of those affected, in a particular locality; this requires a probing of wider sociological and political questions posed by local environmental and infrastructural changes. Chapters 2 and 3 subject what we may term the economic dimensions of glocalization to sociological scrutiny: my respective foci will thereby lie on financial markets, marketization, and other features of our global economy (in Chapter 2), and on contemporary consumerism (in Chapter 3), respectively. Chapter 4 moves the discussion into the much-debated field of migration and local responses to migratory flows. This is followed by two interconnected chapters with a shared focus on urban glocalization: after a discussion in Chapter 5 of how urban sociology has responded to contemporary *flows and scapes*, Chapter 6 traces an emerging methodology for capturing the semiotic dimensions of glocalization. Chapter 7 then argues for a critical social science focused on the power relations and unintended consequences of our digital era.

To meet the far-reaching political and epistemological challenges posed by current changes that are commonly subsumed under the term "globalization," sociology must indeed remember, celebrate and practice "the art of looking," which has been a quintessential part of the sociological craft at least since Chicago School sociologists emphasized this in the interwar period (Lindner 2007: 312, 313). Already at this stage in my argument, it is worth remembering what exactly this Chicago School "art of looking" entailed: a profound, nonjudgmental curiosity for life as lived and interpreted by a specific individual or group; second, the concurrent insistence that while appropriate methods can indeed capture the "emic-" or insider's view, a fuller understanding requires "two sets of eyes," and hence a combination of internal and external "perspectives" that must include but also push beyond the "boundaries of thinking as usual" (quoted in Lindner 2007: 314). We will repeatedly return to this issue, which is of both methodological and analytical significance, for it forces us to think what kinds of questions research participants can be expected to provide answers for, and what else—in addition to such answers—it is the sociologist's task to generate. There is a further similarity between the spirit of Chicago School sociology and the approach(es) sketched in what follows: a shared belief in the profound added value of interdisciplinarity (see Bulmer 1984: 38). While grounded in sociology's qualitative tradition, this book also argues consistently for the importance of interdisciplinary borrowings. In the chapters that follow, such synergies will variously draw on the contributions by social anthropologists, historians, geographers, political scientists, and social researchers grounded in cultural studies. As a first, and at this stage inevitably tentative answer to the question posed by this book's title, one may thus conclude from the outset that one thing sociology needs to be *in times of glocalization* is interdisciplinary.

In addition to exploring methodological and conceptual angles that cross multiple boundaries within the social sciences, another recurring theme in what follows pertains to the challenges of perceiving, noticing and capturing our era's multiple, transnational "flows." Vital though knowing how to look sociologically is, this needs to be complemented by what Les Back describes as an "art of listening" (Back 2007) recalibrated toward an age of global markets, flows, and multicultural heterogeneities. Although equally necessary, this does not singularly suffice either: as we will discover, sociologists have to sharpen all their senses to be able to capture the multiple and contradictory ways in which lives and localities are affected and significantly reshaped by our era's global interconnections. This is a "multi-sensorial" challenge, implicating "sights, sounds, smells, tastes, and touches," as well as what Loïc Wacquant calls a "bodily sociology" that requires the researcher's body as an "instrument of data collection" (Lindner 2007: 320, 321).

What is more, the question will also need to be confronted as to how all our arts of perception may interface with the political status quo: is it enough to record and interpret what we see, hear, taste, smell and otherwise witness? Alternatively, how critical of what we perceive and capture do we need to be? Is there only one possible answer to this? Or might sociology be best advised to cultivate a diversity of answers to the question as to whether or not the present demands that we not only witness, record and interpret, but also criticize? These are, as we shall discover, challenging questions indeed. Moreover, these questions are not new, some of them have been part of the sociological enterprise from its inception. However, the following discussions suggest that present circumstances mean that we must urgently (re)turn our attention to these questions.

A note of modesty and self-reflexive caution is also required from the outset. What this book offers cannot possibly amount to a comprehensive review of all bodies of relevant literature in a huge and rapidly expanding field of scholarship. Instead, the following chapters develop critical outlines of select thematic clusters and a tracing of particular methodological lines of enquiry and innovation within them. One of the threads tying them together can be described with reference to Clifford Geertz. Geertz's seminal, *semiotic concept of culture* continues to resonate with what qualitative sociology strives to understand, namely context-bound "webs of significance," various "frames of meaning," "significant symbols [and] their mutual interference" (Geertz 1973: 5, 28). Surely, in our times of glocalization, sociologists and other social scientists must ask themselves how such webs of significance fare, how they are impacted by multiple global flows, and how this can be captured and illuminated.

Thematically, this book also aims to help broaden our understanding of the scope, complexity, and many manifestations of globalization. Commonsensical understandings of, or—arguably more accurately—associations triggered by, globalization are captured in the following account:

> For every job lost to deindustrialization in Ohio, workers in the Pearl River Delta are drawn to Shenzen, built on [...] once fertile soil. In time, the Pearl River having been depleted, what work there is will move to Vietnam or Bangladesh, and then [...] will reappear in the American rust belt where labor once again is cheap. Workers and their families, productive lands, nature's resource wealth, and much more are mined into bits and fed to the machine of capitalist production—from which surplus values are extracted out of the wreckage of human lives. Capitalism [...] is about the endless accumulation of capital [...] destructive of the very economic (and social) order from which it extracts its profits. (Lemert 2015: 148)

All of this relates to very real experiences in the lives of countless millions. Outsourcing, the privatization of formerly public goods and other dimensions of what we have come to identify with neoliberalism, the ever-deeper structural integration of local lives and economies in transnational markets and supply chains—these are indeed all part of a wide continuum of dimensions that any meaningful attempt to understand globalization must confront. However, the problem is that these are only select parts of a yet much wider, considerably more complex and contradictory range of phenomena that such an attempt and resulting account must also acknowledge and think its way through. An additional problem pertains to the selection: if someone—as many, ironically both on the (far) Left and on the (far) Right of the traditional political spectrum are inclined to do—wants to give an ill-defined shorthand they call "globalization" a bad name, all they need to do is to reduce it to "neoliberalism" and those very real, though by no means exhaustive experiences summarized in Lemert's account above. A sociologically fuller and hence more accurate account of globalization, I will argue, needs to include and critically examine but also push considerably beyond the experiences and structural patterns depicted therein.

Finally, I would like to close this introductory chapter by declaring what is often, arguably too often, left implicit, namely my intentions as the author of what follows. It should be remembered that in speaking and writing we may in fact pursue a variety of purposes. Persuading an audience or reader is only one possible rhetorical aim, albeit a clearly important one. A much wider range of possible rhetorical intentions include the following: to pose questions, to unsettle long-established assumptions, to interject in ongoing debates, to foreground generally overlooked issues, to get oneself and others to reconsider and reflect upon what is often assumed as given; and perhaps to provoke, to annoy, to invite readers to disagree and to defend their potentially alternative positions anew. In different sections of the ensuing chapters, I will attempt to do each of the above. I will not, however, seek to "preach": where I touch on normative and political positions, the intention will not be to insinuate that I am—or anyone else is—automatically "right" and that diverging positions are "mistaken" and in immediate need of revision. Normative and political issues are inescapable, important and at the very heart of parts of the ensuing discussions. But when I touch on those it will be in the spirit of encouraging debate and reflexivity amongst all of us, and to eschew overly simplistic, nonreflexive answers. In many other parts of the following discussions, by contrast, my intentions will be analytical: to sketch methodologically compelling ways of collecting and making sense of (qualitative) data on some of the flows, interconnections and tensions that have come to define our lives in the twenty-first century; and to revisit some of the conceptual and theoretical terrains also required for this. Underpinning the following discussions in their entirety are the formidable and enormously important questions as to what defines the sociological craft and which different forms its application can assume under contemporary circumstances. These are challenging questions indeed. They will not be resolved here. All the present author hopes to accomplish is to open them anew and to thereby encourage much-needed discussion, within and far beyond sociology.

Notes

1 It should be noted that recent research has shown this common juxtaposition of Marx to Weber to have been based on a selective and contestable reading of the latter's work. Oliver Neun has thus shown that the notion of Max Weber as apolitical, or even right-leaning, had been premised on Talcott Parsons' translation of Weber's oeuvre. An alternative reading, one considerably closer to the Marxist tradition, to social democracy and to what we will later encounter as "public sociology," is enabled by Hans Gerth and C. Wright Mills' lesser-known, but arguably more accurate and even-handed account of Weber's writings (Neun 2015). Put simply: the political bifurcation of sociology described here may have been premised on a reading of Max Weber that was partial at best, and positively distorting at worst. Yet, and the arguable distortions written into prominent understandings of Weberian sociology notwithstanding, their impact on the history of the discipline to date are undeniable.

2 The concept of "ideology" is frequently used, in both academic and political everyday discussion, though much less frequently treated with the required conceptual clarity. The working definition employed here (Augoustinos 1998) regards ideology as subsuming language, ideas, and social practices that play a direct or indirect political role insofar as they either feed into the reproduction *or* the subversion of existing relations of power.

3 Depending on the measurements or definitions of globalization employed, other arguments have insisted on a more recent starting point to systematic global interconnections. For example, O'Rourke and Williamson take a "reshuffling" of local/national resources and "commodity price convergence" across distances as measures of globalization; if thus defined more narrowly (and not in terms of the wide range of *flows* and *scapes* outlined here), the "big bang"—or demonstrable start—of "sustained globalization" can be traced to the 1820s (O'Rourke and Williamson 2002).

Chapter 1

FROM LOCALITIES TO *"NON-PLACES"*?

Photographing Social Change

My wife and I recently spent a difficult period of six months living in a previously semirural English location that had since become an infrastructural node in our national and international networks of travel, work, and commerce. Thus, living very near an airport that serves and connects the region in question to the world at large, I used to be woken up every night by heavy air traffic, by cargo planes taking off with ferocious frequency between one and four o'clock in the morning. We had ended up in this location by accident, needing accommodation at very short notice, in a place that would be geographically fairly convenient for both my and my wife's commutes to work. Given the urgency of this at the time, we had to disregard the fact that the area in question had also acquired a reputation for its high levels of Brexit support.[1] Two (self-defining) Europeans moving there, at the height of the furor created by the UK's uneasily unfolding exit from the European Union, was—in hindsight—always going to be difficult. And so it was. However, our problems extended far beyond restless nights and our deep uneasiness with the political positions held by many of our neighbors at the time. What many residents in this particular location, and probably many others like it around the globe, share is a usually unarticulated but locally inescapable experience of being squeezed by changes to the area being imposed from the outside.

The intentions of this chapter are threefold and interrelated. First, I will sketch some of the methodological questions raised by our recent experiences in the locality in question, wishing to point toward some possible ways of capturing recent and ongoing social changes in places such as the one described above and in what follows. Second, this discussion will draw on several conceptual strands in recent sociological theorizing that can help us make sense of the social changes at stake here and of how they impact on local lives. Third, in combining the empirical with the methodological and the conceptual, this discussion shows that examples such as the one that lies at the heart of this chapter strengthen the more general case for a reinvigorated *sociological imagination* and for a *public sociology* (Burawoy 2005) today.

Let me start with a methodological question and note. Early during our temporary sojourn in the locality in question, I began to wonder what a sociologically compelling way of making sense of our experiences there might look like. Quite apart from the usual and obvious arsenal of social scientific methods (i.e., surveys, interviews, focus groups, ethnographic fieldwork), I found myself wondering *how else* local social change could be captured, perhaps less intrusively and with potentially greater sensitivity to the wider conditions that underpin local lives and how those have been altered. Importantly, this is not to be misread as an argument against more conventional social scientific approaches, but as an illustration of how those may be productively complemented. Without in any shape or form pretending that what follows exhausts this complex (epistemological) question, I would like to make a case for the use of photography; more particularly, for the importance of finding the right vantage points[2] and angles, from which aspects of local social life otherwise literally hidden from view or simply overlooked can be gleaned.

The particular methodological rationale I propose to build on is an argument (Sweetman 2009) about the ability of visual methods, photography in particular, to capture aspects of social life that are *both* widely taken for granted (and hence commonly overlooked) *and* the very terrain through which the ongoing reproduction of things as they are is accomplished. Put more simply, Paul Sweetman has proposed that photography constitutes an appropriate means for capturing the domain of what, as was mentioned earlier, Pierre Bourdieu terms the *habitus*. To appreciate this argument fully, a conceptual reminder of what Bourdieu describes through this concept is in order: the habitus subsumes cognitive structures (i.e., classificatory and interpretative patterns), affective dispositions, motivations and practices that are (sub)culturally inherited and shared, widely taken for granted (i.e., nonreflexive), and provide individuals with a cultural commonsense that enables improvised responses to the unforeseen; what is more, the habitus is shaped by existing social structures and in turn plays a role in their reproduction (Bourdieu 1977: 72–83). According to Sweetman, then, photography offers sociologists a way of accessing those aspects of people's lifeworlds "of which they were simultaneously 'unaware' but also knew 'better than anyone'" (Sweetman 2009: 497). This returns us to the epistemologically crucial question, raised by Les Back (2007: 12), as to whether or not we can assume the people we study to be "experts in their own lives." The answer suggested by Bourdieu, subsequently amplified by Sweetman, and endorsed by the present author, is that social actors as the "owners" of their experiences certainly possess a type of expertise, without which sociological insight is impossible to imagine. At the same time, however, everyday, commonsensical knowledge is partial, often nonreflexive, and incomplete. In other words, the habitus, although a crucial part of what qualitative sociological accounts depict, certainly does not exhaust the scope of our analyses, nor is it straightforward to record and put into words. Social actors' expertise of their own lives is real, important, and one of the very "raw materials" necessary for sociological insight; but such lived expertise is also incomplete, and often "lived" rather than reflected upon or explicitly articulated. Sociological analysis is thus comparable to the historian's craft, whose historiography is certainly premised upon but also goes beyond historical actors' accounts of their lives and epochs (i.e., surely we take it as given that historians' perspectives are wider and more systematically arrived at than those held by the people whose histories they write). Not dissimilarly, Bourdieu reserved for sociological enquiry, or "socioanalysis," a crucial additional dimension, namely a making explicit of, and the facilitation of reflexivity on, what is generally taken for granted; this can then "help transform" the latter "into a reflexive, self-critical practice" (quoted in Sweetman 2009: 504). It is against this conceptual backdrop that Sweetman makes the following case for the methodological benefits of using photography:

> [V]isual methods may not only allow for the excavation [...] of the unthought or unstated, but also the recognition and potential transformation of habitus in the same sort of way as Bourdieu suggests can be achieved through socioanalysis [...] [V]isual methods of research may be particularly helpful in revealing [...] aspects of practice that are difficult otherwise to recognize or articulate [...] [and] to uncover [...] way[s] of being in the world, [of which] we may simultaneously be all but "unaware." (Sweetman 2009: 506)

When complemented by the deeply contextualized, and contextualizing, insights that drive qualitative sociology, photography may thus open up new perspectives on aspects of social life that are crucial, though barely noticed, and on some of the environmental and political parameters, within which local lives unfold.

With these general remarks on the potential power and relevance of photography for sociology in mind, let us return to the locality at stake here. Consider, then, the following photographs, which I took toward the end of our time in the locality in question on a narrow, barely frequented footpath between the airport and what used to be farmers' fields until not long ago, now converted into semi-industrial land by and for the logistics centers and distribution hubs of large supermarket chains and department stores.

All taken on the same day, the locations depicted in these photographs are separated by less than two kilometers. As snapshots of the local village, with its late medieval church spire (Figure 1.1), of further capital investment and major infrastructural changes underway extremely close by and encroaching ever further (Figure 1.2), and of some of the many distribution centers in the area (Figures 1.3–1.5), through which some of our countless daily internet orders pass during their journeys to us, these figures tell the story of profound, recent social changes. This is what some of the central nodes in our increasingly global and certainly transnational supply chains look like. Without them, contemporary consumer capitalism would not work the way it does. Without them, consumers would still rely on local shops, in city centers, rather than on online orders and convenient delivery services. What the figures above do not depict are the other major components of infrastructure required. The area in question also enjoys the questionable reputation of being among the UK's "best-connected" towns, notably only for drivers. This entails immediate access—immediate only when not hampered by rush-hour congestion—to motorways and busy A-roads and the already mentioned airport. Conversely, reaching the "local" railway station constitutes a major challenge, unless one drives. (And what absurdity,

Figure 1.1 Photograph taken by the author

Figure 1.2 Photograph taken by the author

Figure 1.3 Photograph taken by the author

Figure 1.4 Photograph taken by the author

Figure 1.5 Photograph taken by the author

when one stops to think about this, it is to have to drive to a railway station!) If there was ever an example of John Urry's depiction (2000: 193) of "car-only environments" that are "swamped by automobility" and prevent pedestrians, cyclists, and those wishing or having to rely on public transport from full or easy participation in the (local) public sphere, this is it. In the particular locality in question, the "cult of automobility" has another dimension: a local race track, generating almost daily acoustic and air pollution that added further misery to our brief sojourn in the area.

Motorways, logistics centers, and the constant stream of workers and goods in and out of the locality have further implications. In addition to the already mentioned and severe traffic issues, entirely disproportional to the number of residents living in and around the town, there are severe environmental issues associated with it: air pollution and the buildup of heavy roadside plastic littering. In sociological terms, what are we to make of places such as this one, similar examples of which can be found throughout the postindustrial parts of our shared planet? Does sociology have concepts and methodologies suitable to the study of places that in many ways bear the collateral damage created by digital, transnational economies and their consumption patterns? Which contextual factors and which historical shifts need to be factored into our attempts to understand how such localities are affected by much wider social forces? While my wife and I left again after six months of sometimes uncomfortable encounters, severe pollution, soul-destroying commutes, and continual infrastructural expansion encroaching ever closer on us and our temporary neighbors, most locals do not have that option,[3] and some do not wish to. What is life lived more permanently in such places like?

Supermodernity's "Non-places" and Their Hinterlands

There are prominent strands of sociological theory generated over recent decades that can help us get a grip on localities like the one just described. At the same time, contextually useful though such theoretical perspectives are, they also require further nuancing, fine-tuning and elaboration in light of the particular empirical realities in question. What the theoretical positions, to which I turn next, have in common is a preoccupation with the impact of an increasingly globalized consumer society on localities and the everyday lives lived therein.

Foremost among the social scientists who have turned our collective attention toward the impact of globalization on space has been the French anthropologist Marc Augé. Augé begins with a definition of globalization, *mondialisation* in French, of relevance to our discussion: globalization, he contends, subsumes two dimensions that we may paraphrase as pertaining to a particular economic and technological system and to a distinctive form of consciousness, respectively. In terms of the former, globalization manifests in an "extension," more or less "over the whole surface of the planet of the so-called free market and technological networks of communication and information"; as for the latter, our era has enabled a novel form of "planetary awareness" (Augé 2008: x). On this premise, Augé proceeds to paint a compelling picture of what he terms *supermodernity*, a novel historical situation defined by "excess" and a "shrinking of the planet." According to Augé, supermodernity has seen the appearance of new kinds of spaces. In addition to long-established "anthropological places," we now also inhabit and navigate a multiplicity of *non-places*: the former have been a feature of humanity's relationship to space throughout our collective history, they refer to particular localities with idiosyncratic histories and in which individuals occupy clear positions vis-à-vis others and in wider social hierarchies and cultural traditions; such anthropological places entail a "culture localized in time and space." Non-places, by contrast, are merely "spaces of circulation, consumption, and communication." They proliferate in the here and now where they enable "transport and transit" (i.e., in the shape of bypasses, motorways, high-speed roads, interchanges, railways, high-speed trains and railway stations, airports, and airport lounges), commerce (i.e., manifesting in supermarkets, service stations, shopping malls, and retail outlets), leisure (i.e., leisure parks and tourist hot spots), and create at most "temporary abodes," either "luxurious" (i.e., hotel chains) or "inhumane" (e.g., shanty towns and refugee camps) (Augé 2008: 24–25, 28, viii, 59, 63). We experience such non-places as anonymous and "non-symbolized space," in which we are temporarily "freed" from cultural moorings, live in a seemingly "perpetual present and encounter with [the] self," and negotiate our routes through "spaces of contemporary consumption" that reference universally recognizable "company logos" and "multinational brand names"; non-places are powered by "cable and wireless networks," while reducing us to "solitary individuality" (Augé 2008: 63–66, 82–86).

In terms of the empirical snapshots that frame this chapter, Marc Augé's analysis provides crucial contextualization related to the wider structural shifts Western-style consumerism, its associated practices, and spatial manifestations have undergone over the last few decades. At the same time, the locality sketched above also calls for a fine-tuning of Augé's framework. What the figures and account above show is that the *non-places* of our age, which are largely places of consumption, also have "hinterlands": those provide the wider and essential infrastructural bases and links that enable and power supermodern consumption. Augé himself points out (2008: 28) that there are "installations needed for the accelerated circulation of passengers and goods (high-speed roads and railways, interchanges, airports) [that] are just as much non-places as the means of transport themselves, or the great commercial centers, or the extended transit camps where the planet's refugees are parked." This having been said, however, there is a mismatch between the attention the "front regions"— in reappropriation of Erving Goffman's terminology (1990)—of our age of consumption have received, as opposed to the relative neglect with regard to their "back regions." Concerning the former, seminal contributions to the sociological literature have done much to illuminate the organizing principles and cultural-symbolic logics of contemporary consumerism, including tendencies of *McDonaldization* (Ritzer 1993) and *Disneyization* (Bryman 2004). Written into those, as well as into Augé's analysis, is a more or less tacit assumption that contemporary consumerism is tantamount to at least a degree of homogenization, be it in the shape of the standardization of products, the global spread of particular signs and sign systems, or what we will encounter in Chapter 3 as the "containerization" (Martin 2016) that enables today's global commodity and transport chains. The locality described above indeed provides ample corroborating evidence of such tendencies toward global sameness. However, it also provides indications of powerful countertendencies and, at times, reactionary localisms that are perhaps particularly likely to manifest in some of the hinterlands to supermodernity's *non-places*. The question thus arises as to which additional conceptual strands are required to complement Augé's account.

Some necessary, additional analytical momentum is provided by the late Zygmunt Bauman's wide-ranging analyses of the characteristics of *Liquid Modernity*: this is essentially the contemporary phase of modernity, in which widening inequalities, chronic uncertainties, hyper-individualism as much as the reactions and frustrations it breeds, as well as a disorientating flux have come to define our lives. Bauman's thinking about the here and now spanned numerous topics and multiple books, which came to define his *oeuvre* during the later phases of his prolific career (Bauman 2000, 2001, 2003). Two central arguments from this formidable body of work are especially pertinent to my argument here. First, Bauman offers an account of globalization and its *human consequences* (Bauman 1998) that centers on a novel disjunction of capital and labor: while in an earlier, solidly modern phase, industrial production was more or less wedged to particular places and their working populations, this former, structural connection has been severed in times of multinational corporations capable and willing to relocate, or "outsource," to where labor costs and taxes are lower and production is therefore more profitable. Bauman (1998, 2000) summarizes the net effect of this disjuncture as a new state of affairs, in which capital has become mobile, or "nomadic," while many lives, and often experiences of hopeless misery, have remained local. While this part of Bauman's analyses of liquid modernity relates to two of the extremes of the contemporary condition (i.e., global riches and the local hopelessness experienced by those left behind and abandoned by fickle capital and disempowered national politics), the second pertinent strand formulates a proposition concerning the cultural-cum-political "logic" underpinning contemporary consumerism. The latter, Bauman claims (1991: 98), constitutes an essentially conservative social practice insofar as it is through our consumption practices and identities as consumers that social reproduction is accomplished; while a generation or two ago individuals derived their sense of identification and belonging from their occupational positions, this has now shifted and been inadequately replaced by often atomizing self-identifications defined by commodities consumed and leisure practices performed. Clearly, Bauman's largely agency-denying account of consumerism can be contested (e.g., Fiske 1989) and the suggestion here is not that his is the only plausible reading of our consumer society. However, his argument poses thought-provoking questions. Consumerism, Bauman has suggested, is a conservative way of relating to the world around us since it seduces us into "docility"; we may paraphrase this part of Bauman's analysis as the proposition that as long as we consume, we are unlikely to question, let alone resist, a social order of steep inequalities and only loosely held together by a culture of individualizing consumerism.

Although Bauman's ideas about liquid modernity are relevant to, and should form part of our analytical arsenal as we approach localities such as the one described above, they arguably do not go far enough in helping us understand the workings and far-reaching effects of capitalist expansion, or some of the local responses triggered by it. For that, we require a longer and distinctly interdisciplinary theoretical lens. Of central significance in this regard is the magnum opus of the economic historian Karl Polanyi. In 1944, Polanyi published *The Great Transformation*, a book of extraordinary reach and scope. In it, Polanyi traces the history and long-term consequences of the industrial revolution and the rise in the nineteenth century of what the author depicts as a historically novel phenomenon, namely a "market economy." This must not be misunderstood. Market exchanges most certainly long predated industrial modernity. However, the sociological or anthropological novelty of the latter, according to Polanyi, consisted of two interrelated and truly groundbreaking developments. Two of the most influential and enduring Polanyian concepts describe those: first, the notion of a now suddenly *disembedded economy*; second, the appearance of particular *fictitious commodities*. The novel phenomenon of a "self-regulating market," Polanyi argued, gave rise to a historically unique disjuncture between formerly closely and mutually integrated domains of life. The result was for the first time a *dis*embedded economy, which Polanyi characterized as follows:

> [T]he change from regulated to self-regulating markets at the end of the eighteenth century represented a complete transformation in the structure of society. A self-regulating market demands nothing less than the institutional separation of society into an economic and a political sphere [...] True, no society can exist without a system [...] which ensures [...] the production and distribution of goods. But that does not imply the existence of separate economic institutions; normally, the economic order is merely a function of the social order [...] Nineteenth-century society, in which economic activity was isolated and imputed to a distinctive economic motive, was a singular departure. Such an institutional pattern could not have functioned unless society was somehow subordinated to its requirements. (Polanyi 2001 [1944]: 74)

Polanyi argued that part and parcel of this era-defining rupture at the heart of the social fabric, only as a result of which our very understanding of *the economy* as a stand-alone (and increasingly dominant) domain of human activity became possible, was the commodification of the three core factors of production, namely *labor*, *land*, and *money*. In formulating his second main proposition, Polanyi of course knew that labor, land, and money had long been part of, and been required for, any systems of production. However, where nineteenth-century market society departed radically from previous eras was in redefining labor, land, and money as "objects [...] for sale on the market":

> None of them is produced for sale. The commodity description of labor, land and money is entirely fictitious. Nevertheless, it is with the help of this fiction that the actual markets for labor, land and money are organized; these are being actually bought and sold on the market; their demand and supply are real magnitudes [...] Undoubtedly, labor, land and money are essential to a market economy. But no society could stand the effects of such as a system of crude fiction [...] unless its human and natural substance as well as its business organization was protected against the ravages of this satanic mill. (Polanyi 2001: 76–77)

This anticipates Polanyi's third proposition, in which his analysis of the long-term consequences of the self-regulating market culminated.

The disembedding of the economy, coupled to the mis-construal of labor, land, and money as commodities, was—according to Polanyi (and in an observation particularly prescient of later environmental degradation)— bound to result in chronic crises that ultimately threatened the very foundations of production and human cohabitation. This led to a number of ideologically highly diverse "countermovements," some of which were in turn mutually antagonistic (i.e., the political polarization between socialist and fascist reactions against capitalist crisis), against a "dislocation [...] [that] would have destroyed the very organization of production [...] the market had called into being" (Polanyi 2001: 136). This is the essence of Polanyi's postulated *double movement*, pitting diverse societal reactions against ever-expanding market forces.

While Polanyi's initial impact was particularly pronounced among economic anthropologists trying to understand the particularities and social consequences of industrial capitalism, his premises and conclusions have certainly not been without their critics (see Karner and Weicht 2016: 6–20). Notwithstanding those, the period since the financial crisis of 2007/2008 has seen a renaissance of interest in and scholarship about Polanyi (e.g., Dale 2010). Among those calling most forcefully for a return to, followed by critical amendments of, Polanyian premises has been Nancy Fraser. In a series of outlines of contemporary capitalist crises, Fraser argues for a "neo-Polanyian" approach (Fraser 2011, 2014). This applies a selective updating of Polanyi's *The Great Transformation*, through which new insights into current circumstances become possible. Avoiding the romanticization of preindustrial societies of which some of Polanyi's critics have accused him (Booth 1994; Karner and Weicht 2016: 9), Fraser rightly insists that exploitative structures and deep social crises are not unique to capitalist modernity only. However, in order to illuminate the particularities of contemporary capitalism in what are often described as its neoliberal manifestations, Fraser argues for a replacement of the Polanyian double movement with what she terms a "triple movement." This revolves around three distinctive vectors of social change, which Fraser calls *marketization, social protectionisms*, and *emancipation*. Marketization refers to the continuing and accelerating tendency toward expanding the scope and reach of what is being commodified (see below). The second continuity with Polanyi's thought emerges from what Fraser describes as various types of social protectionisms—importantly Fraser here distinguishes between "savory" and "unsavory" protectionisms—that constitute contemporary forms of "countermovement" against the dislocations and crises brought about by marketization. Finally, emancipation describes the diverse strategies of struggle and attempted empowerment employed by or for those enduring exclusion either in the realm of the market or indeed at the hands of the "unsavory," often nationalist, social protectionisms that reassert social hierarchies and political boundaries (Fraser 2011). The conceptual line stretching from *The Great Transformation* to such a neo-Polanyian approach becomes yet more apparent when Fraser argues for a carefully historicized and current widening of the concept of "fictitious commodities": this, Fraser argues, enables us to recognize how current crises connect to today's ever-widening market domains; a historically unprecedented commodification of formerly extra-economic realms is arguably indeed at work in today's markets in, for example, carbon emissions, biotechnology, care work, or financial derivatives (Fraser 2014).

With our conceptual apparatus for the present chapter thus in place, I next return to the methodological-cum-analytical claim being made here: that photographs can help us take the step from macro-theoretical propositions to very specific localities, and then—yet more specifically—to little-known, little-used vantage points within them; in another argumentative step, that the theoretical strands outlined here resonate in, and can help us read, what is seen and captured from such vantage points. Finally, and as we shall see, the results also raise considerably bigger questions about sociology's wider societal significance.

Evasive Answers and toward a Reflexively Public Sociology

Several features of my brief sketch of one of the countless localities that have been profoundly reshaped, and continue being reshaped, by the wider dynamics and social forces created by contemporary capitalism warrant revisiting and elaboration. First, what I offered at this chapter's outset was little more than a descriptive account, and one heavily tinged by my own experiences in and reflections on the locality in question. My mere mention of the political leanings of the majority of our former neighbors will suffice to have me accused, in some political quarters, of lacking scientific objectivity, at least in this particular descriptive account. To counter such potential counters, and to thereby make a more explicit case for a particular sociological approach, let me point out the following. At no point did the earlier account suggest that the dominant political leanings in my then surroundings were a priori "wrong," to be ridiculed or beyond comprehension. On the contrary, my self-positioning as a self-defining European in this particular locality served a vital scientific purpose: an example of what sociologists sometimes characterize as *reflexivity*, it served to position my own biography and subjectivity in a particular context, and to thereby draw attention to particular political tensions that are indeed ubiquitous in places like the one I described. In other words, such reflexivity—sometimes associated with *standpoint theory* (e.g., Collins 1990) and its central postulate that we all experience the world from the confines of our particular subject positions relative to wider configurations of power, inclusion, and exclusion—actually enables us to notice facets of social life that would otherwise elude us. It was the tension between my own political positions and those of many around me at the time that helped me ask the key sociological questions in places such as the one described: What are the wider social changes that have impacted on people's local lifeworlds? How have the latter been affected? And might we need to understand local politics in relation to such far-reaching and seemingly unstoppable changes? Crucially, the result can be an engagement with people and places that neither condones nor condemns, instead, it contextualizes.

At the same time, the earlier descriptive account serves as another illustration of an argument that accompanies us throughout this book: namely that contemporary social changes widely associated with globalization challenge us to refine our individual and disciplinary skills at observing, listening (Back 2007), smelling, tasting, and in short perceiving both the subtlety and at times the monstrosity with which social forces and dislocations impose themselves on us. It is precisely this that a sociology of glocalization can and must provide. This is no easy task. It is sometimes not at all clear how we get from a vague sense of our own and other people's disquiet about the scale and direction of current changes to a clear and systematic approach to capturing this empirically. My observations at the start of this chapter are no more than sketches of what needs to be done next. And even such preliminary sketches take time, patience, unusual approaches (like the one taken via a footpath known to only very few in an era dominated by our collective reliance on cars, smartphones, and internet shopping) and setbacks. It was only after five months in the area and many kilometers walked and run in all directions that I finally managed to find the particular vantage point, from which the photographs above were taken. It was this vantage point that enabled me to finally see what I had merely sensed up until then: that the area and the people living in it were suffering, not materially, but environmentally, being deprived of more and more space that previous generations would have taken for granted and that is now confiscated by some of the most powerful actors of transnational capitalism. It was from the particular angle the above photographs were taken from that some of Marc Augé's most memorable postulates about today's transformation of concrete, "anthropological places" and their local meanings became empirically discernible: what the figures above indeed provide snapshots of is the ongoing "reconstruction of places" through "acceleration and de-localization." In the face of the environmental and other "upheavals of the present," Augé continues, "the past" tends to acquire an "illusory [...] stability": "When bulldozers deface the landscape, the young people run off to the city or 'allochthons' move in, it is in the most concrete, the most spatial sense that the landmarks—not just of the territory, but of identity itself—are erased" (Augé 2008: 32, 39). All of this resonates strongly in Figures 1.1 and 1.2 or, more accurately, in their mutual juxtaposition. Where Figure 1.1 shows an "anthropological place," whose long- and short-term histories are known and meaningful to residents, past and present, Figure 1.2—taken a mere stone's throw away—captures what happens once the bulldozers arrive. What the juxtaposition of the two photographs does not portray is the timeline: the way in which multiple building projects have encroached on the original anthropological place, the town in question, from practically all direction for many years, and how they continue to do so. What is left of the original town now finds itself squeezed, or trapped, between the airport, motorways, A-roads, and growing numbers of logistics and distribution centers; of the roads leading into and out of town, only one still opens up—for a short stretch of a couple of miles—onto the kinds of fields seen in Figure 1.1. And even or especially from there, finding oneself right below the airport's flight path and in the immediate vicinity of the often even noisier race track, one is a long way from "the countryside" as we might imagine it.

It was thus only from a very particular vantage point—remember: a little used, fenced-in path between logistics centers and an airport—that I could finally see the full scale of how a small town is being dwarfed, and arguably suffocated, by the infrastructural investments and encroachments made on it from all directions. The nostalgic quest for some sense of "community" that probably never was (Bauman 2001) becomes far less surprising, when seen in this light. One need not necessarily be versed in the details of post- or neo-Marxist theorizing, although it helps, about capitalist accumulation, reinvestment and expansion (e.g., Harvey 1989) to sense what is happening, and its environmental and social consequences, around the world. We need not, and in all likelihood will not, agree on a single political counterstrategy. In the first instance, we need to be able to see, hear, and smell the evidence. The "sensing" and capturing of contemporary changes afoot is already a difficult enough task. Yet, this is a vital step, for which a sociology underpinned by a rich and growing methodological arsenal can be of crucial help. With that in mind, let us reconsider the photographs above, paying particular attention to the scales depicted: the size of the logistics hubs, when compared to how small the town is; the latter's proximity to both the distribution centers and the airport, which—remember—starts just on the other side of the fence and path shown in Figure 1.3. Figures 1.2–1.5 depict the local arrival of what Zygmunt Bauman (1998) describes as today's global, "nomadic capital" and its relative disconnection from surrounding communities, at least when compared to the previous era's local embeddedness of capitalist factory production which then still relied on the availability of local workers. By contrast, note in Figures 1.3–1.5 the two "layers" of fencing surrounding (or protecting?) the distribution hubs whose employees either drive or take overcrowded buses from elsewhere to their place of work. The latter's connections to our wider circuits of distribution are what matters most here, the immediate proximity to the airport and to the national motorway network is of course anything but accidental, and the architecture of the distribution centers reveals (or conceals?) what goes on inside them: these are huge storage spaces for our era's transnationally circulating commodities. These enormous warehouses, as is discernible in parts of Figure 1.3, conveniently open up to multiple docking and loading bays for the lorries that then take those commodities on their onward journeys.

Now imagine what the town (Figure 1.1) nearby and its surroundings might have been like, a generation or two ago. This is not an invitation to legitimize political nostalgia, but merely to put our *sociological imagination* to work: to follow C. Wright Mills' seminal definition of the sociologist's craft as revolving around the ability to detect structures and histories behind the biographical. Finally, try to imagine what life is like, double-glazed windows and all, for the residents of a town located right next to an airport where planes, of the cargo and chartered variety, land and take off all night, every night, all year. To switch back into an analytical register, what Figures 1.2–1.5 also convey is the scale and reach of the commodification of formerly agricultural land in the twenty-first century. Whether or not readers are convinced by the Polanyian conceptualization of land as a "fictitious commodity," the claim that there are locally experienced social and environmental consequences to ever-expanding marketization, à la Nancy Fraser, appears hard to refute in light of the photographic evidence above. What were farmers' fields passed down families' ancestral lines until not long ago, has become meta-commercial space: land sold and bought—by large corporations—and then used for no other apparent purpose than the handling of other commodities. Put differently, these particular hinterlands and distribution nodes required by our contemporary consumption practices are commodified stretches of land whose sole purpose is to facilitate further commodification, or marketization "squared," so to speak.

Finally, my earlier account and what it depicts also raise some crucial questions about Michael Burawoy's (2005) famous definition of *public sociology*. Burawoy encourages us to return to arguably the most important question of all: namely why do sociology? Who or what is it all for? Burawoy's answer is as nuanced and thought-provoking as any ever provided. Reminding us of our multiple audiences (i.e., from students, fellow sociologists, our departments, and associations to the disenfranchised civil societies and policy makers), Burawoy distinguishes four types of sociologies, their mutually enriching forms of knowledge and (potential) contributions to the world. He terms them *professional, critical, policy,* and *public* sociology. Our wider context today, Burawoy points out (2005: 4; 6), is one in which "[u]nfettered capitalism fuels market tyrannies and untold inequities on a global scale" and in which "[g]lobalization is wreaking havoc with sociology's basic unit of analysis—the nation-state." Localities like the one described above can help us see precisely those much larger forces at play, as they "touch" down in and alter particular places and the lives lived therein. At the same time, the specific historical moment I spent in the locality in question also encourages a certain updating of some of Burawoy's observations. Nation-states, which—more than merely yesteryear's chief units of sociological analysis—have also become over the last century and a half the taken-for-granted institutional and symbolic backdrop and setting for their citizens' lives (Billig 1995; Karner 2020a), are currently experiencing a palpable renaissance, a restaging and reassertion against some of the forces of globalization and marketization discussed here. Given the history of nationalism, as the ideology legitimating a (world of) nation-state(s),[4] and the central role nationalism played in the exploitations, polarizations, and atrocities committed throughout the nineteenth and twentieth centuries, such a renaissance should give us very grave cause for concern, especially in light of the historically myopic, neo-nationalist frenzies whipped up at present and across many parts of the world. With the required sociological imagination, standing in May 2019 at the vantage points from which the photos above were taken, this too could be sensed. What is more, in alerting us to the diverse, "social protectionist" counterreactions against marketization in evidence today, Nancy Fraser (2011) provides us with a conceptual category for phenomena such as Brexit, which—as my account above has made clear—formed a crucial part of the overall "picture" encountered in this particular locality, and numerous others like it, in the spring and early summer of 2019. Whether this particular social protectionism is classified as "unsavory" or not will in all likelihood depend on our normative and political positions.

Thus, against the backdrop of the relentless capital and infrastructural investment in an area overwhelmed by the scale of change, local support for Brexit can indeed—following Nancy Fraser's typology—be read as an example of *social protectionism* against marketization and of rigid exclusion of "the other." The photographs above tell parts of the wider story to this.

They do not condone, my self-definition as a European is far too pronounced and my encounters with local Brexiteers were far too antagonistic for me to ever condone their politics, but as sociologists we also have to look, listen, taste, feel, and smell more carefully. We have to push through the pain of confrontation, disagreement, disappointment, and otherwise silently accepted self-righteousness and bewilderment to somehow get to the context. Once we have captured some of the locally relevant context, we ought to ask ourselves which of Burawoy's four sociologies we are able to contribute to and how. In the case of the particular reflections offered earlier, the most plausible answer is that the contextualization provided there has the potential to generate forms of *critical* and *public sociology*. Burawoy (2005: 10) defines the former as the "conscience of professional sociology" insofar as it critically reflects upon the discipline's "foundations—both the explicit and the implicit, both normative and descriptive." This entire book, and within it each of the case studies and phenomena examined, is geared toward such a critical reexamination of the suitability of established sociological paradigms in capturing, depicting, and comprehending today's social changes. With regard to public sociologies, Burawoy (2005: 7) defines those as attempts to bring "sociology into a conversation with publics, understood as people who are themselves involved in a conversation"; such publics are themselves internally highly heterogeneous, comprising a diversity of groupings, associations, and counter-publics of the historically marginalized and oppressed. We should not expect sociology to easily resolve any of the conversations in question, or to act as the final arbitrator. Or in the words of Burawoy, public sociology "has no intrinsic normative valence, other than the commitment to dialogue" (2005: 8). In cases and places such as the one to which I keep returning for the present discussion, there are indeed no simple resolutions, no straightforward alliances between the sociologist and a particular political blueprint or policy suggestion. Sometimes it is our task to emphasize just how protracted, complex, and contradictory the sets of issues around which public conversations unfold are. Sometimes it is precisely the task of public sociology to insist on complexity and to show why there are no simple solutions, answers, or culprits.

In the particular location in question, there is every reason to argue that people suffer from a form of environmental deprivation directly related to infrastructural overinvestment in their area. The earlier photographs testify to this. A public sociology should include an element of *defamiliarization* (Barthes 2000 [1957]) to demonstrate that what may be widely regarded as "inevitable" is the outcome of political decisions and the manifestation of deeply sedimented ways of life and engrained, culturally shared ideas. Sociology needs to record all this, but it also needs to retain its willingness to criticize it, to entertain alternatives. Pointing out the utter absurdity of having train stations that can only be reached by car is a perhaps trivial, but necessary example of this. It could also include pointing out the following: on the little cul-de-sac, one that certainly is not in the more affluent parts of town, on which my wife and I lived for six months, there were considerably more cars than adult residents. In fact, ours was the only household with two adults and only one car. No matter what the infrastructural circumstances, a public sociology—particularly at a point in history when, at long last, growing numbers of people are waking up to the urgency of the climate crisis—needs to be prepared to raise questions about such patterns of car ownership and dependency. Local residents are not just victims of forces and changes beyond their control, they are of course also participants in them. The logistics centers and distribution hubs depicted above are of course structurally directly related to our internet shopping delivered straight to our homes. At the same time, those logistics centers are also a much-needed place and source of employment for large numbers of people across the region. The buses dropping workers off, and collecting them nearby, before and after they make their way—still on foot—to and from the distribution centers at nearly all times of day and night are constant reminders of this.

Before we allow ourselves to get too romantic (and in some cases too self-righteous) about emerging subcultures of green or ethical consumerism or the hopes we may invest in the next generation, there are further critical questions to be asked. Of course, people differ in their carbon footprints, their sense of shared responsibility and potential agency vis-à-vis our shared planet and futures. These differences entail different lifestyles and political choices that matter. At the same time, it is similarly apparent that different parts of the world contribute at highly differential rates to the crises humanity faces today. Put bluntly, the more affluent make by far the greatest contributions to environmental crises in particular, and to them (i.e., "us") therefore also goes the lion's share of responsibility for the state of the world. Change surely must, if not start, then at least go through them, through us, the relatively or undeniably privileged among the world's population. Yet, this is also a trivial and incomplete "truth." It is incomplete because we ought to know that although many of the world's crises are disproportionately due to the actions and lifestyles of the advantaged, many among the rest are aspiring to the same, collective and potentially self-destructive lifestyle, and the postindustrial parts of the world are showing relatively few signs of truly changing, or wanting to change, course. It is at this point in the argument that we might return to Zygmunt Bauman's critical assessment of consumerism as an essentially conservative social force, one that fosters a docile acceptance—and inadvertent participation in, or even reproduction—of the uncertainties, inequalities, and crises of our liquid modern world. As suggested by my brief allusion above to potentially more reflexive consumerist subcultures, Bauman's provocative propositions about consumerism need to be read as precisely that, mere suggestions—rather than declarations of fact—that pose open questions and call for further empirical research. What is at stake here goes far beyond sociological debates and relates to our very collective futures: Can consumerism be ethical, politically reflexive, and critical? If so, where can we discern such critical consumerisms? How is their effectiveness to be judged? These are complex questions that can only be posed here. They relate to localities such as the one that has framed this chapter, yet these questions also go much further. It is my hope that this chapter, and the present book in its entirety, will invite more discussion of these crucial issues of our times.

The just mentioned proposition that even, or perhaps especially, the world's comparatively privileged are showing few signs of willingness to self-critically reflect upon the multiple impacts of our consumer lifestyle is also incomplete because it implicitly works with the idea that history and hence social change are plannable and designable. Instead, we need to remember one of the social sciences' most powerful concepts, that of the "unintended consequences" (e.g., Merton 1936) of our and others' actions. Retranslated into the context in question, we must remember that no one buys a second, third, or fourth family car *in order to* add to climate change, any more than we buy our groceries or books via our smartphone apps *in order to* exacerbate the problem of roadside- and general plastic littering or to hasten the decline of town centers and traditional shops. At the same time, our hyper-technologized world is so full of complexity and unintended consequences that even the most reflexive and ethical consumers cannot help some entanglements in production and distribution chains, and consumption practices, the effects of which run counter to what they intend. It suffices to remember, for instance, how little privileged consumers in the affluent parts of the world know about the (rare) metals, and the conditions under which they are mined, that go into our smartphones and "power" ever larger parts of our lives, irrespective of our professed political positions and ethical leanings.

So what is the alternative, I hear some of my readers mutter. As social scientists, we know that humans have not always lived with our now seemingly overpowering and unquenchable thirst for information, entertainment, and consumption. We know that for long stretches of our species' history, our hunting-gathering ancestors lived with an altogether different ethos, which a famous anthropologist once described as a "Zen road to affluence" and an economy of subsistence and modesty, in stark contrast to our era's obsession with "infinite needs" (Sahlins 1974). Again, for an era to have a dominant ethos is not to deny the laudable and necessary existence of subcultural enclaves that reject precisely such a dominant *habitus*. But the undeniable reality remains that even today's most outspoken and passionate critics struggle to explain if or how our era's central circle could be squared: how to envisage—let alone achieve—a new, sustainable and inclusive growth that could meet ever-growing consumer demands and expectations, that might even ensure employment and dignity for everyone, without inflicting further, potentially irreversible damage to our environment and the coming generations' future. The hunter-gatherer's contentment with the bare necessities cannot provide a viable blueprint for humanity, soon to total eight billion people, in the twenty-first century. On such complex terrain, sociology will certainly not be able to provide all the answers. To think it could, would be naïve at best, and politically dangerous at worst, for we know how the boldest of political promises and blueprints also tend to generate some of the most damaging and dangerous of unintended consequences. What sociology can and must do is to complicate the discussions further, to insist on empirical and structural complexities, where others want to push for purportedly easy answers and solutions. In such circumstances, it is part of the task of public sociology to introduce additional questions, to point out contradictions, and to insist that public debate face up to such complexity.

We have come a long way from a footpath between an airport and commercial distribution hubs. In methodological terms, this chapter has not only made a general case for a reinvigoration of our sociological vision, but it has argued for a *looking for* the most appropriate vantage points, and for a *looking from* select angles that are capable of capturing recent social shifts and dislocations. Thus, the sociological imagination can enable us to see how the photographs above are connected to much wider, structural questions and dilemmas. Concurrently, much of the discussion in this chapter has also begun to point toward our increasingly global economic systems of supply, production, distribution, and consumption. It is yet further in this direction that we turn next.

Notes

1 At the June 2016 "in-out referendum," nearly 61 percent of voters in the area—and hence considerably more than the national average—had voted in favor of Brexit.
2 This also echoes Caroline Knowles' (2014: 15) search for appropriate "vantage-points," which she defines as relevant "viewing platforms," and the use of photography as part of her *travelling methods* along some of globalization's "backroads."

3 Andreas Reckwitz's account (2020: 100–101) of today's conversion of (semi-)rural locations into "flyover land" is pertinent here. The latter, Reckwitz argues, reflects the spatial marginalization endured by its residents; those are typically parts of the "old middleclass" whose loss of status, prestige, and economic prosperity are a feature of our late modern social structure.

4 There is important definitional work to be repeated here. "Ideology," a notoriously vague and often ill-defined term, is here taken to include ideas, language, and behavioral practices that are political insofar as they play a role, acknowledged or not, in either the reproduction or the subversion of existing power relations (Augoustinos 1998). The working definition of nationalism adopted here is Ernest Gellner's seminal description of nationalism as the attempt to make "culture and polity" congruent (Gellner 1983). Both concepts undoubtedly and strongly resonate in the UK's decision to leave the European Union, irrespective of one's potential (dis)agreement with this decision.

Chapter 2

THE (IN)VISIBLE WORLDS OF THE ECONOMY

A One-Hour Survey: Getting a Glimpse of *Financescapes* in Crisis

In his seminal *Banal Nationalism*, Michael Billig (1995: 110–127) reveals the ubiquitous, if largely unnoticed, discursive "flagging" of national identifications through what he terms an "illustrative day survey." Sampling British national newspapers on the relatively "ordinary" day that was June 28, 1993, Billig demonstrates how inescapable the distinctly *national* framing of headline news, political commentaries, sports reporting, weather forecasts and readerships is across the press, and how such daily "homeland-making" is an integral part of the routine reproduction of the institutions of the nation-state and of most of its citizens' widely unquestioned identification with them. Billig's argument continues to resonate in, and indeed depicts, some of the ideological conditions of possibility for features of glocalization such as nationalist counterreactions against global flows and interdependencies. Billig's day survey also poses more general, methodological questions as to how, twenty-five years on, other workings of glocalization and globalization may be captured. For that, it stands to reason that we may need to look to some of today's media with distinctly transnational orientations, international reach, and with a particular focus. Put differently, where are some of the processes and flows underpinning our glocalizing world encountered?

Reappropriating Billig's discursive-qualitative "survey" approach for different ends, we may, for example, wonder what satellite and cable channels exclusively dedicated to (global) financial markets, flows and investors depict and how. This is what I did, and recorded, in a shorter time-window, namely between 1:30 and 2:30 p.m. (GMT) on April 20, 2020. During this hour, as European markets reflected a difficult morning and the stock exchange in New York was getting ready to start its day, Bloomberg ran the following information recorded by the present author:

> The rapidly changing numbers reported from the FTSE MIB, the DAX, the IBEX 35, the EURO STOXX 50, the CAC 40 and the FTSE 100 flicker across the bottom of my television screen. This alternates with current exchange rates—GBP/USD, GBP/EUR, EUR/USD—and their similarly rapid changes, which are interspersed by graphs depicting how those currency exchange rates have fluctuated over recent days. I realize that all this is on loop, constantly changing rates and figures and all: I am next offered the commodity indexes for gold, silver, copper, platinum, zinc, nickel, lead, wheat, corn, sugar, coffee, cocoa, soy beans, natural gas and ICE Brent, accompanied by indications of their recent changes, positive or negative. Similar upward or downward trajectories for aggregate indexes (i.e. global, US, pan-European, for the US corporate sector) are presented thereafter, followed by updates on the most recent changes to the 2-year, 5-year, and 10-year yields on Italian, French, and UK bonds. All along, in a column down the side of the screen, and running in parallel to more detailed oral commentaries on individual news stories, a long list of headlines with a financial and economic focus are displayed and given brief summaries. Here is a selection of some of those headlines: "Singapore's daily virus infections top 1,000 for first time", "Turkey said to weigh capital injection for state owned banks", "Zimbabwe's currency plans upended", "Fitch downgrades Hong Kong as pandemic poses economic shock", "Italy's Conte calls for joint bonds", "Architect of UK austerity says retrenchment needed post-crisis", "Brazil analysts see further rate cuts", "Collapse of Canadian consumer confidence is finally slowing", "Oil rout may well signal bullish turning point for EM [emerging market] currencies", "Fracking crews are falling fast amid oil bust", "With crude oil in free fall, energy stocks also head south", "WTI oil falls 37%—biggest intraday drop since 1982", "US colleges bracing for devastating summer and fall", "Novartis joins bid to vet old malaria drug for Coronavirus". The news speaker now tries to inject "some good news" among all this: viewers are told of the US president's announcement of more aid, of a soon-to-be-expected "reopening of the economy", and of a delaying of some tariff payments. Against the backdrop of the countdown to the opening bell of the NY stock exchange, there are further announcements: of recent Netflix earnings and predictions as to which industries' profitability is likely to be "impaired" by the coronavirus "for a long-time". The news speaker's sobering assessment that it is "brutal in the oil market" is followed

by an interview with a *chief oil analyst* who explains today's top-story of "oil sink[ing] to weakest level since December 1998". Viewers are told that crude's drop is due to a global oversupply, at a time of near-global lockdowns and a veritable stand-still to international travel. With oil storage facilities rapidly filling up, oil is "plunging" and the airline industry is predicted "not to recover in months".

Apart from the very different media at the heart of *Banal Nationalism* and this exercise, respectively, there are other obvious differences between Billig's day survey in June 1993 and my much narrower "hour survey." The former considered all national newspapers published in the course of a day, whereas for the exercise above a single hour spent watching a single channel already yielded a hard-to-manage amount of observations, given that the channel in question offers multiple information flows and a rapid turnover of news items, graphs, interviews and commentaries from multiple contexts, from around the world, and all at once. Further, while Bloomberg's economic and financial focus is thematically much narrower than the British newspapers', its intended audiences are geographically much more widely dispersed. As the channel's repeatedly interspersed self-advertising illustrates, Bloomberg primarily addresses international investors. In between news items focused on global market players and regional economies, the channel reveals its primary intended audiences: claiming to have Europe and other parts of the world "covered," Bloomberg states that it "is analyzing" while "the world is watching"; what this means more concretely emerges from the promise of "interactive brokers [...] providing trading solutions"; emphasizing that investing involves "much more than gold and oil," Bloomberg describes its commodity indexes—for no less than 23 commodities—as enabling "true diversification [...] for your stock and bond portfolio."

Much of the terminology contained in the observations recorded above, as well as the world of stock exchanges and investment portfolios more generally, is likely to appear alien to many of this book's readers and indeed to many a sociologist. It is certainly not my intention here, nor would I be able, to offer definitional outlines or analyses of the financial structures, mechanisms and processes mentioned above. For this, there is a vast specialist literature in the areas of economics and finance. Instead, the observations generated by my one-hour survey serve a sociological purpose. They offer a snapshot of select aspects of our global economy, on a particular day, which—also in contrast to Billig's "day survey"—was anything but ordinary. On April 20, 2020, the world found itself in the midst of the global crisis and as of yet unknown but inevitably enormous economic consequences brought about by the Covid-19 pandemic, to which I shall also return in a later chapter for different analytical purposes. For now, what my summary of Bloomberg coverage in a very short time-window captures is a picture of a globalized economy, its constant flows and shifts, in a moment of profound crisis. Beyond that, the account above also alerts us to a particular, economically and politically enormously consequential social domain driven by specialist terminology and knowledges that lie outside most people's everyday understandings. Put more simply: unlike in Billig's day survey, we here see a specialist, less accessible, and distinctly transnational news medium operating in an extraordinary context. (Later that day, and unbelievably for an age of car-dependency and global trade, oil prices dropped further and even into negative territory, meaning oil producing companies were having to pay traders to take oil off them.) All of this also raises important epistemological and sociological questions.

This chapter and the next focus on select aspects of today's global economy. Contrary to "commonsense" misunderstandings, economies of course involve much more than the circulation of money.[1] When looked at through the lens of economic anthropology (i.e., through a comparative science of humanity focused on the social organization underpinning the allocation of resources and the material survival of groups and individuals), all economic systems involve processes of production, exchange and distribution, and consumption (Ferraro 1995: 151–172), highly contextually variable though those are. In the next chapter, I expand on these dimensions of economic life to also discuss, for example, some of our systems for dealing with waste products, as some of the (unintended) consequences of our economic lives in today's global era, and some infrastructural conditions of possibility underpinning it. In addition, later discussions return to how global financial flows, *financescapes* in Appudurai's terminology, unfold in parallel to other transnational flows: for example, those of people (*ethnoscapes*), ideas (*ideoscapes*) and more. More immediately, however, the present chapter seeks to accomplish two things: first, to discuss how and why the complexities of the domains broadly subsumed under "economics" and "the markets" pose difficult, much wider questions about the nature of social research and about the scale of social actors' knowledge of their own life-worlds; and second, to sketch some ways in which sociological research has begun to capture core aspects of the global economy, including the activities of key financial actors and our transnational chains of production and commodity circulation.

Scientific Detachment? Fuzzy Boundaries? A "Double Hermeneutic"?

By way of a conceptual and methodological grounding for the present chapter, it is worth pondering how the study of (global) economic connections maps onto qualitative sociology's conventional terrains. The allocation and distribution of resources (i.e., issues of wealth and inequality), the organization of production processes, relationships of exchange, and the workings of our consumer society—these are of course core issues in all our lives; they feature prominently in political manifestos, decide elections and shape competing positions that in turn constitute public debate. In other words, issues and phenomena broadly subsumed under "the economy," which in the current era invariably extends to distant places and transnational flows, form central aspects of all our life-worlds and lived experiences. As such, people of course have opinions about the economy, we all experience and interpret how processes and structures of production, distribution, consumption, resource allocation and waste management impact us and shape our lives. At first sight then, capturing such views and experiences—through the conventional repertoire of qualitative research methods (i.e., interviews, focus groups, ethnographic fieldwork)—constitutes an obvious starting point for a sociological engagement with economic matters. However, might we need to also ask ourselves what data thus generated might contain, as well as what it might conceal? Quite apart from people's opinions and experiences, how much do any of us know about some of the underlying structural processes, of which the "one-hour survey" offered above provided a glimpse? And can, or even should, a sociology of today's (global) economy seek to include not only people's views and interpretations, but also some of those wider flows and interconnections that are likely to elude most of us? If so, how might this be accomplished? And how does a sociological engagement with economic flows and interconnections differ from what specialist disciplines, most notably economics and finance, offer? To begin a discussion of these important issues, it makes sense to review long-established, competing understandings of what exactly qualitative social research captures and how this relates to, or possibly differs from, forms of everyday knowledge.

Financial and economic systems are perfect illustrations of the partiality and limitations of social actors' widely (and arguably wrongly) assumed "expertise in their own lives": as Les Back (2007: 12, *italics added*) suggests, a more realistic understanding of what sociology involves is the capturing of "*both* the insights *and* the blindness in the accounts of the people who live the consequences of our uncertain world," ideally tied to reflexive acknowledgement of sociologists' own "assumptions, prejudgments" and constraints. Put differently, and to bring this back to the hour survey above, how many of us—sociologists and non-sociologists alike—know how stock exchanges operate, how today's DAX, Dow Jones, or FTSE 100 are calculated, or what exactly they even are, what they reflect, what they impact and how, and what in turn shapes them? Yet, the far-reaching consequences, or the power, of our globally interconnected markets are impossible to deny. In due course, I turn to a selection of recent contributions to the sociology of economic life in our era of global connections. The particular studies and approaches, individually and collectively, help illuminate some of the multiple social domains constitutive of today's global economy. Further, the contributions discussed later also offer relevant insights into the expanding methodological arsenal required for a sociology of global flows and interdependencies. As a first step, however, what is required is a meta-discussion of long-standing debates about the complex relationship between everyday knowledges and (second-order) sociological knowledge. As already hinted, our era's economic complexities arguably re-inflect those debates in important new ways.

The study of complex systems, such as that of our global system of production, trade and consumption, poses questions as to how much individuals and groups know about the structures and processes that surround them; about how to access such knowledge; and about the relationship and difference between different types of accounts of the social world. In other words, we here come face to face with the epistemological questions as to how we know what we know or, perhaps more accurately, how we know what we think we know about the social world; and about who the "we" in such statements is taken to be (i.e., social researchers, social actors, or both).

There is a fundamental question at the root of sociological work, and at the heart of other branches of the social sciences, which, although often hidden from view, should always be born in mind: *(how) can sociologists come to know more about people and the social realities they inhabit than those social actors know themselves?* This question goes to the heart of the social scientific enterprise and it acquires particular salience to those working in the tradition of qualitative social research whose primary goal is to understand how others live in, experience and interpret their worlds. Constraints of space allow for no more than a sketch of three competing answers that point to intra- or sub-paradigmatic differences.

One position is epitomized by the aforementioned Pierre Bourdieu and his postulate of a fundamental distinction between ordinary social actors' commonsense and sociological knowledge. Everyday commonsense subsumes knowledge we acquire through our upbringing and socialization, it underpins our most taken-for-granted activities and our ability to deal with unforeseen circumstances. It is part of what Bourdieu (1977) calls *the habitus*—the (sub) culturally shared assumptions, ideas, categories, tastes, predispositions and cultural practices that structure our taken-for-granted ways of being and contribute to the reproduction of existing social structures. Such modes of thinking, feeling and acting form the subject matter of sociological reflection but they differ, according to this school of thought, from sociological knowledge: "As Bourdieu put it in *The Craft of Sociology*, 'the sine qua non for the constitution of sociological science' was 'the principle of non-consciousness', the a priori assumption that native agents remained unconscious as to the objective logic of their own practices" (Lane 2000: 96). In an essay entitled "The paradox of the sociologist," Bourdieu adds further nuance by considering the relationship between everyday classifications and sociological classifications, describing the latter as "second-degree classifications" (1993: 57). This acknowledges that all social actors order and interpret their world, whilst sociologists then in turn classify—and make sense of—those first-order classifications. In general, Bourdieu's conceptualization of a science of the social assumes that sociology occupies a relatively privileged vantage point, from which a logic underpinning the social world, one rarely noticed by those who live by it, is made apparent and subjected to (critical) analysis.[2]

By contrast, Zygmunt Bauman, for example, formulates a very different understanding of the relationship between "ordinary" meanings and sociological knowledge. Bauman distinguishes the social- from the "hard-" or "natural sciences" insofar as the latter constitute "discursive formations" with clearly defined and closely guarded boundaries. Put simply, those who are not biologists, chemists or physicists will usually not be able to contribute to those scientific disciplines, for research in the natural sciences tends to take place in separate social arenas, such as laboratories, and hence away from the realm of everyday life. This differs from sociologists who do not monopolize attempts to make sense of the social world. It is arguably a defining human trait to seek to understand the social world we inhabit. While the kinds of explanations generated differ, Bauman (1991: 73) emphasizes that "[s]ociologists, as commentators on human experience, share their object with countless others, who [...] legitimately claim a first-hand knowledge of that experience"; consequently, the "object of sociological commentary is an already experienced experience, coming in the shape of [others'] pre-formed narrative[s]," in relation to which sociologists cannot "make a reasonable bid for the superiority, let alone exclusiveness, of their commentary over the interpretations produced incessantly by the direct 'owners' of experience and by other [...] commentators (writers, poets, journalists, politicians, religious thinkers)." Put simply, Bauman suggests that the boundaries between sociological and everyday interpretations of the social world are porous, since they share their "objects of analysis."

A third position, which we may regard as a partial synthesis of these two contrasting perspectives, is condensed into the concept of the "double hermeneutic." Anthony Giddens (1984: 374) describes this as the "intersection of two frames of meaning" and as a "logically necessary part of social science": namely, first, "the meaningful social world as constituted by lay actors" and, second, "the metalanguages invented by social scientists," as well as a "constant 'slippage' from one to the other [that is] involved in the practice of the social sciences." At its simplest, this reiterates that (qualitative) social scientists offer a secondary interpretation of the lives and life-worlds already made meaningful—and hence interpreted—by the people studied. At the heart of all those scientific disciplines focused on "self-constituting symbolic realities" thus lies a "doubly interpretive process" that implicates what Dimitri Ginev has described as "symbolic self-interpretation" and "interpretive theorizing," respectively: the former pertains to human populations' "self-interpretive dimensions," the "native categories, classificatory schemes, and cognitive models" that shape "norms, rules of behavior, and the reality constructed by that behavior"; the second, or "external hermeneutic circle," meanwhile, involves theoretical abstractions and (re)interpretations of lived interpretations, which are offered by observing social scientists whose research in turn is "only possible within the context of interpretive communities of shared experimental and cognitive practices and specialized languages"[3] (Ginev 1998: 260, 261). This conceptualization reconciles two equally necessary dimensions of qualitative social science: description of how someone—an individual or group – experiences and views the(ir) world; and analysis on a "meta-hermeneutical" level that offers interpretations of interpretations. While the first "frame" contains and captures meanings as lived and told by the people sociologists and other human scientists study, the second, analytical layer makes sense of first-order meanings in their wider contexts and in light of relevant theoretical considerations. This defines sociologists' craft as one that depicts others' experiences and views of the world, in order to then— in a second but vital step—add contextualization and concepts, through which to order, understand and reflect upon that which has been recorded. Everyday commonsense thus feeds into sociological analysis,[4] providing it with some of its "raw data," but it does not exhaust what sociological analysis does and offers.

Much of what this book discusses can, epistemologically, be mapped onto these three different conceptualizations of sociological research: that is, sociological science as an uncovering of processes and logics those subjected to them are generally unaware of; alternatively, sociology as one of multiple commentaries on human experience; or the "double hermeneutic." Yet, each of these positions poses follow-on questions, including these: how can sociologists, à la Bourdieu, (claim to) see what eludes others? Alternatively, how viable or necessary is a science if, as Bauman appears to suggest in parts of his work, it regards its "commentaries" as merely one genre among many possible and equally valid ones? Or, with regard to any double hermeneutic: how are we to judge potential divergences between the two "frames of meaning"? Who is to judge the veracity of the secondary, meta-interpretation? The people whose interpretations are reinterpreted by social scientists? Fellow social scientists? Must there be a process of external corroboration, or triangulation, whereby other relevant data is presented to substantiate the credibility of the analysis being offered? These questions should be borne in mind in our reading of any piece of qualitative social science and the analyses it offers.

The subject matter of the present chapter, however, confronts us with a yet more fundamental question that matters to each of the paradigmatic, epistemological positions just sketched. This more fundamental question relates to *what* exactly social actors classify, interpret and comment upon. In some cases, for instance, in relation to the complex systems of our increasingly global economy, the gap and difference between what any of us think we know about the system and how it actually operates may indeed by very formidable. In such scenarios, what exactly is the rationale for recording everyday, "commonsensical" interpretations? How much and what exactly does social scientific analysis (need to) add to what social actors interpreting and commenting upon complex systems already state, know and do? This in turn arguably makes some of the epistemological positions above more or less plausible than the others. Beyond that, the existence of social domains whose workings elude our commonsensical understandings—just remember how little of the one-hour survey above is likely to be meaningful to non-investors or those not trained in economics—of course also underscores the need for separate social scientific disciplines focused exclusively on the laws, regularities and workings of the domains in question.

What the earlier one-hour survey also provides, then, is a reminder of how the detailed mechanisms and processes of the economy's workings are to many of us largely incomprehensible or at least opaque and not immediately accessible, in some cases invisible, and yet in their consequences they are far-reaching, ubiquitous and fundamental to our age of global interconnectedness. Many of the topics Bloomberg reported on April 20, 2020—from interest rates, bond yields and commodity indexes, to currency reforms and consumer confidence—are part of the intellectual terrain surveyed by economists and those trained in finance. At the same time, and as we shall discover in the next section, there are also distinctly sociological dimensions to the domains of the economy that warrant closer examination. Following Georg Simmel's (2018 [1908]) seminal, though too rarely employed definition of the sociological as comprising *Wechselwirkungen*, which are imperfectly translated as the mutual impact and interconnectedness between different actors and components of social life, such connections and reciprocal effects are also at work at all stages and in all realms of the economy. So-called ordinary actors who are participants in and invariably affected by global markets are likely to be able to offer the kinds of classifications, interpretations and commentaries qualitative sociologists typically pay attention to and which they evaluate, as we have seen, from any of the three epistemological positions summarized above. However, sociology needs to do more than just record such interpretations. Meeting the challenges of our times demands that we also pay attention to other aspects of economic life that reveal sociological phenomena at work. This, in turn, requires a sharpening of our concepts, a testing of our and others' assumptions, and an expansion of our methodological arsenal so that we may capture more than people's commentaries on today's global economy. Put differently, we need to also ask how sociological attention to economic matters can pan out in our current era of global interdependencies and local counterreactions.

It is my contention in this chapter and the next, that the contemporary, global economy presents a prime example of systemic complexity which demands detailed definitional work, fine-grained contextualization, methodological flexibility and innovation of (qualitative) sociologists. To put this another way: the more complex a system, the more partial and incomplete everyday knowledge of such a system is likely to be. This does not make research participants' own interpretations, or the first "frame of meaning" in the double hermeneutic, irrelevant, far from it. However, it does call the "people-are-experts-in-their-own-lives" assumption into question. And it strengthens the case for diverse, multidimensional research strategies that explore, capture and trace systems rather than "merely" asking people about them.

Financial Actors and Markets

Building on the general epistemological discussion of the previous section, we should ask ourselves precisely which economic domains demand our sociological attention. Without making any claims whatsoever to exhaust this big question, I would next like to review important sociological work that has been conducted at *some* key nodes in our global economy. The particular key nodes to be discussed here are the following: financial markets; transnational supply chains; and oil as simultaneously a key commodity in, and the very vehicle or condition of infrastructural possibility for, our era's global economy.

The first of these nodes therefore returns our attention to one of the key domains captured, in part, in my earlier one-hour survey, namely the realm of financial investments and transactions. At first sight, this hugely complex thematic cluster, and a quintessential domain of enquiry for economists and financial analysts, arguably appears rather removed from those aspects of social life most sociologists typically direct their attention toward. This having been said, there is a vibrant sociology of financial markets, some of whose major contributions—particularly until the financial crisis of

2007/08—helped illuminate the workings, decision-making and wealth generation facilitated on financial markets and by their key actors. Since the near-global economic downturn triggered by the crisis of 2007/08, major contributions have shifted the focus toward a critical reexamination of today's financial markets' structural place and wider social impact.

With regard to the former strand of scholarship, its fundamental premise is a recognition of "the role of financial markets as fundamental institutions of advanced societies" (Preda 2007: 506). Committed to uncovering the social dynamics of these institutions, this particular sociology of financial markets in turn underwent a succession of paradigm shifts with correspondingly changing foci. Those have been described as having variously constituted a *structural approach*, a *neo-institutionalism*, and *micro-sociological approaches to finance*. Structural approaches are underpinned by the realization that markets are more than mere places and mechanisms of exchange, insofar as they incorporate and presuppose wider social networks (Granovetter 1985). These include "micro-networks (defined by spatial vicinity on the exchange floor and close-knit relationships) and macro-networks" of wider "spatial distance and looser relationships"; all such networks play core functions in the generation of wealth by acting as channels of information "both about the objects being traded and about trading partners" (Preda 2007: 509, 510). Overall, structural approaches to financial markets thus recognize the importance of social relationships and networks, within which information is shared and trust is established in contexts of uncertainty due to "imperfect," rapidly changing information. In more general, conceptual terms, such structural analyses of the networks underpinning financial transactions and markets may be approached through classics of micro-sociology, from Erving Goffman (1990) and Harold Garfinkel (2004) to more recent ethnomethodological studies of how everyday social practices "do" and hence sustain social relationships and wider structures "bottom-up" (e.g., Lee 2006). In contrast to macro-sociology's focus on "large-scale social patterns" (Sanderson 1991: 2) and their historical transformations, micro-sociology foregrounds the continuous construction and reproduction of social realities through individuals' (inter-)actions. Akin to this, structural approaches within the sociology of financial markets illuminate the daily interactions and ongoing collaborative practices performed between individuals as the *conditio sine qua non* for the functioning of financial transactions. Markets certainly require the analyses, calculations and specialist knowledge provided by economists and finance specialists. At the same time, however, there are also sociological phenomena at work in what are generally recognized as economic realms; the daily interactions and underpinning networks constitutive of the economic domain of financial markets are precisely such sociological phenomena. In stating this, I invoke, as was anticipated earlier, Georg Simmel's famous recognition of the sociological dimension behind a wide range of phenomena that are primarily "claimed" by other social science disciplines: for example, space by geographers, political parties or voting behavior by political scientists, markets by economists. However, each of these also include distinctly sociological dimensions, which Simmel located in interactions, mutual dependencies or interpersonal impacts— all subsumed by the semantically rich German word *Wechselwirkungen.* What happens on trading floors, between brokers and investors, or more widely between interdependent and enduring economic partners cooperating over time, as well as the financial and social implications of such networks—or *social capital,* referring to relationships of reciprocity and trust—all also make for rich sociological terrain.

Neo-institutional conceptualizations, by some contrast, broaden the scope of enquiry yet further by locating financial markets within wider political institutions and culturally shared belief-systems: with regard to the former, neo-institutionalism examines "how financial markets shape modern societies" more generally, thereby extending Max Weber's insights that "financial markets are political institutions" in their own right, which demand a conceptualization of power as "the reproduction of specific (group) interests;" further, the state and its constitutive institutions are here shown not to be "the antonym of markets, but as deeply intertwined with them" (Preda 2007: 512, 515, 516). Second, by locating financial markets in their wider institutional and political contexts neo-institutionalism also offers a rethinking of economic behavior. Instead of a narrow and "a-historical perspective on economic rationality" as being exclusively about maximizing monetary benefits and minimizing costs, economic transactions are here recognized as being inseparable from "rituals, symbols and belief-systems"; consequently, the pursuit of "personal gain" is shown to be informed by "more than one reason" (i.e., the purportedly universal profit motif of *homo oeconomicus*) and to be culturally embedded in "broader worldviews" (Preda 2007: 512, 514). Projected back onto our starting snippets offered by the earlier one-hour survey, such a position acts as a much-needed corrective and contextualization of processes and realms that too often seem opaque and far-removed from our lived experience: shrouded in specialist terminology and knowledge and seemingly inaccessible to many though financial markets and processes may appear to be, their sociological study in its neo-institutionalist variant traces the structural and ideological lines of connection between this seemingly separate economic realm and some of the political institutions and cultural ideas that affect and surround us all.

The next sub-paradigmatic shift mentioned above, namely toward micro-sociological studies of finance, shifted the research emphasis (back) toward the production, circulation and stabilization of financial knowledge: in departure from the arguably narrow, structural emphasis on the implicated social networks, the focus was now extended to examine the roles played by individuals, collaborating groups, as well as by new technologies in the generation and circulation of the information enabling financial transactions and markets. Reflecting the complexities of twenty-first century financial flows in their "transcontinental trading environment," work produced by this more recent approach has foregrounded the uses of "formal models in trading," regulators' work, and—crucially—the "expansion of computer-supported trading" (Preda 2007: 521, 522, 526, 527). Projected back onto the observations generated by the one-hour survey that frames this chapter, this third sub-paradigm in the sociology of financial markets thus reveals the complex social worlds (rather than "merely" the economic structures, mechanisms, and processes) that also underpin the surface signs and information flows circulated via media such as Bloomberg: what appears as opaque but important and potentially intimidating financial data to the noninitiated, is thereby shown to be the result of the complex and ongoing decisions, collaborations and negotiations among different economic actors; of fluid market conditions that offer—by definition—the potential for both enormous financial gains and losses; and of specific regulatory environments and technological infrastructures.

The recognition of the impact of new technologies on financial markets, in particular, also reveals the need for careful historicization. Like all institutions, financial markets need to be located and analyzed in their specific technological environments and historical moments. Alex Preda's (2007: 525) insistence that "sociology's task [is] to analyse how (financial) markets connect with other social institutions (e.g., the state, the media), how they affect people's lives in ways other than economic and how they are perceived by larger society" further underscored the need for the financial realm to be contextualized more widely and more critically. This was subsequently shown most powerfully during the fallout to the financial crisis of 2008, which has been described as "not merely economic" but "structural and multidimensional" (Castells, Caraça and Cardoso 2012: 1). Driven by sociologists and others, critical contextualization of the events since 2008 has also led to a renaissance of interest in Karl Polanyi, whose magnum opus *The Great Transformation* was mentioned in the previous chapter, and in the questions associated with him. More accurately, some revival of interest in Polanyi actually predated the 2008-crisis. As early as 2001, two prominent forewords added to a new edition of *The Great Transformation*

(1944) already underscored the contemporary relevance of central Polanyian tenets. None other than Joseph Stiglitz (2001: x), recipient of the Nobel Prize in Economic Sciences the same year, observed that "the myth of the self-regulating economy" was already "virtually dead," that the enduring importance of Polanyi's work lay in its identification of "a particular defect in the self-regulating economy that has been brought back into discussion [of] the relationship between the economy and society [and] of the importance of social relations" as reflected in recognition of the far-reaching consequences of social capital (i.e., people's social networks of mutual trust and reciprocity). Fred Block, meanwhile, elaborated on the economy's wider, "social embeddedness" by returning to Karl Polanyi's argument concerning the disastrous consequences of turning land, labor and money—which had prior to industrial modernity not been treated as objects for purchase and sale—into *fictitious commodities*: according to Polanyi, "creating a fully self-regulating market economy requires that human beings and the natural environment be turned into pure commodities, which assures the destruction of both society and the natural environment" and triggers political counterreactions (Block 2001: xxv). As we saw in the previous chapter, the post-2008 context has seen further analytical developments along neo-Polanyian lines that have identified the marketization of formerly largely non-commodified realms (e.g., other elements of the natural environment, higher education, relationships of care) as the core of contemporary crises (e.g., Fraser 2014).

Casting our minds back, once again, to my earlier observations of Bloomberg's news items and information flows directed primarily at investors, much of the critical economic sociology since 2008 has insisted on a critical, structural contextualization of our financial markets. What to the intended audience is information enabling potential investment decisions, and to the non-invested (pun intended) may be no more than hard-to-follow, numerical measures of a purportedly distant and disconnected realm of activity (i.e., stock markets, commodity indexes, profit margins, bond yields, and currency exchange rates), has been shown to be premised on an underlying cultural logic that is neither "natural" (and hence unavoidable) nor—by any stretch of the imagination—harmlessly inconsequential. Parts of this critical literature draw relatively straightforward connections from Polanyi's original discussion—of how industrialization had ultimately led to the mutually antagonistic counterreactions that were fascism and socialism, respectively—to the situation post-2008. Gareth Dale (2010: 1), for instance, observed that once again "[s]tock markets [were] in meltdown. Trade, investment, output and employment graphs all point south. Protectionist stirrings are in the air. The prescriptions of free market liberalism are revealed as recipes for chaos." Polanyi's enduring relevance, so the argument continues, lies in the following:

> Its premise is that transforming land, labour and money into fictitious commodities endangers nature, human beings and business respectively, leading to grievances, resistance and imperative of protection [...] Through the extension of the freedom of contract to land [...] nature is transformed into an object of commercial exploitation. Turning labour into a commodity transfers control over people's livelihoods to "artificial" and volatile market forces and strips away all protection. (Dale 2010: 60)

Other parts of this critical economic sociology cast their conceptual web more widely, to investigate the entanglements of culture and the economy under specific historical circumstances. This can help locate today's economic flows and financial transactions in their wider social contexts, to problematize their conditions of possibility and (unintended) consequences. Insisting that "culture and institutions are the foundation of any economic system," Castells, Caraça, and Cardoso (2012: 4), for example, have argued that just "as the period of triumphant global informational capitalism was linked to [...] a culture of unrestricted individualism, economic liberalism, and technological optimism, any substantial socio-economic restructuring of global capitalism [will require] the formation of a new economic culture." In drawing our attention to how any economic system is embedded—in Polanyian terminology—in its particular cultural beliefs and values, this also enables us to put some important questions to our twenty-first century global economy. Some such critical questions, which can only be raised here, may include the following: What are some of the consequences, locally and globally, of the commodification of practically all natural resources and raw materials?[5] What are we to make of the profits generated by interest on someone else's debt? How sustainable is this? How legitimate and justifiable is the power given to rating agencies, whose judgments and predictions of a national economy's performance and trajectory impact not only bond yields but also millions of people's lives and futures?

Much of the particular genre of sociological writing, which I have described as a critical economic sociology, moves on epistemologically difficult terrain. Its focus on systemic aspects of our global(izing) economy means that long-established, qualitative strategies for collecting data based on asking people and giving them a voice are unlikely to suffice. After all, only very few of us can legitimately claim to be "experts" in the economic and financial aspects that power our global economy, nor in their equally opaque but undeniable entanglements with our era's cultural, technological and political (/ regulatory) dimensions. This does not mean, of course, that experiences of and perspectives on those dimensions are not worth recording and analyzing, they most certainly are, but it appears doubtful that this will be enough to sustain the kinds of discussions or to enable the types of insights concerning the *structural* features of our global economy mentioned in this section.

There are, however, other propositions in the literature that go a long way toward capturing *widespread perceptions* of the economic facets of glocalization. Some such propositions can help frame ethnographic and other qualitative attempts to understand some of the common discontent with globalization that we repeatedly encounter in this book. An example of such a framing is provided by Stephen Gudeman's (2012) argument that all economies subsume two different dimensions, which he describes as the realms of market competition and community/ "mutuality," respectively. Economies, Gudeman argues, are characterized by a "tension" between "competition and mutuality," "antagonism and community," implying that economic systems, when seen in their wider political contexts and social entanglements, "encompass more than most economists and everyday dogmas allow, and [are] more complex than most anthropologists [and sociologists] realize." More specifically, this means that there are two realms that sit alongside, though often not in easy articulation with one another: the market realm of "impersonal trade" in which "individuals live from competiti[ion over] goods, services and money that [is] separated or alienated from enduring relationships"; and a domain of *mutuality* or *community*, in which social relationships are "made, mediated and maintained" and where other—ideal typically non-commodified— "things and services are secured and allocated, by means of continuing ties, such as taxation and redistribution, through cooperation in kinship groups, households, and other groupings" (Gudeman 2012: 4, 5). However accurately Gudeman's account may capture the structural features of any particular economic system, there is no doubt that his distinction reappears in countless people's perceptions of the global economy. If we listen carefully enough, today's recurring discontent with allegedly overpowering market forces, in contrast to nostalgic accounts of yesteryear's purported (and now lost) "communities" (see Karner and Weicht 2016), testifies to this.

As merely one type, albeit a prominent and enormously consequential one, among the many nodes that constitute or enable economic flows and interdependencies, financial markets and transactions thus point both to the complexity of our global systems and to the epistemological challenges of researching them. There are numerous other such complexities and challenges, some of which relate to the sphere of contemporary production. It is there that we turn next.

From Transnational Chains to Their "Lubricant"

It is stating the obvious to point out that the complexities of today's global economy far transcend what a single book, let alone one of its constitutive chapters, can survey. My intentions here are far more modest: namely, first, to draw attention to concepts and associated clusters of scholarship that help illuminate some of the core junctures, phenomena and characteristics of today's global economy; and, second, to highlight the methodological headway required of, or already being accomplished by, such scholarship. While more modest, this undertaking still demands considerably more space than is offered by the present chapter. To counteract this, I thus now turn to a particular thematic cluster that will extend into the following chapter. The cluster in question relates to aspect of economic production today, its logic and conditions of possibility. The observations and arguments offered in this section should therefore be read as providing some of the required conceptual groundwork for the more elaborate discussions developed in the following chapter.

International system of production and distribution, as arguably most powerfully symbolized by multinational corporations (MNCs), are perhaps what most people associate most immediately with the term "globalization." It is this unhelpful reduction to merely one of its multiple and much more complex cross-border flows and transnational interdependencies that has given "globalization" its bad press of late, as was documented in the observations, with which I set the stage to the introduction of the present book. As we are about to discover, even with regard to systems of production, the trope of the all-powerful MNC constitutes an oversimplification; or more accurately, MNCs themselves need to be rethought as merely one possible manifestation of a bigger and considerably more varied phenomenon. The latter is what the specialist literature has variously defined as *global commodity chains, global value chains, global production networks*, or *global supply chain capitalism*.[6]

By way of a definitional starting point, a commodity chain comprises a "network of labor and production processes whose end result is a finished commodity" (Lee 2017: 1). On a very basic conceptual level, this describes any division of labor, within and between firms and other groups of organized economic actors, that structures and directs the systematic transformation of raw materials into items for sale and purchase. It is a function and sign of a globally increasingly interconnected economy, then, that such inter- and/ or intra-firm networks span greater distances and acquire transnational dimensions. Or, in the words of Coe, Dicken and Hess (2008: 274), the "interconnected nodes and links" of globalizing networks of production increasingly "extend spatially across national boundaries and, in so doing, integrate parts of disparate national and subnational territories." Reflecting the fact that the basic motivation of any capitalist enterprise orients it toward the generation of value, or profit, the associated terminology subsequently came to shift from (global) commodity chains to *global value chains*. Concurrently, and the focus on the "global division of labor and its functional integration beyond national boundaries" notwithstanding, research on this core dimension of today's economy is also fully cognizant of the fact that steep asymmetries of power and an often highly unequal "distribution of gains" and—in structural terms—of access to different stages of the production chain divide its "multiple nodes" (Lee 2017: 7, 2, 3). Translated into some of the basic terms of sociological theory that are often unhelpfully presented as mutually exclusive alternatives, *both* a functional division of labor *and* systems of inequality and exploitation coexist within, and define, the production processes accomplished in our epoch's organizationally complex and geographically far-reaching commodity-/ value chains. What is more, work in this area also addresses the wider question about the historicity—whether already "pre-modern," "modern, or distinctively "postmodern" (e.g., Martell 2017: 32–55)—of globalization. When applied more narrowly to geographically dispersed structures of production, it has thus been pointed out, for instance, that alongside the established view (e.g., O'Rourke and Williamson 2002) that "capitalism has been gradually globalized since the nineteenth century [...] the production activities [of] two major commodities"—namely ships and wheat flour—had "already spanned the globe [...] in the period from 1590 to 1790" (Lee 2017: 4).

Apart from such wider questions about the timing of the deeper historical shifts that have enabled the creation of economic networks across geographical distances, existing research on global commodity and value chains has been effective at capturing some of the relations of power and inequality structuring such production (see Lee 2017). Two paradigmatic examples suffice to illustrate this. Between them they illustrate how global value chains are hierarchical structures, in which market access, infrastructural capabilities, the "distribution of gains" or the ability to "upgrade from low to high-value activities" are highly unequally distributed and in some cases monopolized by the structurally most powerful economic actors implicated: the first study showed this with regard to the "global tuna chain," an increasingly competitive industry, in which—since the late 1980s—dominant Japanese and US multinationals have concentrated on distribution and retailing, leaving Pacific Island countries' fishing industries, located at an earlier "node" of the value chain, often with disappointingly low profit margins. The second example, again paradigmatically, relates to changes to "fresh vegetable value chains" against the backdrop of shifting consumer demands and expectations in the privileged parts of the global North since the mid-1980s. UK supermarkets, for instance, have since "begun to compete for a year-round offering of quality produce with a greater variety in rotation, and food safety concerns have demanded more control over suppliers' farming activities," leading to a growing reliance on "large contract farmers" to the exclusion of small-holders in Africa and elsewhere (Lee 2017: 6, 10).

Such direct interdependencies—examples of Georg Simmel's abovementioned *Wechselwirkungen*—between producers, suppliers and consumers also explain the terminological and conceptual broadening reflected in what have come to be called *global production networks*: such an approach extends from commodity or value chains to the full "nexus of interconnected functions, operations and transactions through which a specific product or service is *produced, distributed and consumed*" (Coe, Dicken and Hess 2008: 271, *italics added*). This broadened perspective also underpins Anna Tsing's (2009: 149–150, 156–157) influential conceptualization of *supply chain capitalism*. Under this she subsumes commodity chains that operate through mechanisms of "subcontracting and outsourcing," in processes that "span the globe [and involve] fragmented but linked economic niches." New technologies, "new regimes of profitability" (i.e., directed toward stockholders' expectations), and mechanisms of "super-exploitation" are all characteristic of this current phase in global capitalist production, for which Tsing considers Walmart to have provided "the model." Supply chain capitalism, Tsing argues, cuts labor costs and disciplines workforces across distances and boundaries, and across "ostensibly independent" but structurally and ideologically closely enmeshed and asymmetrically dependent entrepreneurs. Essentializing gender ideologies and stereotypes about purported cultural characteristics play their role in locking workers in exploitative conditions and in driving a supply chain capitalism, which works "not by coercion alone" but also by "tapping [into] performances of so-called noneconomic features of identity":

> Supply chain capitalism makes use of diverse social-economic niches through which goods and services can be produced more cheaply. Such niches are reproduced in performances of cultural identity through which suppliers show their agility and efficiency. Such performances, in turn, are encouraged by new figures of labor and labor power in which making a living appears as management, consumption, or entrepreneurship. These figurations blur the lines between self-exploitation and superexploitation, not just for owner-operators but also for the workers recruited into supplier enterprises. Through such forms of exploitation, supply chain capitalism creates both great wealth and great poverty [...] National and colonial histories—rather than "economic" functional requirements—explain the divergent trajectories of the chains. (Tsing 2009: 171)

In synthesizing attention to *both* structural *and* cultural features, and by examining asymmetric global connections in their very specific historical moment, Tsing's conceptualization illuminates more than merely supply chain capitalism. It also directs us to some constitutive dimensions of glocalization more generally. Put differently, we here encounter an example of social scientific thinking about the interplay of historical, structural, and symbolic conditions that possesses much wider pertinence to this book in its entirety.

By way of a conclusion to this chapter, it is vital to also remember some of the infrastructural and technological conditions of possibility underpinning the global chains and networks of production, value generation, and distribution that form a vital part of the transnational economy. In other words, what drives and enables systems of production across long distances and geographically disparate, but structurally interconnected "nodes"? Simply put, one of its quintessential conditions—or quite literally its very source of energy—is oil. In our current historical age, and given its technological logic and constraints, it is oil that powers many of our global flows, most certainly including core facets of today's transnational production networks, distribution circuits and markets. Caroline Knowles, in her study of some of the "backroads" of globalization to which I will return at greater length in the next chapter, makes the case yet more forcefully:

> Oil is not just central to globalisation, a fundamental, if fragile, vector of translocal connection, it literally constitutes it. To say that oil is globalisation is not an overstatement. Oil is fundamental because it makes globalisation possible. Providing the energy that transports people and objects around the world, oil is responsible for the time-space compressions that define globalisation. Global politics is shaped by the scramble to secure oil and distribute it around a shifting matrix of regimes. This central constituent of globalisation is also fragile [...] Growing militancy in the Middle East, also the location of the world's largest remaining oil deposits, disperses local sources of uncertainty globally. The rapid industrialisation of China and India, making them oil-hungry on an unprecedented scale, upsets existing calculations of global oil demand. Fluctuations in oil prices and supplies up end delicately balanced subsistence in the global South, by raising the price of basic foods [...] impacting balances of payment, while securing record profits in oil-producing countries. Oil constitutes the substance of globalisation itself. (Knowles 2014: 22)

This condenses core characteristics of the world in the early twenty-first century: our collective, systemic reliance on a slowly diminishing resource;

today's global inequalities and interdependencies—true *Wechselwirkungen* in Georg Simmel's terminology; geopolitical tensions and uncertainties; the multiple, far-reaching, economic and political consequences of fluctuating oil prices and their vastly different impact on different regions and localities. Oil is indeed and unquestionably a necessary and constituent feature of today's globalization, but it is not the only one, as the present book aims to show. Oil is part of the very base of resources and infrastructures that enable globalization, it is arguably the metaphorical power house of it all, the lubricant that makes the cogs of our global system turn. As we shall see in later chapters, however, there is yet more to the power house. Today's digital economy requires oil, among other technological and infrastructural preconditions. And our systemic reliance on oil has long been recognized, at least by the scientific establishment and by (global) citizens concerned about the climate crisis as a(n unintended) consequence of our oil-dependency, as also creating profound risks. If alternative technologies and sources of energy are to facilitate a profound and necessary shift in production and transportation in the years ahead, then this will undoubtedly alter economic systems and cultural practices the world over. Our environmental crises demand nothing less. But it seems highly unlikely that such a potential paradigm shift would simultaneously disable globalization in all its facets, that all global flows and interdependencies would cease along with a move away from oil. Put more simply, Knowles captures much about globalization, though not all of it.

To return, one final time, to the one-hour survey with which I started this chapter, I am of course writing these lines (i.e., in May 2020) against a backdrop that has changed profoundly since Caroline Knowles penned her insightful words about oil and globalization, relatively recent though this still is. The current Covid-19 pandemic has changed the parameters very suddenly and very profoundly, however temporary this change is likely to be. The sudden, dramatic drop in the oil price, as well as its far-reaching impact on our financial markets, were the big, global news on the day in question. The long-term consequences of this are as yet uncertain as I am writing this. But a version of the question just alluded to has suddenly indeed arisen: if we take Caroline Knowles' argument to its logical conclusion, we may need to wonder if in a situation when oil stops moving, whether globalization temporarily then stops, too. Are the current, pandemic-induced lockdowns tantamount to a temporary interruption to globalization? This would seem highly unlikely, or at least an oversimplified reading of the extraordinary circumstances captured in the one-hour survey above. Instead, and to anticipate a theme that will be explored in more depth and detail in a later chapter, it seems more plausible to shift the discussion from globalization toward glocalization and to recognize that various "blockages," of which the current crisis is a most dramatic example, are part and parcel of our "glocalizing" world.

As has already been hinted, this chapter needs to be read in conjunction with, and as a necessary thematic and conceptual springboard into, the following chapter. Jointly, the present chapter and the following one attempt to capture and illuminate some of the *economic* characteristics and dynamics—some of them prominent and well-known, others much less visible or easily accessible—of our current era of glocalization. Thematically, this chapter has therefore cast its glance in a range of directions: from financial markets and transactions, to global production chains and the centrality of oil to our global economy. At the same time, and in keeping with this book's overall focus, I have here also taken up the epistemological issue as to how sociologists and other social scientists can lay claim to knowing and understanding the complexities of our global systems. This, in turn, subsumes questions of both method—the *how* we go about identifying and collecting relevant data—and of conceptualization (i.e., the frames of interpretation and analysis then to be applied to the empirical materials thus collected). On this epistemological level, parts of the discussion in this chapter have begun to argue that the conventional, qualitative recording of people's experiences, opinions, values and interpretations, albeit all relevant, will not suffice to illuminate complex systems. For the latter (i.e., in order to illuminate the structural dimensions underpinning our social world rather than the culturally shared meanings amenable to being captured by a double hermeneutic), a wider and more innovative range of methodological approaches is needed. In the next chapter, our engagement with social phenomena that are, broadly speaking, part of our economic realm, will continue. The trajectory of the argument will take us yet further into this epistemological and methodological direction, in order to enquire how exactly some of the most innovative contributions to recent social science have attempted to bring the complexities of today's economic flows and interconnections into view. Taken in their entirety, the arguments presented in this chapter and the next resonate with observations first offered by John Law: namely that methodological adjustments in the social sciences are necessitated by the recognition that our era has "decentered subjectivities" (i.e., resulting in individuals with complex, shifting and multiple identities), that new "geographical complexities arise when intimacy no longer necessarily implies proximity," and that our "global flows are uncertain, unpredictable and indeed chaotic in the mathematical sense." "Many now think," Law continues, that "ethnography needs to work differently if it is to understand a networked or fluid world. The sense that knowledge is contexted and limited has become widespread, and feminists have talked about situated knowledges, while anthropologists have explored writing and receiving culture [...] So the world is on the move and social science more or less reluctantly follows" (Law 2004: 3).

In the next chapter, we continue to trace recent vectors and manifestations of social change and some particularly promising attempts by social scientists to "keep up" with the associated movements and flows.

Notes

1 Sociologically, money functions as a generalized medium of exchange/ payment, as a means of storing wealth and as a measurement of value (e.g., see Bohannan 1990: 262).

2 A different and stronger version of such an approach, and one informed by a different theoretical tradition, is encountered in the work of the French Marxist Louis Althusser. A structural Marxist, Althusser (2014) saw the workings of capitalist *ideology* in a wide variety of institutions, from the family to the church and media. Moreover, Althusser considered the capitalist mode of production (i.e., bourgeois ownership of the means of production and a proletariat forced to sell its labor power) to be, taken on its own, insufficient to guarantee the reproduction of a capitalist social formation. Such reproduction, he argued, required ideology, for without the aforementioned institutions capitalism would not be transmitted over time. In an Althusser-ian framework, social actors' purported *false consciousness* is juxtaposed to the epistemological privilege of the Marxist theorist allegedly able to detect and unmask the workings of capitalist ideology.

3 What exactly the secondary, social scientific layer of the "double hermeneutic" adds to the primary, lived interpretations recorded depends on the specific research questions and settings and on the theoretical-analytical perspectives being adopted.

4 This partly resembles important arguments about the complex, "intimate interplay" between "common-sense" knowledge and social scientific enquiry (O'Connell Davidson and Layder 1994: 2–3). While I concur that everyday- and social scientific thinking do not constitute hermetically sealed epistemological domains, the present and ensuing discussions place greater emphasis on the particularities and analytical additions generated on the second layer of the double hermeneutic.

5 It is here worth considering long-standing concerns about the commodification of water, for instance, or the range of commodity indexes (i.e., for a total of 23 different commodities) mentioned in my one-hour survey.

6 Current constraints of space do not permit a fuller discussion of important differences in conceptual emphasis between these only partially overlapping approaches. Alongside some central, shared concerns, paradigmatic shifts in focus from commodity chains to value chains, production networks and (global) supply chain capitalism have also redirected some of the analytical attention from a preoccupation with productive processes towards a wider remit that also includes questions of distribution, consumption, information flows, disparities of power, and issues of regulation, management and control. For a comprehensive account of those differences and shifts, see Pick (forthcoming).

Chapter 3

OF "GLOBAL OBJECTS" AND "TRAVELING METHODS"

I do not like shopping. Department stores quite literally tire me. I find trips to supermarkets, though necessary, tedious. And I have caused many a family disagreement with my inability to enjoy the practice of walking city centers and comparing similar items of ultimately the same thing. Buying souvenirs has always been my least favorite part of traveling, and I have often been embarrassed by the fact that my gifts to others are more modest than theirs for me. Neither has online shopping made purchasing commodities any more enjoyable for me, thoughts about what happens behind the scene (or behind the screen) prevent this, though they have not prevented me from joining the global ranks of online shoppers. Email requests to provide customer feedback on items just bought annoy me more than I can say: why does an economic transaction no longer suffice, why does this now get symbolically protracted into pseudo-reflexive "satisfaction-ratings," I regularly ask myself. (I know why, of course, to help sellers' self-advertising via their social media channels and, perhaps, to help potential future customers make their decisions. The problem is that I do not find those answers convincing, so I just routinely ignore the emailed feedback requests.)

These confessions of an arguably "flawed consumer" (Bauman 2005), or perhaps merely an overthinking one, still leave room for occasional surprises. Months ago, in a furniture shop I had no interest in visiting myself, I spotted an object that caught my attention and imagination: an incredible work of craftsmanship, sturdy yet elegant, a nostalgic invocation of premodern rurality that would, even I was immediately convinced, enhance its future owner's quality of life and aesthetically enrich any twenty-first century living room. The object in question was a sofa, one we did not need and did not buy. Yet, I found myself doing two things I would usually be extremely reluctant and unlikely to do: I asked the shop owner about the sofa's history, its materials and production; and I even took a picture of this particular piece of furniture. What was so beguiling to me was more than the object's apparent beauty. More fascinating was a deep contrast between its appearance and its history:

the sofa oozed authenticity and local belonging. Made of Harris tweed and leather, it materially and semiotically referenced the Outer Hebrides. Yet, this turned out to be a far more cosmopolitan object than its appearance and celebration of Scottish traditionalism first suggested. The sofa's other main component, as pointed out by the shop owner in question and subsequently corroborated on the website of another "vintage" furniture shop that includes the same item in its catalogue, is Italian aniline leather. Put simply: a commodity that speaks the semiotic language of traditional craftsmanship and localism turned out to be an amalgamation of materials from very different places. Such global connections behind a purportedly local and traditional product becomes yet more apparent when we trace the history and production of its second constitutive material, namely aniline leather, further. A relevant website informs potentially interested customers that this product—"made in Italy, of course"—combines "nuance" and a more "natural" appearance than those of its competitors, with "long-lasting strength" (i.e., being the "most resistant and strongest" type of leather). All this, the description continues, is the result of "deep knowledge" of the material and the application of trademark protected "traditional techniques": invented in Tuscany, those use "vegetable ingredients" in their method of tanning. Yet, here again, a regional history of craftsmanship intersects with distinctly contemporary concerns and with producers in many other parts of the world:

> In a global world, our hide too is global. It comes from different countries and the entire process is certified. From the breeding to the tannery. As a result we know that no animals are killed just for their skin. The cowhides that we use are the by-products of the food industries. (https://www.meridioband.com/what-is-italian-leather-10-things-you-should-know/)

Put differently, a commodity—the sofa—that is sold, at least in part, on the basis of its allegedly authentic Scottishness (i.e., as conveyed by the Harris tweed, as a regionally protected and certified material) turns out, at closer inspection, to combine elements from very different parts of the world. Its aniline leather, in turn, involves production and supply networks that span yet much further around the globe. If this applies to a commodity that is sold as a purported sign of rustic regionalism, what might other commodities without the veneer of local traditionalism reveal? In conceptual and methodological terms, *what can the qualitatively oriented social sciences contribute to our understanding of commodities, their production, circulation and transport, as well as their consumption and disposal?* Building on the previous chapter(s), the present discussion expands my engagement with the structures, processes and spheres of activity that jointly comprise our global economy today. In addition, and also in keeping with the analytical tone of the preceding chapters, what follows again entwines a discussion of some central empirical themes and core issues with conceptual and methodological reflections on how some innovative approaches in the social sciences have responded to the epistemological challenges created by global flows and their impact on localities.

The Case for Looking Widely and Globally

The previous chapter began to make the case that a conventional, qualitative approach toward capturing people's experiences, perspectives and perceptions in their own words is unlikely to suffice for a sociology of complex structures and interdependencies that elude most of our presumed expertise "in our own lives" (Back 2007). This earlier argument was partly framed in relation to existing sociological paradigms that view the relationship between people's own accounts and sociological meta-accounts in one of three ways: as a relationship of radical difference, à la Bourdieu and others who regard everyday knowledge and social scientific knowledge as fundamentally different in kind; alternatively, as coexisting and potentially intersecting attempts to make social life meaningful; or, in line with the concept of the double hermeneutic (Giddens 1984), as a two-step process whereby social actors' own interpretations of their life-worlds are collected and then subjected to secondary reinterpretations by the social scientists doing the recording and analyzing of experiences already made meaningful by the "direct owners" (Bauman 1991: 73) of those experiences.

In the present and subsequent chapters I propose to push these existing arguments and epistemological positions further. If we take the double hermeneutic as an attempted synthesis of the first two positions just resketched—insofar as it takes everyday knowledge profoundly seriously but also insists that sociological analysis needs to offer more than a mere recording of others' lived interpretations of their realities, then this still leaves a number of crucial questions to be addressed. In other words, there is no room for false self-satisfaction with the mere notion of a double-hermeneutic. First and at the very least, we need to ask ourselves what exactly needs to happen on the second interpretative layer of the double hermeneutic, *what defines the craft of (some) sociologists?* While my proposed answer to this complex question only emerges from this book in its entirety, in this chapter, I will argue that two interrelated features *necessary for* sociological analysis (but merely optional or very occasionally encountered in everyday, "commonsensical" knowledge) are careful contextualization and the ability and willingness to "look widely." I will illustrate this through select but seminal recent contributions to the study of some defining features of our era's economic flows. As we will see, the latter need to be traced from the securing of raw materials, through complex chains and networks of production and the transport logistics and infrastructures they require, to the points of consumption, potential re-usage and waste disposal. Having touched on the crucial issue of oil already, I start this thematic, conceptual and methodological "journey" with another necessary condition of possibility for today's transnational supply chains.

The phenomenon in question is what is known as "containerization." Craig Martin describes the "global rise" of the shipping container over the last fifty years as tantamount to a logistics revolution that has facilitated the "seamless" transport of goods across vast distances, across different stretches of our supply networks, and between different means of commodity distribution. What is more, shipping containers offer a wider "lens," through which to "look at a range of [...] social and culture shifts from the mid-to-late twentieth century to the present day," including the expansion of globalized trade networks and their impact on local workforces and occupational groups the world over (Martin 2016: 3–4). Containerization thus adds to those facets of globalization that seminal contributions to the literature have depicted as forms of standardization. Other postulated manifestations of such standardizing include the world's purported "McDonaldization" (Ritzer 1993) or "Disneyization" (Bryman 2004): whether they place their analytical focus on a quasi-Weberian rationalization of production and consumption practices (as in the former case), or on the global spread of a way of branding certain kinds of consumption spaces (as in the latter), what such works share is their proposed distillation of homogenizing forces from the complexities of economic life today. However, as we have also already begun to see, and as we will explore in more detail in due course, such homogenization is far from uncontested. In the first instance, the workings and implications of the "container revolution," as traced by Craig Martin, need extensive outline.

An example of "tertiary packing," the purpose of which it is to enable the mechanized transfer of "other commodities around the globe," standardized, so-called intermodal containers are quickly and efficiently moved between ships, trains, trucks and, looking ahead, increasingly even planes;[1] they are the organizing unit of our era's distribution and supply chains, as reflected in the fact that some 90 percent of today's goods get transported in sealed containers; being passed from one operator to the next (i.e., from manufacturers to freight forwarding companies, shipping agents, rail network operators to road hauliers), it is containers that ultimately get commodities from producers to consumers (Martin 2016: 8, 28, 33). We may in fact describe shipping containers as micro-vessels of globalization, as the conditio-sine-qua-non for the transnational circulation of commodities. Fittingly, Craig

Martin describes containers as *world-objects*, as "*the* representative object" or even "icon of present-day capitalism." The scale of their use and circulation explains why. By 2016, some 6,000 container ships with a total capacity of nearly twenty million containers were crisscrossing our oceans, leading Martin to propose a corrective addition to Arjun Appadurai's (1990) conceptualization of globalization as comprising a number of *scapes* and *flows*: Martin speaks of a new, "global containerscape" to capture how "the globe is [now] envisaged as a vast logistical surface of containers being moved in huge container ships before being moved onto rail and road networks" (Martin 2016: 57, 61). As already hinted, the significance of containerization goes beyond the central infrastructural role it has come to play in our global economy. Along with other world objects, such as those tied more squarely to the digital revolution of recent decades (e.g., the internet, telecommunication satellites), containers play an important part in the production of the essentially compressed "spatial and temporal relationships" typical of our "global age": to illustrate this further, Martin invokes some of the greats and the good of contemporary social theory to show that our transnational "containerscape" adds a further and vital dimension to Manuel Castells' conception of the world today as comprising a *space of flows*; and building on David Harvey's acknowledgement of containerization as a facilitator of global production networks and hence as a necessary precondition for economic globalization per se, Martin traces the crucial role containerization has played within the wider structural shifts, observed since the mid-twentieth century, from Fordist mass-production (formerly concentrated in a small number of "core countries") toward a "post-Fordist economy of outsourced, flexible production" (Martin 2016: 61–67).

Focused on a particular (world) object (i.e., the shipping container) and its associated institutional and infrastructural changes (i.e., standardization in the transport and circulation of commodities), Martin's analysis of the processes of containerization reveals how globalization challenges the social sciences and how the latter, in turn, may respond most productively. To elaborate on terminology already used, Martin's is an example of social scientific contextualization and the willingness to "look widely." With regard to the former, a convincing qualitative social science cannot be content with the mere depiction of meanings, or—important though this is—with descriptive accounts of, for instance, experiences, ideas, beliefs, practices, relationships, or institutions. Instead, sound analysis of social phenomena calls for their historical, geographical, and political contextualization, for an embedding of the things we observe and record in their wider settings; and such contextualization in turn enables insights into both the social, political, economic, and cultural circumstances, out of which a given phenomenon has emerged, and into its wider consequences, planned and unintended. Related to this, proper contextualization demands a wide lens: as sociologists we ought to know that most, if not all, meanings and interpretations are contestable and contested, that social fields are places of struggle and disagreement; that social phenomena can be viewed from a number of angles; that unintended consequences of actions and decisions are everywhere; and that objects often have multiple uses. "Looking widely" means that we try to capture as much of this diversity as possible, and that our assumption is *not* that we will find simple answers to complex questions.

In Martin's case, looking widely involves him following the world object that is the shipping container along as many of its routes as possible. Some of the insights thereby generated may indeed appear surprising, for they point toward some initially unanticipated reuses of this arguably most emblematic of all icons of global capitalism. Instead of conforming to the intentions of the object's inventors and its many economic beneficiaries, some such reappropriations take us far beyond processes of standardization and logistical planning. Conceptually, this resonates with John Urry's case for the relevance of "complexity theory" to contemporary sociology: foregrounding "chaos, unpredictability and non-linearity," this argument insists that we need to acknowledge the messiness and complexity of the social world, and its frequent refusal to fit "neat" accounts of simple causality or clearly discernible functions. Instead, a sociological invocation of "complexity theory" allows us to capture how social actions also frequently generate, albeit unintentionally, "unexpected, unpredictable and chaotic outcomes, often the opposite of what the human agents involved may seek to realize" (Urry 2000: 206, 207). In the specific terms provided by our present empirical example, this manifests in some of the initially unintended, illegal uses, to which shipping containers have also been put, from the smuggling of tobacco, drugs or contraband to "people trafficking." Elsewhere, and in a perfectly legal though no less initially unanticipated domain, shipping containers have also been reappropriated in a number of other ways, often as part of the leisure or the creative industries: the particular examples Martin traces include a Danish "cultural collective" and a Scottish residency center, in which shipping containers have been turned into studios and accommodation for visiting artists (Martin 2016: 76–91, 101, 1).

These reappropriations for different contexts and purposes of what was initially produced as an item for "tertiary packing" also raises more general questions, to which we turn next: namely how exactly something becomes a (global) commodity and whether—in a manner of speaking—there may be "life" beyond commodification.

"Commodity Situations" and "Trails"

Previous chapters have already introduced the observation that our epoch's hallmarks include tendencies of *marketization*, which refer to the transformation of an ever-widening range of objects, social phenomena and relationships, as well as (raw) materials into commodities for sale and purchase. To weave this analytical thread further, it bears dividends to next explore conceptual questions about such commodification in greater depth.

For this purpose, and to push beyond working definitions of commodities as simply items sold and bought in market settings, we may turn yet again to the cultural theorist Arjun Appadurai. In his introduction to an influential collection of essays, Appadurai opened new ground: challenging "naturalizing" conceptions of particular items as objects that can purportedly only be, or can only be seen as, purchasable and sellable, Appadurai reconceptualized commodities as the context-bound outcome of specific social and economic relationships and practices. Or, in his own words, rather than reifying commodities as "objects of economic value," our focus should shift toward *"the commodity situation in the social life of any 'thing'"*; it is precisely and only in such commodity situations that the object's *"exchangeability (past, present or future) for some other thing [becomes] its socially relevant feature"* (Appadurai 1988: 3, 13, *original italics*). Elsewhere in the same volume, Igor Kopytoff elaborates on this reconceptualization of commodification as a process that defines only a particular "state" in an object's longer "biography":

> For the economist, commodities simply are. That is, certain things [...] are produced, exist, and can be seen to circulate through the economic system as they are being exchanged for other things, usually in exchange for money [...] From a cultural perspective, the production of commodities is also a cultural and cognitive process: commodities must be not only produced materially as things, but also culturally marked as being a certain kind of thing. Out of the total range of things available in a society, only some of them are considered appropriate for marking as commodities. Moreover, the same thing may be treated as a commodity at one time and not at another. (Kopytoff 1988: 64)

If the commodity situation is thus merely a particular phase in an object's life cycle, important follow-on questions arise: How are such commodity phases created for any particular "good"? How do such enabling (or commodifying) conditions in turn vary across historical and social contexts? Before turning to some recent literature that begins to answer these important questions with regard to very particular commodities in our glocalizing era, we ought to take note of another strand in Kopytoff's line of argument. Not only do commodities always have to be made, culturally as much as economically, but there is another anthropological constant to be mentioned here: or what Kopytoff terms a cultural "counter-drive" to the "potential onrush of commoditization," whereby parts of a society's natural and symbolic environment is "set apart" and hence marked—in Emile Durkheim's understanding—as "sacred," and hence defined as being "precluded from being commoditized" (Kopytoff 1988: 73). Put more simply, commodities are not always and perennially "for sale," but their exchangeability for money only defines a particular context and stretch of time; further, cultures impose limits to what can or—normatively speaking—should be able to enter into the commodity situation. Arguments already mentioned about today's tendencies toward widening *marketization* (Fraser 2014) suggest that some historical epochs, in particular our own, allow commodity situations to expand more than other eras have done; and, concurrently, that such marketization tendencies unfold alongside (much) less prominent cultural "counter-drives" that sacralize certain domains as lying outside (potential) commodification. Approached as a set of propositions to be tested empirically, rather than as statements of fact, these arguments frame parts of this book. For more immediate purposes in this chapter, however, questions about a particular object's creation as a commodity, or about the commodity situation as only one phase in the longer "biography" of a particular "social thing," require further illustration.

Some rare books, an example of which I turn to next, epitomize not only how the sociological imagination can be put to critically productive use in the early twenty-first century but, in the process, they also sketch new conceptual terrain and pioneer some novel methodological approaches that are demanded by the particularities of our historical moment. Caroline Knowles' study of the ubiquitous, albeit generally taken-for-granted and hence overlooked commodity that are flip-flops is a case in point. Conceptually, Knowles challenges and modifies the "scape-and-flows-view" in the study of globalization, which also provided a starting point to this book. Knowles' alternative is to recognize that globalization and its much lesser known, though structurally highly significant "backroads" comprise "journeys" and "frictions": the former refer to "episodic and continuous sequences of movement" by people, objects and materials alike that, when examined systematically, are capable of "revealing the operation of social worlds"; frictions, meanwhile, foreground the global economy's "instabilities and fragilities," recognizing that "rather than flowing, objects lurch along, stopping and moving [...] along a shifting, untidy, inchoate network of routes and trails" (Knowles 2014: 7–9, 13, 119). What Knowles offers is nothing less than a paradigm shift away from two equally simplistic, though mutually exclusive conceptions of globalization: first, Knowles challenges the (quasi-neo-functionalist) trope of the purported "global village"; second, and concurrently, Knowles also encourages a critical, more nuanced rethinking of views of globalization that regard "it" as little more than a system of super-exploitation driven by "nomadic" capital (Bauman 1998). Instead, we are here again encouraged to confront the "messiness" and contradictions of contemporary social life. As social scientists, this forces us to recognize "the ephemeral, the indefinite and the irregular," not to assume the "repeatable" and "stable"; instead we need to adjust our methodological lenses to "heterogeneity, variation [and] displacement" and to recognize that our world today may just require new metaphors of understanding such as those of a "maelstrom or a tide-rip [...] filled with currents, eddies, flows, vortices, unpredictable change, storms [...] and moments of lull and calm" (Law 2004: 4–7). Knowles' particular, highly original methodological response to such conditions is what she terms *traveling methods*: a focus on "traveling objects"—in this case the transported materials that go into the incremental production, distribution and consumption of flip-flops—and their implicated "matrix" of "multiple intersecting trails of people and objects" demands multi-sited ethnography across vast distances. As Knowles illustrates, such "translocal social research" requires flexibility and a diversity of "vantage points" or "viewing platforms"; it is by definition a collaborative endeavor, relying—in each setting—on local actors' local knowledge and language skills; and while tried and tested methods for capturing local everyday lives (i.e., photography,[2] "interviews on the hoof," and walking research participants' "habitual landscacpes" with them) play a vital function, the tracing of the traveling objects' long-distance journeys also necessitates an "ad hoc patchwork" of pragmatic decisions, the ability and willingness to follow materials *en route* (Knowles 2014: 14–18).

Putting her traveling methods into action, Caroline Knowles thereby manages to trace the full "biographies" of the materials that go into the making of flip-flops as well as the life cycle of the commodity itself. What is more, by following one particular "flip-flop trail"—in a wider, global network of multiple trails, which "splinter into thousands of routes" (Knowles 2014: 59), from raw material extraction, global production networks, transnational distributions, localized consumption practices and waste disposal—Knowles captures yet more than some flip-flops' journeys around significant parts of the globe. She also teases out, with ethnographic skill and the careful contextualizing required for this, how individuals' personal stories of migration, work and struggle intersect with, and enable, particular stretches of the flip-flop trail. More accurately, Knowles' research documents the following phases and locations along the trail: the oil fields of Kuwait, for oil is of course the quintessential raw material required for the plastic that goes into the making of flip-flops; the petrochemical plants in Daesan, South Korea, where oil is turned into "low value plastic pellets"; from there, Knowles follows the trail to Fuzhou, China's coastal "plastic city" and, more particularly, to the middlemen and bosses dominating parts of the competitive, flexible and geographically shifting industry that is flip-flop production. Next, Knowles (2014: 83) travels to one of the actual "production centers," namely a "patchwork of rural-turned-industrial villages" south of Fuzhou, where she pays particular attention to local biographies and migrant workers enabling the functioning of this "plastic village." Turning to one particular factory floor next, where flip-flops are made—and hence, in our broader conceptual terms, enter into a more easily recognizable "commodity situation," Knowles documents a total of ten production steps that are delivered in the course of noisy shift work structuring twenty-four-hour operations. Her next recordings of the flip-flop trail trace the objects' journeys, inside the aforementioned world objects that are shipping containers, from Fuzhou and Shanghai via Singapore and Djibouti to Ethiopia. This part of Knowles' journey implicates new actors, organizations, and locations, from warehouses, "mega-hub ports," seafarers, international shipping companies and distribution networks; as such, this part of the trail reveals the centrality of logistics, as "globalisation's connective substance" that facilitates the transport of objects "from place to place." As Knowles' traveling methods also show, during this next stage of the journey, the transnational distribution of flip-flops also entails "new uncertainties" and encounters with some of the "fragile textures" of our global economy: in this particular case, this manifests in regular "attacks and seizures" experienced by container-ships in the Gulf of Aden, where Somali pirates, military escorts, private security firms, and shipping insurance companies have become conspicuous groups of actors implicated in the trail (Knowles 2014: 119, 124, 125). Flip-flops' entry into Ethiopia, Knowles shows next, happens via one of two routes, though these can in turn at times "intertwine": legally, through Djibouti; or, in the form of smuggled contraband, via the Somaliland coast. From here on, Knowles picks up the trail again, in local markets in Addis Ababa: the local appeal of flip-flops as the cheapest of all available shoes is here connected to a range of commercial activities (i.e., from wholesale to retail), whose "translocal vectors"—Knowles (2014: 139–145) demonstrates—in turn require contextualization, namely in relation to the historical, geopolitical and economic connections between China and Ethiopia. The penultimate step along the trail sees Knowles (2014: 157) turn to local consumption practices, in the course of which "flip-flops finally make it onto [the] feet" of research participants; some of their biographical journeys—in the course of intra-Ethiopian urbanization, of daily routes around the home and neighborhood, or as part of domestic workers' transnational migrations— are shown to constitute further intersections with the flip-flop trail. Finally, and in anticipation of a theme (i.e., waste) to which we shall return to in due course, Knowles follows the trail right to its end: in this particular case, to a 36-hectare landfill to the south-west of Addis Ababa, where discarded flip-flops merge with much of the city's other rubbish that is the object of a glocal "business in waste management." At this stage, flip-flops have moved out of the actual commodity phase as cheap shoes; yet, there is still economic value to be derived from them. In the setting in question, discarded and ubiquitous plastic can be turned back into cash, namely by some of the most marginalized, so-called "scratchers," who collect plastic and sell it to factories that use recycled materials (Knowles 2014: 177–179).

Translated back into the conceptual terms that have framed the present section, in following some of globalization's "backroads," namely those that constitute a particular flip-flop trail, Caroline Knowles corroborates Appadurai's and Kopytoff's proposition that commodities only become such during a particular stage, phase, or situation in particular "social things'" more protracted and complicated "biographies." What is more, Knowles provides powerful empirical illustration of just how global some of those material routes and life cycles have become. Something as seemingly banal as a flip-flop has become almost unthinkable, or at least for now apparently unproduceable, outside the global interconnections that define our economy today. Yet, economic globalization is here shown to be much more and much more complicated than a system of transnational production and commodity circulation. Each of the nodes along the trail, Knowles shows us, is also profoundly local, shaped by regional histories, inequalities and struggles:

Globalisation's fragilities [...] weave their way through people's lives along the trail as incommensurable, personal [...] precarities [...] Globalisation is lived in houses and in neighbourboods. It is lived through work [...] What stretches these things beyond the local [...] is a chaotic patchwork of movement, on different scales, by different people, by objects like flip-flops, by materials like plastics, and by substances like food [...] [G]lobalisation is made in little, hyper-local sections, all of them connected [...] to the next stage [...] on the trail. At no point, and this would seem to be crucial [...] is an entire trail, or even a large section of it, revealed. Globalisation is not what we think it is. (Knowles 2014: 190, 193)

The importance of Knowles' empirical insights, and the methodological innovations underpinning them, can hardly be overstated. Neither can the significance of her conclusion: if globalization is indeed "not what we think it is," if its countless trails and routes never reveal themselves in their entirety or their complex interconnectedness, a crucial epistemological note of modesty follows. Simplistic statements about globalization will not do. Our knowledge of globalization, or more accurately of glocalization as it is only in (and in interaction with) localities that "it" can be sensed and captured, proceeds by necessity in piecemeal fashion. Seeing longer stretches of its trails requires time, effort and considerable methodological inventiveness.

Narrowing our focus to the specific stretch that is the "commodity phase" in particular objects' "biographies" next, there are further, important questions about commodities to be explored. I propose to do so through a selection of other, methodologically innovative contributions to the social sciences.

Commodities: Signs, Senses, and Skills

If Appadurai's and Kopytoff's earlier quoted conceptual contributions provide necessary definitional groundwork enabling us to see commodities as a temporally bounded phase or physical state in the longer life cycles of various "social things," an important follow-on question relates to whether or not the length and relative importance of commodity situations differ across successive historical epochs. Since the 1980s, prominent debates in the social sciences and humanities have answered this in the affirmative. For some, consumption lies at the heart of the "move into postmodernity" (Bocock 1993: 4), as consumption practices have "replace[d] production as the central mode of social behaviour from which standpoint [our] society can be interpreted" (Kellner 1989: 19). Others take the argument yet further in postulating that "if our ancestors were shaped and trained by their societies as producers first and foremost, we are increasingly shaped and trained as consumers first, and all the rest after" (Blackshaw 2005: 111). Acknowledging that consumption involves more than just "material objects" with a "simple, direct, utilitarian usage" and instead extends to ideas, images, and the articulation of meanings (Bocock 1993: 52), some prominent social theorists of recent decades have interrogated the wider implications of the cultural centrality of consumerism in the contemporary era. To Zygmunt Bauman (1991, 1998, 2000, 2005), consumerism furnishes an essentially "docile" mind-set, one that underpins the reproduction of a social order defined by enduring hierarchies and growing insecurities. What is more, Bauman (2003) suggests that a consumerist mentality has seeped into other domains, leading, for instance, to a purported change in attitude toward intimacy, a commodification-of-sorts of human relationships that are now increasingly approached with a "best-before mentality" that demands "instant gratification" from humans as much as from commodities purchased. To others, conversely, consumption also offers more of an emancipatory potential: for commodities can also be critically reappropriated, as "goods to speak with" (Fiske 1989: 31), in the articulation of oppositional politics.

The arguably most pervasive impact of consumerism has been claimed for the realm of people's self-understandings and publicly performed identifications. Building in part on Jean Baudrillard's (1993: 23) notion of the "mobility and endless structural play of signs," many commentators have argued that commodities function as "symbolic signs" in a historically novel "mix-and-match" approach to people's ongoing identity-work (Bocock 1993: 52). Put differently, collective and individual identities, so the claim, are no longer seen as permanently ascribed by virtue of class, gender, ethnicity or status group; instead, our period of "late" or "reflexive modernity" has allegedly seen the rise of a "post-traditional order" (Giddens 1991), in which individuals draw, to a significant extent, on consumption (practices) in their ongoing "identity-play" and self-constitution. Although this unquestionably captures parts of the contemporary experience, at least for the relatively affluent sections of the world's population, there are also obvious limits to this line of argument. Not all identifications can be picked, chosen and discarded at will; not all ascriptions can be renegotiated; not every aspect of our individual and (sub-)culturally shared biographies is mediated by, or articulated through, commodities and consumption practices. Most importantly, the subject positions of class, gender, ethnicity, race and status group continue—for many millions of people the world over—to provide "ways of seeing" (Brubaker et al. 2004) and, most importantly, "structures of action" (Karner 2007a) that lie outside the realms of what people reflect upon or can change. These important limits to the reach of people's identity-negotiations notwithstanding, discussions of the symbolic workings and expressive potentials of commodities are also acutely relevant for a sociology of glocalization. Put differently, not only financial flows and commodities routinely cross-national borders, connecting localities in different parts of the globe; so do signs, and commodities as signs.

A more recent study of the semiotics of a particular commodity, and of its transformations in an era dominated by multinational capital, is provided by Claudio Benzecry. The at first sight perhaps somewhat surprising object of analysis for Benzecry are the football jerseys, in their diachronically variable designs, of the Argentinean team Boca Juniors. Placing an "object and its [multiple] uses" in its different, over recent decades increasingly global "circuits of fabrication, production and consumption," Benzecry (2008: 49) also inadvertently enables a critical engagement and partial refinement of Kopytoff's (1988) earlier-mentioned opposition of "commoditization" to the cultural "counter-drive" of "sacralization." In the case of Boca Juniors' jerseys, this reappears in the shape of a chain of interrelated oppositions that structure much talk and thinking about football in an age defined by the "hyper-acceleration" of the global "flows of capital and labor." Such oppositions frequently pit "tradition" against technology, "authenticity" against "global modernity," reciprocal community-relations against "the market," and "totemic" identifications (i.e., with collective symbols, such as a football club's colors and jersey) against commodification (Benzecry 2008: 49, 51, 70). Yet, as Benzecry's carefully contextualized reading of the (recent) history of the club, its fans and merchandise shows, the real story is more complex, more nuanced, and better captured by well-known social scientific insights into the "invention of tradition" (Hobsbawm and Ranger 1983) and the "fabrication of authenticity." Showing that "value is attached to a football jersey in many different forms," that its meanings thus "shift" contextually, and that the object itself can become a "site of contestation," Benzecry identifies a range of actors and organizations that have participated in shaping the "many social lives" of the Boca Juniors jersey: fans, the club's administrators, the Argentinian Football Association (itself part of the international body, FIFA), designers, but also—since the market's transnationalization in the 1990s—multinational corporations, particularly Nike International and its "outsourced," under-paid workers in Thailand (Benzecry 2008: 70, 52–55). By retelling Boca Juniors' (recent) history, and by placing it in its wider and shifting economic contexts, Benzecry is able to demonstrate that—instead of an overly simplistic dichotomy juxtaposing "community" to market-relations—it is more accurate to speak of a somewhat blurry "continuity between [...] totemic moments" and marketed football. The former, in turn, have spanned "sacralizing" occasions as politically diverse as the Pope's "blessing of the team's jersey"; formerly, "Che" Guevara's support of Boca Juniors, with whom the number eleven (i.e., traditionally left-wing attackers' number in football) continues to be associated; and the "gift-giving practice" of particularly loyal players—as opposed to those frequently denigrated as the "hyper-mobile mercenaries" of recent decades—throwing their jerseys toward adoring supporters in the stands. Closer to the other end of the spectrum, meanwhile, one might locate the selling of "counterfeited jerseys with fake Nike logos" or an emerging market of football jerseys as part of tourists' consumption practices. Further, there are also some more unexpected uses: those include the articulation of diasporic connections and identifications among Boca supporters abroad; or, in an apparent display of just how contradictory some of the jersey's uses and meanings can be, Nike itself has participated in a nostalgic consumerism by also designing and selling "retro-vintage," 1935 jerseys, thereby offering "an imagined pastoral past" the company has, in fact, helped displace. (Benzecry 2008: 71, 60–64, 69, 59).

In capturing all this, Benzecry (2008: 59) demonstrates that it is indeed "possible to read globalization from a football jersey" but also that the emerging picture is decidedly more complex than a simple juxtaposition of commodities (i.e., products "made for exchange") to "totem[s] (an unchangeable product that shows the boundaries of a community") acknowledges. While it may still be partly accurate to speak of some "last realm[s] of sacredness" in an "otherwise hyper-commodified market" (e.g., the national team colors and jerseys, although those are of course also a source of revenue), in between those poles or end-points of a continuum of meanings and practices there is indeed much room for "blurring" in how commercialized objects are used, reappropriated and debated. This, in turn, only begins to sketch, as Benzecry acknowledges (2008: 65), the complexity of the question as to "what consumers do with their goods" and hence what the "social life of goods" after their acquisition entails.

From the semiotic domain (i.e., the realm of signs and the meanings they transport), it is worth turning back again to an earlier phase in particular commodities' biographies. It is in specific, local market-places that distinctly glocal "sensescapes" (Rhys-Taylor 2013) are at work and can be captured in all they reveal about global interconnections with local lives. A powerful illustration of this is provided by Dawn Lyon and Les Back's "multi-sensory ethnographic research" conducted at Deptford market, in East London. As all other contributions to the social sciences mentioned in this book, Lyon and Back start by providing the necessary historical and structural contextualization. This particular locality reflects the longer history of the British empire as well as today's multicultural "super-diversity" (Vertovec 2007). In demographic terms, more recent migration flows to the area have included those by Turkish Cypriots in the 1970s, by Vietnamese refugees a decade later, by West African arrivals during the 1990s, and Eastern European migrants post-2004 alongside South Americans. (Infra)structurally, meanwhile, the earlier-discussed phenomenon of "containerization" since the 1960s has also had a major local impact, displacing some of the traffic of goods that had previously been shipped up the Thames to Deptford and which could from then on be off-loaded at seaports—such as Dover—and be transported on by road from there (Lyon and Back 2012: 4.3, 4.1). It is against this backdrop that Lyon and Back trace how "global connections are threaded through the local economy" at Deptford market, and they argue that this calls for methodological innovation. Instead of an often un-reflexive "over-reliance" on interviews and their undeniable danger of "at times select[ing] the means ahead of the questions," Lyon and Back (re-)broaden the repertoire of ethnographic methods of data collection, while setting out a clear rationale for this in the particular setting of their fieldwork: they thus combine more traditional methods for recording daily conversations at local fishmongers, that is, pertaining to "fantastical fish tales" and talk with customers over "price and quantity," with photography and "sound recordings" (i.e., of the "background sounds of work"). Wanting "to listen as well as to look," Lyon and Back (2012: 2.2–2.4) argue that tapping into the visual and the aural holds the promise of accessing "areas of social life" that are part of people's *habitus*, "beyond or on the edge of consciousness," and hence "difficult to verbalise."[3] It is thus by bringing together photography, sound recordings and more traditional encounters and conversations in the field that Lyon and Back (2012: 8.1; 4.3–4.4) capture the "sensuous and embodied realms" of two fishmongers' flexible "tactics suited to [London's] changing cultural dynamics" in general, and to the "agora of multiculture" that is Deptford market in particular. The two fishmongers in question, whom we will encounter a second time in a later chapter, are "Charlie" and "Khalid": heir to a 100-year family business, Charlie performs his job with a "deep sensory connection to fish as the material, object and product of his labor," applying his craft to fish imported from all around the world as he "works the crowd" of potential customers. Khalid, meanwhile, was born in Kashmir and is a relative newcomer to the local market and the business. His particular skill, as a "craftsman of urban multiculture," is his "ability to pay attention to changing consumption patterns and the tastes of the area's multicultural inhabitants"; consequently, Khalid's shop has become a veritable "map of the local ethnoscape," a space not of "romantic utopia" but of "multiculture at work." Khalid's distinctive economic niche[4] is based on his recognition of, and catering to, customers' diverse backgrounds and associated consumption preferences (Lyon and Back 2012: 5.8–5.9, 6.5, 6.8, 7.2).

Deptford market thus reveals local intersections of economic and migratory flows with particular biographical trajectories. This also anticipates a theme, to which we shall return in later chapters. For our more immediate purposes, Lyon and Back's methodological broadening highlights further complexities in the *social life* of "things" that become commodities at a particular stage and play a range of roles in the lives of those who sell, purchase and consume them. And as Lyon and Back demonstrate most compellingly, all of this involves "the global" as well as "the local."

Waste and Some Concluding Reflections

By way of a penultimate analytical step in the present chapter, let us next turn toward the end of various trails that stretch from the extraction of raw materials, to complex, transnational production (or value-generation) networks, via supply and distribution chains, to local markets, diverse consumption practices, and eventually to rubbish heaps. Building on a thought-provoking definition of waste as "every object, plus time," Brian Thill paints a picture of the centrality and scale of waste that is deeply unsettling in terms of what it says about the impact of our civilization's unintended by-products:

> There is no human-made object so well-traveled, so ambient, as waste. It fills the oceans and the highest peaks. Our waste lays thick blankets of our chemical age across the entire planet [...] It's in the air, in the water [...] and piling up in immense mountains of garbage [...] The soil itself is part of a new geology, as the beaches have been remade [...] their sands mingled with the pulverized microplastics of our petroleum age. The genes of sea creatures that ingest these incredibly small fragments of our trash are mutating [...] With our waste we have reordered space and place [...] if one of humankind's desires has been to put its stamp on the world, waste is the most compelling and universal way in which it has accomplished its mission. Every landscape is a trashscape. (Thill 2015: 3–4)

Thus, we are offered another conceptual refinement relevant to our discussions in their entirety: in its global reach and ramifications, waste also flows across distances and boundaries, furnishing another *scape*—namely what Thill identifies as the "trashscape"—of our global age. Thill's account of this is primarily focused on the environmental costs and dimensions of waste. Other important parts of the literature complement this sociologically, by approaching "rubbish as 'social archive,'" in Caroline Knowles' terminology. What in the context of her work is primarily focused on Addis Ababa possesses much wider relevance. Starting from the definitional premise that *rubbish* refers to "objects, materials and substances that no longer have any use or value," Knowles shows how waste also provides another "lens" or "vantage point" from which to view social life: rubbish provides an "inventory" of sorts of a locality's "material life," it reflects social inequalities and thereby provides, if we take the time and care to decipher it, a "visual commentary" on people's behavior, on the "efficacy of municipal governance," as well as on the "social content and fabrics of everyday life" (Knowles 2014: 174–176).

As recent controversies over where and how to dispose of the plastics that increasingly overwhelm our planets' ecosystems have shown, *trashscapes* are profoundly transnational and deeply political. With container ships full of plastics heading from the world's affluent parts to the much less privileged (i.e., in a deeply problematic outsourcing of environmental damage to the marginalized and cash-strapped), and with some plastic-carrying container ships now being refused entry and returned to where such waste originated from, we come face-to-face with the globalization of waste. In the narrower conceptual terms of the present chapter, rubbish constitutes yet another phase—one that usually follows the "commodity situation"— in the *biography of things*. Thus, waste needs to be seen in its wider context and hence also as a separate stage in the much longer chains of value-creation, consumption practices, and that which lies beyond them.

In an illustration of both the sociological and the global dimensions of waste, Zsuzsa Gille develops the concept of a "waste regime." This starts from the premise that economies are more than value-creation chains: instead, "value also begets waste, waste also begets value […] and waste begets waste," in complex "waste chains" that operate across different geographical scales (Gille 2013: 27, 28). In other words, to move from merely noticing toward analyzing our transnational trashscapes, we need to recognize that waste always "constitutes a social relationship" in which "macro-entities," that is, institutions, and "conventions" shape the three defining dimensions of a given "waste regime": first, the *production* of waste, which invariably reflects social relations of hierarchically distributed power, privilege and marginalization (i.e., questions as to who produces waste, how, where, and how much); second, the *representation* of waste, which relates to the issue as to how waste is defined and talked about and the "bodies of knowledge and expertise" implicated therein; third, the *politics* of waste that extend to the question as to "who is mobilized to deal with waste" and where and under which conditions they do so (Gille 2013: 29). Gille also shows that while economists may regard waste as merely belonging to the domain of "opportunity costs," a sociological approach will foreground structural contexts and illuminate the production of waste as an "unintended consequence" of larger processes and systems (i.e., this also means that the "locations" and "causes" of waste must not be "conflated"). Further, recognizing waste chains as implicating social relations also alerts us to the fact that waste translates into unequally distributed risks: bringing her contextualization and analysis of waste chains full circle, Gille (2013: 31) shows that the "ability to shield oneself from risks and to increase another's exposure to them is a key source and result of power." Most relevant for our wider understanding of *glocalization* is Gille's (2013: 42) demonstration that all three dimensions of waste regimes, namely the "production, representation and politics of waste," reveal structural connections between "local, national and global scales." Thus, once again, we are brought face-to-face with the sociological as comprising *Wechselwirkungen* à la Georg Simmel, or inter-relations between actors, institutions, and phenomena that impact on one another. In this particular scenario, we need to recognize that all our rubbish heaps and other by-products created at any stage of any process of production, circulation and consumption (i.e., the economy, broadly defined) implicate others elsewhere. Waste—how it is created, managed, "outsourced," talked about or simply not noticed—is a profoundly *social* phenomenon: it can only be produced, handled, displaced, politicized or forgotten in specific settings and within existing social hierarchies. And those settings and hierarchies, in turn, are intrinsically transnational, as our era's many "waste chains"—for example, those pertaining to plastics, food waste, environmentally hazardous substances, or indeed our carbon footprints as arguably the most ubiquitous of all by-products of twenty-first century living—show.

This chapter, building on the previous one, has touched on vast and complex terrain. It has done so on the basis of select, recent contributions to sociological research and theorizing concerning key dimensions of the global economy today. Given the geographical scales and conceptual complexities involved, I certainly do not claim to have offered a comprehensive discussion here. Instead, this chapter has reflected on illustrative examples of how select social scientists have attempted to empirically capture and analytically make sense of some of our era's transnational economic flows and interconnections.

More specifically, building on important recent research (e.g., Knowles 2014) our discussion has also extended to some of the methodological innovations proposed therein. Such innovations trace, for instance, (commodified) material objects along their complex, "biographical" (Kopytoff 1988) trails and across multiple social domains. The challenge, as we have seen, lies in capturing and understanding resources, commodities and other objects as "embedded" (Polanyi 2001 [1944]) in now increasingly global "circuits" (Benzecry 2008) of production, distribution, exchange, consumption, use and disposal. Some of the questions confronted here thus lie in the interface of economic and cultural sociology: at stake are the (transnational) production and exchange of commodities and, inevitably, the global structures of inequality implicated therein; as well as the long-distance (re)appropriations of commodities as goods, signs and identity markers. Put differently, this chapter has continued my engagement with a global economic sociology that began in the previous chapter. However, my focus here has been more specific, namely on the question as to how some such commodities become commodities in our globally interconnected economies, in particular contexts, and for a variety of material and social purposes. To partly re-appropriate and build on classical Marxist terminology, we need to also ask how particular objects produced for global markets come to possess *use* and *exchange value*, as well as *significatory value*. Put differently, questions arise as to the different ways in which particular objects matter to people: as objects with discernible practical applications in their lives; as commodities with a monetary value under current market conditions; and as signs through which their users also communicate other messages and ideas. More concretely, in discussing and building upon important work on "containerization" (Martin 2016) and Knowles' pioneering "traveling methods," we have begun to see the challenges and rewards of a transnational tracing of particular commodities and their complex reappropriations and uses in specific, local life-worlds. Extending our focus further, we have also sketched how emerging social scientific work follows objects and materials as they leave the "commodity situation" and, ultimately, become waste.

In terms of wider epistemological debates, this discussion also picked up and further developed a crucial question already raised in previous chapters, namely how to define the qualitative sociologist's craft and its relationship to other types of knowledge of the social world. The argument developed in this respect thus far has been that sociological work—or the methodologically rigorous application of the sociological imagination—requires at least two features that can, but often do not, appear in other accounts of social life and "social things" (Lemert 2005). Sociological analysis, I have argued, simply *has to* be underpinned by careful and systematic *contextualization* of the phenomenon under investigation. In other words, sociological work demands that we embed the things we observe and record in their wider settings, drawing attention to the historical, political, economic and cultural circumstances, out of which they have emerged. Related to this, contextualization demands of us that we "*look widely*" rather than isolating and detaching the phenomenon in question. Our axiomatic, disciplinary premise should be that social fields are places of debate, contest and struggle. We should therefore be prepared to look and search widely for data that variously corroborates *and* challenges our own secondary interpretations (if, that is, we adhere to the notion of qualitative social research as revolving around a double hermeneutic). We need to capture social fields in all their diversities, as realms comprising contradictory forces, competing politics, and alternative interpretations.[5]

As our discussions so far have also demonstrated, while contextualization and "looking widely" are nonnegotiable, necessary conditions for a sociology adequate to the task of illuminating contemporary circumstances, they are not automatically and singularly sufficient. Our discussion has already shown that glocalization involves a range of phenomena and shifts that call not only for methodological recalibration but also for conceptual innovation. In other words, and as the following chapters will elaborate further, a sociological analysis of glocalization also demands the application and refinement of existing theoretical frameworks and conceptual categories. What is more, and as we shall also see, complementing wide-ranging contextualization with a focus on *theory* (i.e., a set of propositions, categories, claims, assumed connections etc. that we bring to bear on data in order to make sense of it) does not yet tell the full story of what defines successful sociological analysis either. The final condition for this, I will argue, is *reflexivity*. In the next chapter, we take further steps in exploring these features of sociological work while also taking a thematic turn, namely toward migratory flows and attempts to block them.

Notes

1 For a futuristic example of containerized air-cargo, see, for example, http://www. logisticsmatter.com/2016/02/09/boeing-just-patented-an-aircraft-that-picks-up-and-carries-regular-containers/

2 For a fuller sense of Caroline Knowles' use of photography in conjunction with ethnographic contextualization along the "flip-flop trail," also see www.flipfloptrail. com/.

3 Also important to note here are Lyon and Back's responses to the ethical issues raised by such an approach. They refer to this, in part, as the "moral maze of image ethics" and they explain that their strategy for negotiating this was to keep "returning to our participants to check repeatedly for both accuracy and consent" (Lyon and Back 2012: 2.5).

4 Importantly, in inadvertent corroboration of research findings in similar urban settings concerning inter-ethnic economic rivalries and the local importance of entrepreneurs' social capital (Karner and Parker 2011), Lyon and Back reveal not only *convivial multiculture* (Gilroy 2004) but some deep "ambivalences and rivalries" that also define places like Deptford market: Khalid and Charlie were thus originally directly competing rivals, with the former being "frozen out" by Charlie's networks, until Khalid "mobilized" his own relatives and contacts in other parts of London to support his emerging business and distinctive niche (Lyon and Black 2012: 6.6).

5 Consequently, as sociologists we should generally be wary of statements such as "this group of people thinks x or does y", for we know – or should know – that while many individuals may indeed think x or do y, others will not, or will at least not want to.

Chapter 4

FROM MOBILITY TO "LIMINALITY" AND *BLOCKAGE*

There is strong case that social scientists ought to keep diaries. The keeping of a field diary is an intrinsic part of the ethnographic craft. It is where and how ethnographers have long captured the steady stream of events and impressions they encounter and experience in the course of their fieldwork; further, field diaries enable reflexive accounts of how the field impacts the ethnographer as well as, vice versa, of how the ethnographer—as a participant observer with a background and history of their own—impacts back on the people and settings around them. Diaries can also serve other purposes. C. Wright Mills famously demanded that sociologists "keep a journal" as a core part of their *intellectual craftsmanship*: in the sociologist's journal, "personal experience and professional activities, studies under way and studies planned" join; it is there that we reflect upon both what we "are doing intellectually" and what we are "experiencing as a person"; we give ourselves space to relate our quotidian to our "work in progress" and to "capture 'fringe thoughts' [...] [or] ideas which may be by-products of everyday life, snatches of conversation overheard [...] or [...] dreams. Once noted, these may lead to more systematic thinking" (Mills 2000: 196). More recently, in advice directed primarily at PhD students but relevant to all social scientists, Les Back (2002: 3.5) has made a similar case for our ongoing recording of life around us and our reflections on "it." Often in the "the middle of a creative drought," Back (2002: 3.5) argues, "you will be doing something else [...] and an idea will come into focus. My advice is be ready for this unexpected visitor. Carry a notebook all the time, keep a record of these ideas. You need to devise a system to record how your thinking evolves over time."

In this spirit, and in continuation of a long-tradition of sociological journal-keeping, let me set the scene for this chapter with an extract from my own diary recorded in March 2020:

> For years, I have been thinking and writing about our era as a time of multiple crises. Yet, how unprepared this still left me for what is happening now!? I am writing this against the backdrop of several crises that are

already pushing local and regional communities as well as national, transnational and global structures to the brink. And perhaps for the first time in living memory, certainly for the first time in my generation's experience in the world's comparatively privileged parts, we realize that we do not know how things are likely to pan out. An until recently still lingering sense of optimism and belief in the future is quickly giving way to truly dystopian imaginings. What are those crises? Along with many others, I find myself profoundly worried and shocked, although not surprised, by events currently unfolding on the Turkish-Greek land border, by the arrival, organized or at least encouraged by the Turkish government, of thousands pushing for, but denied, entry to the European Union. This unfolds in parallel to the continuing arrivals on already hopelessly over-stretched Greek islands in the Eastern Aegean. Refugees stranded, living in dire conditions and unwanted on both sides of a closed border; local communities whose former livelihoods and lives—tied to a fragile tourist industry—also lie in tatters; are there solutions anywhere in sight? If there are, I can't see them, all I can see at present are clashing visions for the future, competing claims for rights and entitlements, which—though they certainly should all be guaranteed—are currently widely seen as being mutually exclusive, as creating cruel zero-sum games, in which all sides, and ultimately all our humanity is likely to lose out. All one can say with certainty is that these are locally endured, inadvertent consequences of violent conflicts elsewhere and of extreme global asymmetries in wealth and opportunity that appear to go beyond our individual and collective capacities of comprehension, action or remedy. The second crisis has been with us for years, celebrated by some, dreaded by many others: Brexit, whose impact—psychological and bureaucratic - on us Europeans making our living in the UK has been tangible and damaging for nearly four years now. The economic fall-out is very likely to manifest over the coming years. The full political consequences of the centrifugal, nationalist forces possibly still to be unleashed by Brexit, for a historically war-torn continent pacified and held together by the institutions of the European Union, are impossible to predict at present. European history provides ample reason to be very fearful of those long-term consequences. And yet, alongside, all of this is currently being pushed from view by a further, truly global crisis. I am writing this in a condition, already shared by countless others across numerous nation-states, of cautionary or publicly enforced social distancing and self-isolation. Put differently, we are almost entirely house-bound. In the space of a few weeks, days really, the global coronavirus pandemic has changed everything. Thousands have already died, many thousands more are likely to follow, tragically. The daily increase in infections and deaths, recorded across the world, is frightening. Borders have closed, local and national infrastructures across many countries are increasingly, in some cases hopelessly overstretched. There are now daily runs on, and queues outside, supermarkets. Politicians' calls for calm, for rational shopping, and reassurances that supply chains are and will remain intact do not appear to convince everyone. My wife and I can't fly home to see our elderly parents, who are considered to be among the most vulnerable. I found myself on the phone to my embassy the other day, in a conversation that quickly turned very personal, about home, and not getting there, at least for now. Not only is this a crisis whose full death-toll we will not know for who knows how long. It is also a time when sociability, social order, social structures and our beliefs in their durability are being tested profoundly. (In a moment of theoretical abstraction, I realize that this could sustain ethnomethodological studies of how everyday interactions make, or "do," social order for many years. Sociology, in general, could experience a huge renaissance against the backdrop of this crisis. Once taken-for-granted social relationships and structures are suddenly experienced or perceived as missing or partly disintegrating, or they are already missed by countless people, as the domain of the social—or in Georg Simmel's terminology of "Wechselwirkungen," only imperfectly translated as mutual interactions or interplays—is being called into question or at least being redefined.) As for globalization, "it" is already getting the blame for this pandemic in some political quarters, as was to be predicted. More helpfully, we are going to have to rethink what globalization entails: in Caroline Knowles' (2014: 13) words, the latter is not all about "flows," it has always also contained numerous "frictions." The closing of borders we are currently seeing, the shutting off of countries, regions, or households adds another dimension: not only flows and frictions define our globalizing moment, but also—suddenly—some powerful blockages. This is what we will need to comprehend: our era's globalization subsumes systematic transnational inter-connectedness and constant cross-border flows on the one hand, as well as political counter-reactions indicative of widespread "frictions" and, particularly in moments of acute crises, emerging and growing blockages, on the other. The crises we are facing at present are tantamount to a Socratic moment, in which we come to know that—with regard to the future—we "know nothing," or at least, very little, in terms of what precisely lies ahead or how to get out of our profound present conundrum. This is not to even mention something that can be predicted: the inevitable economic downturn lying just around the corner. Concern about a massive slump in oil prices has quickly been overtaken by the far-reaching economic fall-out of the pandemic. The full extent of this remains to be seen, economists variously predict at least a global recession, others a full-blown depression. Perhaps never before have the multiple, deep "entanglement[s] and [our] interconnectedness" (Beck and Grande 2010: 419), both global and (g)local, become so apparent, so quickly. One crisis is threatening to at least temporarily sever countless connections, and will jeopardize countless dreams and plans. The economic ripple effects of this health crisis seem impossible to predict or comprehend at present. In just our immediate circle, I am thinking of Greek friends who have of course also had to close their deli as part of the social distancing measures introduced to deal with the COVID-19 pandemic. No-one knows at present how long the measures will have to stay in force. On the last morning before the closure we bought their last Greek pasta and honey from them. Wanting to hug them, which I couldn't, I think I saw us all fighting back the tears, from a distance. And then there are the young martial artists, who have done so well to start a very successful gym, they are doing everything they can to rescue their business by switching into online-mode: can they really teach kickboxing to kids and adults via social media? They are certainly trying, my wife and I had our first online, personal training session via skype earlier today; my "home-office" has become a part-time gym. On the much larger stage, which feels strangely close and unusually distant both at the same time just now, there are enormous questions this moment will raise with additional urgency: how will we respond, any of us, anywhere in the world, to this deeply unsettling time? With a new-found, undeniably needed cosmopolitan consciousness—à la Ulrich Beck -, or with nationalist retrenchment? Or, more likely, in which combination or amalgamation will these political orientations manifest?

My starting-point to this book, following seminal existing understandings, was a conceptualization of globalization as defined by transnational *flows* and ever-growing, structural inter-dependencies that span geographical distances and national boundaries. In this chapter, I turn to the particular flow that garners more attention and political debate than any other. It is the flow of people. Contrary to a tacit assumption underpinning much public discussion of the issue, migratory flows are not just a hallmark of our era. Far from it, all human history has known migrations and the ensuing encounters between heterogeneous individuals and groups. In some ways, today's preoccupation with globalization can be historically myopic, as discussants often work with the implicit but misleading assumption that what they are describing is a novel phenomenon, thereby overlooking previous era's global inter-connections. At the same time, there are certainly reasons to conclude that today's globalization is qualitatively different, and structurally more wide-reaching than previous era's global flows. When it comes to human migrations, and the way those are commonly debated and problematized, the charge of historical myopia is yet more relevant. Ideological complaints about, and opposition to, migration have led to the most consequential electoral decisions and political shifts of recent years. Although anti-migration politics do not suffice as a singular *explanans*, without anti-immigration sentiments Donald Trump's election, Brexit, and comparable shifts to the Right in other settings would not have occurred. Common to them all is a profound, and historically short-sighted nostalgia (Karner and Weicht 2016) that assumes that (im)migration has only recently begun to affect localities and that constructs the impact of inward migration as a problem, an unwanted imposition, and as a purported threat to local populations and their "way of life." Leaving aside, for now, the profound ethical problems written into such political claims, they distort history. Large-scale migration and multiculturalism are certainly not novel phenomena, neither are other dimensions of globalization. The period between 1870 and 1914, for instance, can be characterized as a "first globalization of finance and trade" (Piketty 2014: 28ff.) and through concurrent, migration-induced social changes in many parts of the world. Neither does the claim, common to today's neo-nationalisms (e.g., Gingrich and Banks 2006) that inward migratory flows threaten the future viability of welfare states and the economic prosperity enjoyed in the world's more affluent nation-states stand up to more careful scrutiny: for demographic trends in those very same, most affluent states often point toward aging and declining populations, while the long-term durability of welfare states and continuing economic growth will generally require larger proportions of young, economically active tax-payers. Put more simply, far from being an inevitable danger, inward migration often turns out to be an asset, when viewed in longer historical and wider structural terms.

It is against this backdrop that the present chapter examines some of the migratory flows as well as some of the often-negative local reactions against them from the epistemological angle that defines this book. I thus here ask how, over recent years, sociologists and other social scientists have approached *migratory flows and neo-nationalist opposition* to it. Which methodological approaches and conceptual frames have been found to be useful? What are the particular challenges scholars of migration and of nationalism face in the twenty-first century? What is at stake here are indeed some of the core-questions of our era. It will therefore come as little surprise that what is needed is inter-disciplinarity, and hence the willingness to learn from other disciplines' methodological arsenals and traditions. Rather than offering comprehensive overviews of large and continually growing bodies of research, however, I will illustrate my argument with reference to a small number of very specific studies. Those have been selected on the basis of, first, their relevance to the issues discussed here; and, second, because of their methodological innovations or particularities. My discussion, then, focusses on key-moments and key-characteristics of migratory flows, and of the localist, often outrightly nationalist reactions to them, which partly define our glocalizing era. At the root of the discussion are three concepts already alluded to—namely the roles played by *flows* (Appadurai 1990), *frictions* (Knowles 2014) and *blockages* in our current form of globalization. This is complemented by another concept that has historically been most prominent in social anthropology: the notion of *liminality*, to which I turn next.

Thinking about "Thresholds" and (Enduring) Crises

In contrast to much political rhetoric on the issue, important contributions to the academic study of migratory flows have come to view migration not as extraordinary and problematic but as an "integral aspect of social life"; and as a "complex process" that takes very different forms for different groups of people migrating under vastly different circumstances in different contexts, all of which, however, implicate "both structural factors and human agency" (Easthope 2009: 61, 62). A sociologically comprehensive engagement with migration cannot be content with examining migrants' routes only, enormously complex and diverse though those are in their own right (i.e., think, for instance, of the vastly different experiences separating the globe-trotting and almost generally welcomed business elite from the exclusions imposed upon some of the world's most marginalized who embark on forced migrations in the hope of being granted asylum elsewhere). What is also needed, then, is an engagement with the different types of "reception" offered to different groups of migrants, and with the structural conditions and mechanisms behind such receptions. Put differently, sociological discussions of migration implicate, almost by definition, not only those who migrate but also those who "receive" and respond to them, in a variety of different ways. One consequence of this is that migration studies have come to examine "both mobility and place attachment" (Easthope 2009: 75), and the latter—as well as potential changes to it—among migrants *and* so-called "receiving societies." Although all of this provides a useful starting point for what follows, the interface of mobilities, place attachments and local discursive-political reactions to migration do not capture the full picture either. One may ask, for instance, how we might make sense of another prominent dimension: the blocking of particular migratory flows and its impact on those who find themselves "stuck" where they did not want to be, namely somewhere in-between "here" and "there."

A conceptual strand to be introduced at this point revolves around the anthropological concept of *liminality*, which was first formulated by Arnold van Gennep in 1909, and subsequently developed further by Victor Turner, to capture the "middle stage" in rites of passages that enable a social actor's movement into a new status (Thomassen 2015: 39). Put simply, the liminal stage follows one's ritual separation from a previous structural position and precedes their societal re-integration in a new role and with a new social identity. The recent rediscovery of this concept, which on a higher level of abstraction therefore pertains to "threshold and boundary experiences," has postulated that "liminal conditions have come to shape the contemporary" in many ways, not least as manifest in the "uncertainties created by globalization processes" (Horvath, Thomassen and Wydra 2015: 1, 8). Other elaborations on the concept have made it yet more immediately relevant to our discussion in this chapter. Bjorn Thomassen thus argues that what in some form may be universal, namely the temporary experience of being "at a boundary or in an in-between position," of an individual or group "standing [...] by choice or assignment [...] on the fringe of 'normal structures,'" can in some circumstances become a permanent state of affairs: liminality, in its temporal dimension, can thereby extend over very lengthy periods of time. Equally relevant are some of liminality's spatial crystallizations, for instance in borderlands. Long associated with experiences of ambivalence, uncertainty or even danger, if liminal experiences are prolonged, this can translate into negative emotional-affective responses (e.g., "resentment, envy and hate") and their potential politicization (Thomassen 2015: 40–52). Another distillation of liminality's relevance to contemporary circumstances ties the concept to crises, which—akin to the ritual structure the term initially described—begin with the "dissolution of order but [can also be] formative of [new] institutions" (Szakolczai 2015: 34). However, Szakolczai (2015: 26, 27) adds an important novelty: unlike the always temporary liminal phases in rites of passage, crisis-induced, collective liminality is "not necessarily [...] followed by a return to normality [but] can be perpetuated endlessly." Drawing on Gregory Bateson's term, Szakolczai characterizes such permanent liminality as a form of "schismogenesis," in which structural unity is broken, yet the resulting "schismatic components are forced to stay together, producing an unpleasant, violent, truly miserable existence." Finally,

Szakolczai also returns us to a spatial setting most pertinent to our present discussion: concurring (with Thomassen) that modern borders are liminal locations (i.e., thresholds between the territories controlled by different nation-states), he observes that some "human beings can be stuck on them almost permanently" (Szakolczai 2015: 22).

Liminality thus reconceptualized can help alert us to what Beck and Grande (2010: 427–430) describe as "new units of research" that enable a "methodological cosmopolitanism"; the latter does not "neglect the national" but it certainly insists on pushing beyond it. As we shall see next, there are contemporary experiences of migration that undeniably call for such a methodological cosmopolitanism, which is in turn enriched by what the concept of liminality enables us to see and name.

"Forced Immobility" as Negative *Liminality*

There has been growing recognition of migrants' actual journeys (i.e., of humans *en route*) as crucial domains of experience, most obviously for the people going through them but also for researchers attempting to capture and understand the diversity of contemporary mobilities. William Walters (2015: 469–478), for instance, has made the case that the "mobilities turn in the social sciences" should recognize the epistemic value of "roads and routes" and of migrants' complex "entanglements" with things (i.e., objects) that include the vehicles that transport them. Walters argues that this matters particularly against the backdrop of our "mediascapes of migration" that commonly reduce would-be asylum-seekers' migration to images of dangerous border crossings, while leaving other important dimensions of their journeys unacknowledged (e.g., borders manifesting in new ways, such as in asylum-seekers' "reception centers," the "microphysics of border control," as well the appearance of "mobile commons" and attempted contestation of the power exercised on some of the most marginalized of migrants). What this implies is a necessary broadening of the lenses and research sites for scholars of migration. Walters (2015: 483) concludes that to "the public square, the detention center, and the border wall, research now needs to add the boat, the plane, the bus, the train and their routes," all of which are places of "meaning making and struggle." For the purposes of our analysis, it should be pointed out that each of these are quintessentially liminal sites.

As has already been mentioned, sociological discussions of migration must start from the fundamental premise that the motivations and experiences characterizing different flows of people differ so vastly that we should, in fact, really only speak of migrations in the plural.[1] Asylum-seekers escaping political oppression, war, economic destitution, or environmental destruction comprise one type of migratory flows; financially (and by implication politically)—powerful business travelers constitute a very different type of international mobility; the global tourist industry (e.g., Bott forthcoming)—in all its variants—is also part of our *glocalizing* world. Structurally and experientially entirely incomparable, these three types of *flows* of people certainly do not sketch the full spectrum of the many, highly diverse mobilities in the twenty-first century. What they illustrate, however, is that it is extremely difficult to distill commonalities that cut across the full spectrum: aside, that is, from the act of crossing (international) borders; and, as Julie Chu (2016: 404) reminds us (by invoking Marc Augé's concept), from the fact that travelling generally puts people in "non-place[s] [...] where everyone is a stranger" and "no one is expected to feel quite at 'home'." Immediately, however, the vast differences separating whom Zygmunt Bauman (1998) characterized as "tourists" and "vagabonds" respectively manifest: "flowing" across borders is a routine, barely-noticed and entirely unproblematic act for the world's powerful and privileged. By contrast, it is forced migrants hoping for refuge elsewhere, who find themselves often in a prolonged state of liminality. And it is some of their experiences that constitute my main focus in this chapter.

Focused on a well-documented case of "Chinese transmigrants from Fuzhou" being smuggled "along transoceanic shipping channels," Julie Chu (2016) makes three points highly relevant to this discussion. First, in reporting how such human smuggling made use of the "standard metal containers" originally designed for the global, and globally standardized, transport of commodity cargo, Chu inadvertently corroborates Craig Martin's (2016) observations of some of the clandestine reappropriations of the central object at the heart of our era's "containerization." Second, Chu makes the basic, though no less important point that different "flows" differ profoundly, that the flow of people does not compare to the flow of goods. In other words, the stark juxtaposition of two hallmarks of our times—namely that of a "liberal regime for expanding 'free trade' in goods and the illiberal one for restricting the movement of people" respectively—challenges prominent (and sometimes self-congratulatory) "assumptions of a world of smooth and speedy circulations" (Chu 2016: 405, 406). The third point Chu makes redirects our attention to political reactions and attempts to control some such migratory flows. By tracing how the control of borders and state surveillance have responded to unauthorized migrants being smuggled inside containers, Chu documents a relatively new "politics of olfaction"[2]: this manifests in how, since the late 1990s, "immigration officers and customs inspectors have [come to] rely on [new] techniques and technologies for detecting the olfactory signature of human waste [...] in the policing of contemporary migration" (Chu 2016: 413, 414). As we have seen, liminality can typically be experienced as a state of uncertainty, anxiety or even danger. Tragically, recent, well-documented cases of unauthorized migrants suffocating while locked in containers or lorries have underscored quite how dangerous their lengthy journeys often are. Three recent contributions to the academic literature enable us to see how many forced migrants experience a negative, (semi-)permanent liminality that can variously be dangerous, frustrating, dehumanizing, and truly "schismogenetic" (Szakolczai 2015: 26).

The first contribution to be discussed is Ruben Anderson's ethnographic study of the West African "migration circuit" and the "policing of the Euro-African borderlands" between the Sahel and Spain. Anderson's multi-sited fieldwork with various African police units, with employees of aid organizations, and importantly with migrants themselves, spanned the following strategic locations along shifting and dangerous routes where migrants' "classification and illegalization"—Anderson calls this an "illegality industry"—occurs: the beaches of Dakar in Senegal; the town of Rosso at the Mauritanian border; a holding- and deportation-center in the north of Mauritania; the vast desert between Mali and Western Sahara; and the Moroccan town of Fnideq near the Spanish autonomous city of Ceuta. Anderson's ethnography is a powerful reminder that in our age of globalization it is not only production processes that are (cost-effectively) "outsourced," so are the policing of (some) borders and the attempted control of "clandestine" migratory flows.[3] More accurately, Anderson demonstrates—when moving from his rich ethnographic description to analysis—that the EU's border agency Frontex and, more particularly, Spain have developed an "intricate gift economy" with police forces and organizations in Senegal, Mali, Mauritania, and Morocco. Gifts, as anthropologists have long known, create enduring "social bonds" by establishing an "obligation to reciprocate." In this particular case, European/Spanish development aid, cash flows, but also infrastructural and organizational "gifts" ranging from "policing gear, vehicles and computers [...] to training courses" and "fingerprint-reading equipment" are intended to ensure the "subcontracting" of border controls and the curtailment of migratory flows long before they reach Europe (Anderson 2014: 126, 136). As importantly, those processes also illustrate a phenomenon to which we shall return in due course, namely the longer histories of highly unequal, oppressive power relations and their continuing impact (though in partly reconfigured fashion) on the present. Anderson thus demonstrates that the "Spanish-African gift economy" of border patrolling contains "echoes from the colonial encounter" and manifests—for instance through deportations and crackdowns aimed at sub-Saharan, black Africans in Mauritania and Morocco—in a renewed "politics of skin color" that still reflects the "legacy of slavery" (Anderson 2014: 127, 134, 141–144). Most relevant to the present analysis is Anderson's ethnographic skill in capturing migrants' own experiences of being en-route. This is a process that bears all the hallmarks of a negative, in some instances decidedly "schismogenetic" liminality. It can take years, it involves periods of "aimless wandering," subjects migrants to a "circle of fear and forced mobility," and eventually makes them internalize the "deportability," "illegality," and the dehumanizing alienness and "thing-likeness" external power-structures impose on them (Anderson 2014: 135–141). Unlike in traditional rites of passage, migrants' liminality can be extremely prolonged, and its outcomes are anything but certain. In particular the long "limbo" many migrants are forced to endure whilst attempting to cross Africa's "internal sea" that is the Sahara impacts their physical and mental health extremely negatively. This is barely surprising, given migrants' "circular world of detentions and ignominies, deportations and empty pocket[s]," and their chronically "liminal state [of being] present yet absent from the jurisdictions they traverse, at turns visible and invisible to the border forces that chase them" (Anderson 2014: 135, 130).

Anderson's ethnographic journey concluded in Morocco, which also constitutes the focus of the second study to be discussed here. Like Anderson, Inka Stock has conducted long-term fieldwork among some of those migrants finding themselves "stuck"—sometimes for years— in a geographical and structural "in-between," neither here nor there, in an often almost unbearable, schismogenetic liminality. Stock's ethnography, unlike Anderson's, focuses on one particular locality only. In the Moroccan capital of Rabat, over a period of 10 years, Stock conducted semi-structured interviews with numerous sub-Saharan migrants and with employees of relevant organizations, complementing this with document analyses and participant observation in a wide range of pertinent local settings: in migrants' homes and neighborhoods, churches, workplaces, with NGOs, at football matches, social events, and at a summer school for children and women (Stock 2019: 15). Stock's central insight relates to the fact that many migrants have now got stranded in a situation of "forced immobility": "stuck" in Rabat for "indeterminate" periods of time, they are not only "stripped of the possibility to participate meaningfully in economic, political and social life," but their biographies are on hold in a "no man's land" where they "gradually lose their name, their status, their home, their past and their future"; theirs is a "space between worlds, where the normal rules and codes through which we recognize the humanity of others are in suspension" (Stock 2019: 2, 3). The structural context, and this echoes Anderson's analysis, is provided by the increasing fortification of the EU's external boundaries and its "externalization" of migration control policies. The Moroccan government also plays a key-role. Migrants' "stuckness," characterized by their classification, "criminalization and control," means that it is often equally impossible for them to continue to Europe as it is to return to their country of origin, while making them vulnerable to the violence used by the Moroccan police and military (Stock 2019: 23–29). By giving some among the generally silenced a voice, Inka Stock (2019: 57) demonstrates the complexity of many migrants' motivations for, and experiences of, migrating, and the contestability of any rigid distinction of "regular" from "irregular" migration; their stories thus reveal a "complicated interplay between moments of 'forced' and 'voluntary' movements as well as 'legal' and 'illegal' stays and crossings, [making it] difficult to say at which point 'illegality' actually begins."

At this point, it is worth emphasizing quite how blatantly such structural *blockage* and "forced immobility" fly in the face of our era's self-understanding as a period of transnational flows. There is certainly much that routinely crosses international borders in our age of glocalization, but concurrently enormous wealth and political energy are invested in attempts at blocking certain human flows of mobility. It is not overstating the case to conclude that the "forcibly immobile" live by a rhythm and in a structural position "out of sync with modernity," for the "indignities of waiting in a culture of the instant, of flows" exclude them from a world "only the privileged, liberal subject has access to" (Stock 2019: 150). As Stock's ethnography shows, the long-term, "existential consequences" of lives lived "in limbo" (Stock 2019: 19) are severe. In an account that inadvertently comes very close to matching Arpad Szakolczai's (2015: 27) depiction of *schismogenesis*, Stock captures how her sub-Saharan research participants "felt they had lost their past" and that they were "living a useless present"; their undeniable clinical depression was underpinned by feelings of loss (i.e., "having lost their place") coupled to an "incapacity to comply with social obligations"; while the past and present are experienced as being "meaningless, the migrants [in question also] have increasing difficulties in focusing on a brighter future" (Stock 2019: 96–99). Particularly important to the present discussion are those analytical strands, through which Stock herself interprets her research participants' experiences through the lens of (negative) liminality. Thus, she invokes Giorgio Agamben's notion of the "state of exception" to illustrate how her research participants are turned into practically rightless "non-persons": their forced and tightly controlled immobility imposes on them a "status of abjection, in between places, neither within the system nor outside it." Consequently, "being stuck in Morocco" is experienced as "liminal times" insofar as these sub-Saharan migrants cannot, for instance, "exchange their time against money on the market by seeking formal employment." Further, Stock draws on Albert Camus definition of the absurd as something "unexplainable through reason and religion"; this applies to Rabat's involuntary immobile who cannot make sense of their liminal lives through their "previous values, beliefs and feelings of belonging" (Stock 2019: 65, 80, 83–85, 103).

Liminality, as initially conceptualized in the anthropology of religion, was a positively connoted concept, which described an intermediate phase supporting an individual's (or a group's) transition from one status (e.g., generational, legal) to another, functioning—in a manner of speaking—as a ritual lubricant at key-stages in people's life-cycle events. Liminality as reconceptualized here, in light of prominent migratory experiences among some of the world's most marginalized, emerges as a very different kind of negative condition, as a (semi-)permanent, stifling, often-times deeply damaging experience with uncertain outcomes. Such negative, schismogenetic liminality is accurately captured thus:

> Liminality['s] [...] fundamental ambivalence creates a time "out of the ordinary when anything can happen" (Cwerner) [...] Old values and ideas lose their meaning while new ones are not yet found [...] [T]he most basic references to what it means to be someone [...] are severely undermined [...] Forced immobility creates marginality and dislocation. (Stock 2019: 104)

The third study to be mentioned in this section moves our geographical attention to the Eastern Mediterranean. The study in question adds to our understanding of the severe structural constraints imposed on forced migrants, while complementing this with an exploration of forms of agency the latter also exhibit. Dimitris Papadopoulos' and Vassilis Tsianos' (2013) qualitative research was conducted prior to the subsequent, further intensification of migratory flows to Greece and it was focused, in part, on three Greek camps (in Pagani, Igoumenitsa, and Mytilini) for transmigrants. By way of structural contextualization, Papadopoulos and Tsianos help us understand, inadvertently, the political function performed by the liminal states created by migration controls; for the latter generally operate to "transform ungovernable streams to governable subjects of mobility that adjust to the needs of local labour markets" (Papadopoulos and Tsianos 2013: 180). Importantly, this underscores that the political reactions to migratory flows ought to be seen as related to other, local or national interests and political contests, such as those over policies pertaining to housing, health care, education, or—as pointed out in this case—employment. Concurrently, however, Papadopoulos and Tsianos also show that transmigrants themselves are not merely passive "objects" of policies not of their own making: severely constrained though they are by political decisions and structures that are imposed on them, transmigrants also exercise remarkable individual and collective agency during the prolonged periods of liminality they endure. In the cases reported by Papadopoulos and Tsianos (2013: 178), this manifests in the "sharing of knowledge," in social and digital "infrastructures of connectivity," and in "affective cooperation, mutual support and care among people on the move."

For the purposes of our present discussion, it bears analytical dividends to view such support structures created by transmigrants through a conceptual lens associated with the cultural theorist Michel de Certeau (1984), who coined the term *tactics* to describe a range of everyday practices through which generally disempowered social actors temporarily manage to slip through the "web of power" that surrounds and entraps them. Tactics, in other words, are the form that constrained human agency takes. Quite how applicable this is to transmigrants' lives emerges from Papadopoulos' and Tsianos' (2013: 185, 187) basic observation that the very decision to migrate can be understood as an "exercising of agency from below in the diffuse conditions of globalization"; transmigrants' resulting "tactics" to "escape [...] [and] confront the regimes of mobility control" can take a variety of often dramatic forms, from being "smuggled" on a vessel, to "using false papers, crossing hundreds of miles of snowed mountains [...] changing one own identity, by destroying the skin of one's own fingertips with acid and a knife to avoid identification, [to] overstaying a visa, an au pair contract, or the regular tourist period of stay." Lest any of this be misread as corroborating common stereotypes of undocumented migratory flows, Papadopoulos and Tsianos go on to demonstrate quite how structurally entangled all our lives are with transmigrants' presence, whether or not "we" are prepared to acknowledge it:

> The spectre of migration will always be with us, among us, more real than anything else: cleaning your home, cleaning your office, cleaning your roads, cleaning your buses, taking care of your kids, fixing your computer, fixing your car, providing sex, providing care, providing baby sitting, ironing your shirts, answering your phone calls, doing your gardening, building your house, collecting your strawberries, living in the flat next door [...] imperceptible to history. (Papadopoulos and Tsianos 2013: 187)

Put differently, some of the most cruelly maligned of all migrants—namely the generally most impoverished and those who, out of sheer necessity, are most prepared to take the gravest of risks in attempts to "change [their] conditions of existence" (Papadopoulos and Tsianos 2013: 188)—are not only already here, but they are also needed. When we consider the often hostile reactions among many in so-called receiving societies, this illustrates what Ulrich Beck

(2017) describes as a contradiction between some locals' political sentiments and their "frames of action": anti-migration opinions thus stand in blatant, if unacknowledged contradiction to the transnational flows and connections on which local lives also depend.

Crucially, Papadopoulos and Tsianos return, once again, to transmigrants' severely constrained but vital agency, as it manifests in their tactics of solidarity and social capital[4] building under extremely difficult, liminal conditions. In a basic sense, such tactics show that transmigrants "do not do the politics we expect them to [and] do not behave as victims should" (Papadopoulos and Tsianos 2013: 190). By building connections and trust with transmigrants over a three-year period, Papadopoulos and Tsianos were able to delve much deeper and to reveal the following: an "infrastructure of connectivity" and knowledge-sharing among migrants, which, often enabled by digital technologies, spans long distances; and, locally, a "politics of care" and a "gift economy between mobile people," through which informal economies can be accessed and periods of negative liminality can be survived. Building on E. P. Thompson's terminology, Papadopoulos and Tsianos (2013: 190–192) describe this as transmigrants' "moral economy of migration" and their "mobile commons."

The important, qualitative studies discussed in this section corroborate that liminal "threshold and boundary experiences" indeed include a variety of contemporary circumstances, such as some of the most troubling and damaging ones (Horvath, Thomassen and Wydra 2015: 7, 8) endured at key-locations along some widely discussed migratory routes. At the same time, evidence of transmigrants' agency, tactics and mutual solidarity also partly resonates with another concept tied to liminality: Victor Turner's (1996) notion of *communitas*, with which he describes nonhierarchical, egalitarian forms of solidarity that are typically encountered during liminal phases spent at the margins or outside of ordinary social structures. With this in mind, we turn to similarly pertinent, sociological insights into some common experiences further along some of today's "migration circuits."

Between (Post-)Liminal "Homemaking" and Nationalist Exclusions

Our next step in this discussion explores the localization of select transnational migratory flows, and specific political responses to them, in various settings further along particular (forced) migrants' "routes." We thus begin to touch on the much bigger question as to what happens on some migrants' arrival elsewhere. Not surprisingly, there is no singular answer to this important question. Contextual variation and context-specific insights are, as so often, crucial here.

One such act of contextualization is provided by Janina Stürner and Petra Bendel whose research locates questions of migration and human rights in the context of another core-feature of the contemporary era: the fact that we now also live in an undeniably "urban age," as indicated, for example, by the proportion of the world's population that now inhabits cities and metropolitan areas.[5] Against this backdrop, Stürner and Bendel demonstrate that a range of cities across Europe, in the US and beyond have come to play a prominent role in migration governance and to push for their more active involvement in policy-development pertaining to migration on both national and international levels. Stürner and Bendel describe this as a process of the "two-way glocalization of human rights" involving two core-dimensions: first, cities and political actors on municipal levels creating "soft law to ensure local reception and integration policies [that are] grounded in fundamental international and European rights"; and, second, through emerging networks cities have begun to "lend legitimacy to EU and UN strategies, [to] advocate rights-based migration governance [...] [and to] push for a place at the international table" (Stürner and Bendel 2019: 215). In methodological terms, Stürner and Bendel develop this argument on the basis of a close analysis of a diversity of relevant documents, charters, and emerging institutional initiatives. They are thereby able to demonstrate quite how crucial city-specific initiatives are in terms of migrants' local reception, societal integration and in the safeguarding of migrants' rights: local organizations and institutional support structures with regard to housing, health care, education, language teaching, employment and vocational training, lived multiculturalism, and the provision of "advice on family reunification, asylum-claims and naturalization" (Stürner and Bendel 2019: 220) all demonstrate this. In other words, some cities are shown to play a central role in "glocalizing" migrants' rights in two ways: by creating effective support structures locally; and by advocating migrants' rights in a "bottom-up" fashion, with growing confidence and often in opposition to wider political forces, especially on national level, that are dominated by "increasingly isolationist" and xenophobic sentiments (Stürner and Bendel 2019: 226).

While such a contextualizing focus on city-level initiatives and support structures for (forced) migrants is useful, it cannot tell the full story. For that, we also require methodologies capable of capturing migrants' lived realities in specific urban settings. Recent sociological studies have made considerable headway in precisely this direction. Some such research has focused, in particular, on asylum-seekers' and refugees' "homemaking practices" (e.g., Kim and Smets 2020) in select European neighborhoods. In the terms of our present discussion, such work enables us to critically assess the relative effectiveness of the post-liminal phases in some forced migrants' routes: akin to rites of passage that conclude with an individual or group moving into a new social status, migration is generally conceived or planned (not least by most migrants themselves) as eventually leading to societal reintegration, albeit in an entirely different social environment. The research to be discussed next allows us to query the extent and relative success of some migrants' post-liminal integration in specific empirical settings; what is more, this also allows us to reflect back upon how far the analogies and analyses enabled by the concept of liminality can be extended to social domains other than the ones it initially captured (i.e., life-cycle rituals).

In a study focused on young Syrian refugees' "(micro)homemaking practices" in an innovative and multiethnic housing project in Amsterdam, Kyohee Kim and Peer Smets have combined a number of methods for collecting data: semi-structured interviews with Syrian, Dutch and Eritrean residents of the housing project in question; informal ethnographic conversations; participant observation at a range of local events; and the use of photography to help capture Syrian refugees' use of familiar cultural products, food and rituals in their reproduction of a sense of familiarity and "home" in Amsterdam. Kim and Smets (2020: 621–623) thereby show the importance of "bonding capital"—or of intra-ethnic connections, support structures and flows, both locally and diasporically across long distances—whereby fellow Syrians aid each other's "homemaking" in a new environment: this happens through the "sharing of information, experiences and emotions," through "leisure activities, consumption- [and] homing practices" that center on familiar products and objects; but also through "virtual spaces and online content [that is] accessible through mobile devices" and, by definition, spans *here* and *there*. Although this indicates quite how entangled human stories of migration are with culturally shared objects and information, it also shows— once again—how uneven globalization's various constitutive flows can be: information travels digitally and hence instantly; commodities are traded routinely across long distances; human migratory flows, by contrast, often move at a much slower pace and encounter far more substantial, sometimes insurmountable institutional obstacles. Further, Kim and Smets also point toward some current limits to these Syrian refugees' new "homemaking." In doing so, Kim and Smets invoke Robert Putnam's (2000) second type of social capital, namely "bridging capital" that refers to meaningful ties across ethno-religious boundaries and which can arguably, in the terms of the present discussion, be interpreted as an indication of (post-liminal) societal integration. In the housing project that is their empirical focus, and notwithstanding some interethnic couples and existing language-learning opportunities, Kim and Smet also report limited participation in wider social events (e.g., sports competitions, cultural exchanges) and express some doubt about the extent of "bridging social capital" connecting the area's Syrian and Dutch residents at present (Kim and Smets 2020: 616–622).

A similarly pertinent piece of research focuses on what its authors term the "architectures of asylum" and examines asylum-seekers' "spatial agency" and homemaking[6] in central Berlin: Anna Marie Steigemann's and Philipp Misselwitz's (2020) "spatial ethnography" of a "temporary container village" known as "Columbiadamm" where Syrian, Afghan and Iraqi asylum-seekers have been accommodated since 2016 while awaiting decisions on their applications for refugee status. Steigemann's and Misselwitz's findings connect in several noteworthy ways with the analytical trajectory sketched in this chapter. First, they demonstrate that asylum-seekers frequently continue to live in a liminal state on arrival; or, in the authors' own words, their research participants are shown to inhabit a "state of permanent temporariness," of "chronic crisis," and "permanently temporal gray spaces" (Steigemann and Misselwitz 2020: 629, 644–646). Second, the municipal (re-) use of standard containers (i.e., three 2.5 × 6 meter containers are used to form an "apartment unit") (Steigemann and Misselwitz 2020: 636) underscores, yet again, the ubiquity and widespread reapplications of containers as one of our era's "global objects" (Martin 2016). Third, Steigemann and Misselwitz also invoke, among other conceptual leads, Michel de Certeau's above-mentioned notion of *tactics*. They do so to demonstrate how asylum-seekers who face "extensive everyday bureaucracies" simultaneously employ a variety of "spatial practices"—ones that "hybridize" cultural elements from their place of origin, "experiences made during the flight," and materials from their new surroundings—to achieve a "sense of dignity, safety and comfort [allowing them to] escape, albeit momentarily, a situation of being permanently surveyed and controlled" (Steigemann and Misselwitz 2020: 628, 631, 644). Put differently, in a situation of continuing structural liminality at the threshold of their hoped-for new lives, asylum-seekers' "homemaking in Berlin's emergency accommodation" is shown to take a variety of forms: from "remodeling the furniture" in their allocated containers; to "adding decorations, [...] renegotiating daily routines [...] offering hospitality, [...] planting a garden, [or] the initiation of a local youth center" (Steigemann and Misselwitz 2020: 644).

With all this in mind, let us return to a core-part of the backdrop to all our discussions in this book: the neo-nationalist, exclusionary discourses that are important political factors in our glocalizing era. Both in the introductory chapter and in chapter one, we have already touched on how, across different contexts, the recent "nationalist turn" (Valluvan and Kalra 2019: 2394) can be read as an inward- and often nostalgically backward-looking reaction against local experiences of rapid social change, against global "flows" and (perceived) dislocations. By way of a conclusion to this section and the present chapter, it is worth paying some more attention to some of the discursive characteristics of today's neo-nationalisms. This is especially relevant since the often profoundly negative, liminal experiences of prolonged exclusion endured by many forced migrants need to be seen in the context of the "mainstreaming"—undeniable since the momentous political decisions of 2016 at the very latest—of "reactionary and particularly racist, Islamophobic and xenophobic political movements, agendas and discourses" (Mondon and Winter 2019: 510).

On a very basic level, it has been argued (Stavrakakis 2017: 530) that exclusionary (i.e., nationalist) forms of populism revolve around a national or ethnic/ racial ingroup that is constructed in essentialist terms as a nonnegotiable, ascribed and unchanging category of belonging for some, and exclusion for all others. Further, today's nationalist populisms implicate members of locally dominant ethnic majorities formulating "narratives of [alleged] loss, disenfranchisement and victimization," as exemplified, for instance, by rightwing politicians bemoaning a purported "loss of white male Christian privilege" (Mondon and Winter 2019: 514, 521). It is important, however, not to mistakenly conclude that all nationalisms today only mobilize the comparatively powerful in defense of their historical privileges. Locally, as for example comparative research of populist nationalisms in northern England and Hungary has recently shown (Thorleifsson 2021), it is often the less privileged, those most directly impacted by the "dissolution of industrialism" and by highly insecure employment who invest the most in nationalist promises. This echoes a longer established assessment of neo-nationalism as revolving around two key-features: its "cultural pessimism" (i.e., a bleak assessment of the status-quo, often contrasted to an allegedly better past); and its "economic chauvinism" (i.e., the claim that socioeconomic privileges and rights should be strictly tied to citizenship status and local belonging) (Gingrich 2006). It is, in other words, more accurate to argue that it is in (local) conditions of "economic restructuring [...] recession, austerity and marketization"[7] that the nationalist attribution of "primary culpability for significant sociopolitical problems, whether real or imagined [...] to various ethno-racial communities" (Valluvan and Kalra 2019: 2393, 2394) generally acquires the most pronounced political traction. Context remains central, of course. The question as to how exactly some of today's experiences of globalization lend apparent plausibility to nationalist narratives can only be answered empirically, in specific contexts (e.g., Karner 2020a): such contextual investigations, in turn, need to focus on specific experiences of social change, on locally available cultural memories, and on nationally active populisms that purport to explain a present that is widely found wanting and to offer "easy," allegedly better alternatives. Concurrently, and important contextual specificities notwithstanding, there is also a deep structure that recurs across today's neo-nationalism: parts of that deep structure consist of "the refugee and the migrant becom[ing] the primary objects of political discourse and the border the primary solution" (Valluvan and Kalra 2019: 2401). And it is, in turn, this discursive "logic" that drives, to a significant extent, the border and policing regimes discussed above. Forced migrants' negative liminality and the politics of nationalist exclusion must, from a sociological perspective, therefore be discussed in tandem.

Concluding Remarks

The discussion in this chapter has corroborated that the world is indeed "far from being a global village" (Martin, Metzger, and Pierre 2006: 500). For all our transnational entanglements, despite some tendencies toward standardization—as shown by processes of "containerization" (Martin 2016), for example—and despite the "possibility of ubiquitous competition around the globe," the issues examined here certainly confirm that globalization ought to be seen as comprising "multiple, often contradictory projects" (Martin, Metzger, and Pierre 2006: 503–506). We have begun to explore some of our era's contradictory vectors through a discussion focused on the negative liminality that defines many forced migrants' experiences both "en route" and on arrival. In moving our overall discussion in this direction, we have been able to see that "flows" are not the only characteristic of our age. There are also important *blockages*, such as some migrants' "forced immobility" (Stock 2019), to be considered.

Liminality captures a particular type of structural experience, that is that of being on the threshold between one social status and another. By way of a conclusion to this chapter, it bears analytical dividends to offer some historicization for our era's forced migrants' negative liminality. It is worth asking what kind of historical understanding or, more accurately, the absence of which other historical understandings help sustain, in part, the politics of exclusion and the border regimes discussed above. For this purpose, Gurminder Bhambra's (2007) meta-sociological reflections on significant lacunae in existing social theories are highly pertinent. Bhambra shows that dominant, sociological analyses of modernity have been chronically Eurocentric and have thereby "silenced" many of the global entanglements, such "as colonial encounters," that have been constitutive parts of modernity since its beginnings. I would like to build on this to argue that what is true of social theory, namely this ethnocentric historical shortsightedness, applies at least as much to wider societal self-understandings. Bhambra offers a way out of this dead-end. She argues that modernity has to be reconceptualized as "formed in and through colonial encounters" and a series of other, deep historical connections across long distances that show that (Western) societies "do not exist as 'closed' entities but [have long been] part of a much wider global context." Conceptually, Bhambra makes this argument with reference to the historian Sanjay Subrahmanyam's concept of *connected histories* which are used to theorize "mobility between places [...] connections across boundaries [...] [and to] rescue history from the nation" (Bhambra 2007: 77; 31–33). Among the most consequential of such global connections was the history of the "triangular trade" between Britain (and France), Africa and then colonial America: its "capital accumulation" involved the profitable exchange along the African coast of "a cargo of manufactured goods" from the "home country" for enslaved Africans who were then "traded on the plantations, at another profit, in exchange for a cargo of colonial produce to be taken back to the home country"; this provided a major "stimulus" for the British economy and also "contributed to the financing of the Industrial Revolution" (Bhambra 2007: 137).

Once such "connected histories" are properly acknowledged, our perspectives on current global inequalities and the transnational flows of people, as well as their widely attempted blockage, are likely to appear in a rather different light. In particular, the present-day legacies of much deeper and longer historical entanglements pose ethical and structural questions that rarely, if ever, are factored into today's politics of border control and migration "management." Put differently, we may indeed ask ourselves what our immigration (and other) policies might look like, if the connections between today's inequalities and the much longer histories of our global connections were considered. Or approaching this from the opposite angle: the fortification of external boundaries in the comparatively affluent and geopolitically powerful parts of the world appears to rest, at least in part, on an overly narrow and highly selective historical consciousness, one that denies or simply does not know our globally "connected histories." The resulting, and highly self-serving "memory nationalism" (see Karner 2021a) is ethnocentrically myopic and among the conditions of possibility for the structures of negative liminality many forced migrants find themselves in.

In the next two chapters, we turn toward some urban settings and their everyday, lived realities of ethnic pluralism. As we have seen, transnational migratory flows are highly heterogeneous. They ought to be seen in their specific, and often much longer historical contexts. As we shall discuss next, the interface of the urban and the global, an important sociological theme for some time, warrants further methodological and conceptual reflections.

SOCIOLOGY IN TIMES OF GLOCALIZATION

110

Notes

1 The enormous diversity of migratory experiences and highly heterogenous structural positions implicated are captured, for instance, in the International Organization for Migration's definition of a migrant as "any person who is moving or has moved across an international border or within a state away from their habitual place of residence [...] regardless of 1) a person's legal status; 2) whether the movement is voluntary or involuntary; 3) what the causes for the movement are; or 4) what the length of the stay is" (Quoted in Stürner and Bendel 2019: 216). In what follows, I will make frequent reference to a much more specific subset, namely to groups of "forced migrants": this terminology is intended to acknowledge the in turn diverse conditions (i.e., from war and political persecution, to chronic poverty and environmental destruction) that compel people to migrate by necessity rather than choice; this is a larger, considerably more nuanced and flexible classification than the narrower, legal(istic), and often restrictive categories of "asylum-seekers" or recognized refugees (also see Karner 2007a: 128–139).

2 Although Chu's point pertains to the "politics of olfaction," it is also at least indirectly relevant to a methodological development—an *olfactory turn*, of sorts, in social science methods—which we shall encounter in parts of Chapter 5.

3 It is worth noting that Anderson's study predated the much-discussed "refugee crisis" of 2015/2016 (e.g., Krzyżanowski, Triandafyllidou and Wodak 2018), which centered on the Eastern Mediterranean, on what came to be known as the "Balkan route" to the heart of Europe (Karner 2020b), as well as the "moral panics" (Cohen 2011) and political polarizations this triggered across the EU.

4 The definition of "social capital" invoked here is Robert Putnam's (2000) who regards it as social networks of mutual trust and reciprocal support either within (i.e., "bonding capital") or across ("bridging capital") ethnic boundaries.

5 In this spirit and partly for this reason, the next two chapters will turn their attention very specifically toward particular city spaces, the impact of global flows on them, and emerging methodological attempts to capture the contemporary interface of the global with the urban.

6 The research reviewed in this section is part of a recent, broader turn toward "homemaking practices" as an important site for sociological research. Similarly worth mentioning here is a pertinent contribution by Anna Pechurina (2020): focused on structurally very differently positioned migrants, that is often long-established Russians in the UK, Pechurina examines the role of "diasporic objects" in their homes. Such objects are shown to communicate both culturally shared meanings and biographically idiosyncratic memories. Inadvertently, this echoes an influential anthropological conceptualization of symbols as channels for such coexisting meanings and memories, some grounded in cultural traditions, others highly personal and idiosyncratically tied to family- and life-histories (Sperber 1975).

7 It is precisely in such geographical contexts and historical moments that Nancy Fraser's (2014) argument cited in previous chapters about various "social protectionisms" reacting against the forces of marketization acquires particular relevance.

Chapter 5

RUNNING IN THE CITY, CAPTURING URBAN LIFE

Austrian sociologist Roland Girtler (2004) specifies ten principles for ethnographic fieldwork. These include the taking of public transport, walking or cycling around a chosen location for fieldwork (rather than retreating to the isolation of a car); the visiting of local cemeteries (i.e., ideal for biographical glimpses relevant to the locality in question) and of high vantage points (i.e., to appreciate its fundamental geographical parameters). On one of my recent returns home, to the city in which I grew up, which I know better than any other place in the world, and which features in some of my previous research (Karner 2007b, 2011, 2021b), I stumbled—almost literally and quite by accident—across a methodological dimension to be added to Girtler's principles. This addition offers, so my claim in parts of this chapter, surprising benefits to the sociologist of any "global-local-nexus." It also, however, presupposes considerable amounts of prior local knowledge.

There is no established name I know of for my proposed methodological innovation yet. Bizarre though it may appear, I propose to term it the *historically informed jogging-method* (or, in inter-textual allusion, *insights-and-memories of the long-distance runner*).[1] Running is part of my life, almost as much as sociology is. Without long and regular runs, I am not sure how or where I would generate new ideas for potential research projects, nor how I would manage to finish older projects. On one of my recent runs, in Austria's second city, it suddenly dawned on me, quite fortuitously, that running might provide yet more than merely momentum for new or developing ideas. What if running, in certain places and under specific circumstances, could metamorphosize into a form of auxiliary, quasi-ethnographic data collection?[2] Here is an extract of a field diary of sorts, jotted down soon after my return from running that day:

I run along the river that structures some of my earliest memories [...] of cold winters when this river was almost frozen over. This hasn't happened since. Along long stretches, the previously dense river-woodlands have recently been destroyed, causing great local controversy, to make way for the mayor's "prestige project," a new hydroelectric power-station. Aware of the many objections, the council has put up public information signs promising that eventually the power-plant will generate "green energy" and "be in harmony with nature." Not for the first time, I get angry when I see this sign, against a backdrop of environmental destruction, before remembering that, despite my and many others' objections, our growing technological dependency requires ever more electricity, on which we all rely [...] I now follow a rail-track, passing by a scrap yard that has changed little over the last thirty years. There is the prison to my left, recently its outer walls were used for an art collaboration whose intentions are explained by a bi-lingual plaque. The juxtaposition of CCTV, barbed wired walls and art would have been unthinkable until not long ago [...] I arrive at the multi-storied block of flats where my late grandparents lived, where at first sight I still know every corner, every turning, and where memories come flooding back to me. I spent my happiest childhood summers here. I look at the names of the building's many residents, now ethnically more diverse than back then, yet the demographic change—discernible in surnames that in this part of the world are often (and sometimes stereotypically) "placed" geographically and linguistically—is not as far-reaching as much local discourse about immigration and its purported impact on neighborhoods like this always claims [...] I pass by my late granddad's former allotment, I was happy here, those allotments still exist, but only in part. Parts of where we used to grow beans and cucumbers have since become a cycling path [...] I now cross what used to be a patch of inner-city woodland and is now a car dealership, followed by a petrol station, a bus stop, and another car dealership. I then arrive at another block of flats, this is the one I lived in for the first eight years of my life, until my parents could afford to move to the suburbs. The playground is almost as it was then, but seems much smaller. Here, the residents' names have become more diverse, in ethno-linguistic terms, suggesting a more substantial demographic change and "turn-over." The kindergarten is still there, so is the church, which now also houses an association for "Austro-Rumanian cultural exchange" [...] I now run through the city's most diverse district. Long considered "shady," the area is now variously praised or criticized as an example of "successful" or "failed" multiculturalism, depending on the respective commentators' political leanings.

When I reread this a few days later, the richness of these reflections—when complemented by local, historical knowledge—dawned on me. The above account suddenly appeared to offer much more than merely a few nostalgic contrasts between "then" and "now" in the place I consider "home." On second sight, these reflections seemed to say much more, almost as though they might operate as an emerging prism through which to view social change in the locality in question. Environmental, technological, and climate change, as well as some of the local political controversies generated in their wake, changes and continuities with regard to social control, the use of public space for commercial, artistic and other purposes, consumerist lifestyles and expectations that define the biographies of many, the gradual transition from an industrial to a postindustrial society, growing ethno-cultural diversity, plus the anxieties and exclusionary strategies with which they have been met by many—all of these phenomena also surface in my "running-diary." However, what gives these reflections their sociological value is the fact that these are not merely descriptive points. The above observations also offer insights through comparison and contextualization. Nostalgic though some of the former might appear, when combined with proper contextualization and local knowledge, observations-cum-reflections such as the above can capture important truths: about an area's past and present, about outsiders' and insiders' perceptions and misperceptions, as well as about the contestable or, in some cases, positively spurious political claims being made about a locality and the vectors of social change impacting on it.

City spaces have been major foci of sociological attention and analysis throughout the discipline's history. In what follows, I first turn to some of the most influential previous and existing schools of sociological thought, whose attention has rested primarily on how migratory flows, diversity and demographic shifts impact on urban contexts. This is followed by a discussion of if, and how, such existing paradigms may help us understand the particular urban context and its recent changes that served as the setting to my *running field notes* above. I conclude this chapter with further reflections on other recent contributions to the literature, which have pushed and enriched our methodological imagination as to how global flows and their crystallization in urban spaces can be recorded and analyzed.

From Chicago to Los Angeles and on to (Post-Secular) "Diasporic Spaces"

Before returning to methodological issues, it bears conceptual dividends to revisit some of the propositions about urban modernity associated with the Chicago School of the inter-war period, as well as with later paradigms it helped generate. Chicago School sociologists Robert E. Park, Louis Wirth, and Ernest W. Burgess are known for some of the most influential ideas about the city, and the kinds of social shifts urban life purportedly spurs, that have been formulated in the course of the discipline's history. Similarly relevant are the contrasts between these early formulations of the 1920s and 1930s, subsequent shifts toward the LA School of the 1980s and 1990s, and, yet more recently, research focused on the "post-secular city" and on transnational connections.

The large body of urban research produced in Chicago by a long list of eminent scholars in the inter-war period was given empirical and conceptual coherence by a methodological preference for ethnography (Lal 1990: 2) as well as by paradigmatic propositions made by leading representatives of the Chicago School. Some of the latter have a strongly generalizing ring (see Braude 1970; Glick Schiller 2005: 54), speaking about "urban life," "urbanism," or "the city" in terms that transcend the specificities of time and space (i.e., ethnically heterogeneous Chicago in the 1920s and 1930s). Chicago School ideas relevant to the present discussion thus include: Robert E. Park's (1928: 892) postulate that migration results in "a cultural hybrid," people "on the margins of two cultures"; Louis Wirth's understanding (1938) of cities as defined by "size, density and heterogeneity," and of urbanism as displaying a particular "ecology," "social organization," and "social psychology" (i.e., tolerance, a loosening of tradition, "largely anonymous" relationships held together by the "pecuniary nexus," anomie, and secularization); and Ernest W. Burgess's "concentric" model (1928: 106–108), capturing Chicago's (former) spatial organization and the associated process of "radial extension," or ethnic population movement over time, "from the center to the periphery" (1928: 112). Such general claims invite comparison with other geographical and historical contexts (Gidley 2013).

A later framework in urban sociology and urban geography, the "Los Angeles School," has since the 1980s taken LA as paradigmatic of a shift toward "postmodern urbanism" defined by the spatial consequences of post-Fordist economic restructuring and a new urban logic epitomized by, though not restricted to, contemporary southern California. With "hinterlands now determin[ing] what is left of the center" (Dear and Dahmann 2008: 266; 270–272; 278), the LA-model detects late capitalist "city-regions fractured [...] into innumerable sociospatial pieces," defined by the ubiquity of difference, and giving rise to both "reactionary and progressive" politics (Nicholls 2011: 189). An understanding of these altered city spaces, and the very different power geometries and economic systems of (transnational) production of which they are a part, demands different sources of conceptual inspiration: where the Chicago School drew on Durkheim and Spencer, the LA School builds on Marxism and poststructuralism to theorize cities as "radically diverse, radically conflictual, radically open," producing "constant breakdown, crises and change," "destabilize[ing]" and "hybridiz[ing]" traditional identities (Nicholls 2011: 190, 194).

While ethnic diversity and urban life have long been considered deeply and structurally intertwined phenomena, it is also worth noting that much classical urban sociology, particularly within the Chicago School, was premised on the assumption that cities were secularizing spaces, in which the social force of religious ideas and institutions was bound to diminish. This has been challenged by recent developments and scholarly attempts to capture them. An emerging paradigm is discernible in a range of scholarship that has rediscovered the centrality of religious ideas, practices and institutions across diverse urban settings. Reflecting on "Religion in the city," Callum Brown (1996: 373) reported in the mid-1990s that secularization theory had become "untenable." Subsequently, an edited collection returned to Chicago to capture the effects of post–World War II urban restructuring on organized religion, including the growth of "individual autonomy and the moral legitimacy of personal choice," further demographic diversification, postindustrial shifts, and the "erosion of neighborhood ties" in the context of growing "economic polarization and spatial dislocation" (Livezey 2000: 6–7; Numrich 2000: 239). This echoes LA School insights, but shifts the analytical focus firmly in the direction of the religious domain. Elsewhere, the (re) discovery of urban religiosity has focused on its social capital generating and sustaining role (Coleman 2003; Smidt 2003; Warren 2003) as part of a reexamination of faith-based social action in city settings, often gathered under the label "the postsecular city" (Orsi 1999; Kong 2010; Beaumont and Baker 2011). Such scholarship has been given additional impetus by a German-funded program of urban studies conducted under the heading of *metroZones* and involving local researchers across the global North and South. The findings of this transdisciplinary project (Becker et al. 2014) question religion's "alleged disappearance in Western industrial cities" and the "secularist gaze of Western urban research" that is arguably ill-equipped to deal with defining features of the postindustrial city (Lanz 2014: 19–21). Advocated instead is a focus on urban religion, or "religious urbanity," through which faith and the city are shown to continually and "reciprocally interact, mutually interlace, producing and transforming each other" (Lanz 2014: 26). This deconstructs long-established heuristic oppositions between cities and capitalist modernity on one hand, and faith on the other. Instead, the religious realm is recognized as "expand[ing] into all (supposedly secular) areas in the permanent production of the urban" (Lanz 2014: 42).

More generally, there is widespread recognition that many of the world's cities are quintessential "diaspora space[s]" (Brah 1996: 16), defined by multiple "local and global connections" (Boutros 2010: 120, 121) that intersect in urban localities and lives. This has led to powerful calls to transcend the social sciences' long-established "methodological nationalism"

(Wimmer and Glick-Schiller 2002), or their paradigmatic assumption that the institutional boundaries provided and guarded by nation-states also delineate the main social scientific units of analysis. The search for new approaches better suited to an era of intensifying global interconnections and interdependencies has included calls to "move away from the nation-state/immigrant paradigm" and to focus on "transnational societal spaces" (Pries 2005: 169), instead. Particularly influential has been Peggy Levitt and Nina Glick Schiller's development of a "transnational social field perspective." This involves a far-reaching recalibration of how social scientists might define our areas of enquiry, their spatial coherence and complexities, and their geographical extensions. According to Levitt and Glick Schiller, recognizing that people increasingly inhabit social fields that span long distances and routinely cross multiple boundaries involves two separate, though interconnected dimensions. They define those as transnational "ways of being" and "ways of belonging" respectively: the former refers to cross-border "social relations and practices [...] institutions, organizations and experiences"; transnational "ways of belonging," meanwhile, are active, reflexive identifications with, or "conscious connection[s]" to, a particular diasporic group (Levitt and Glick Schiller 2004: 1010). Twenty-first century cities around the world indeed epitomize such transnational social fields in both their institutional and ideational workings.

These successive frameworks therefore differ significantly in their mapping of urban spaces and in the social forces and phenomena they detect in them. Instead of seeing these as competing paradigms, however, we might consider them to be mutually complementary interpretative lenses, which alert us to different facets of urban lives lived at the intersections of different global flows. Put differently, contemporary urbanity, as captured in my earlier "running-diary," for example, contains elements that span these different schools of thought. Today's "global-local nexi" may indeed require analytical strategies that draw on such a diversity of approaches to urban life.

Returning Home

Qualitative sociology is at its most powerful when it combines descriptive detail, contextualization, and the analytical process of making sense of data through pertinent theoretical concepts and propositions that are in turn refined by the empirical materials in question. Returning to my reflections on running through parts of the city of my childhood and youth, and in light of the various frameworks in urban sociology just reviewed, which insights might such a process of critically reading an empirical account through relevant conceptual frameworks generate?

To begin addressing this question, let me start with further context. Consider the google map of the city in question(Figure 5.1), in which the run[3] reflected on earlier is marked:

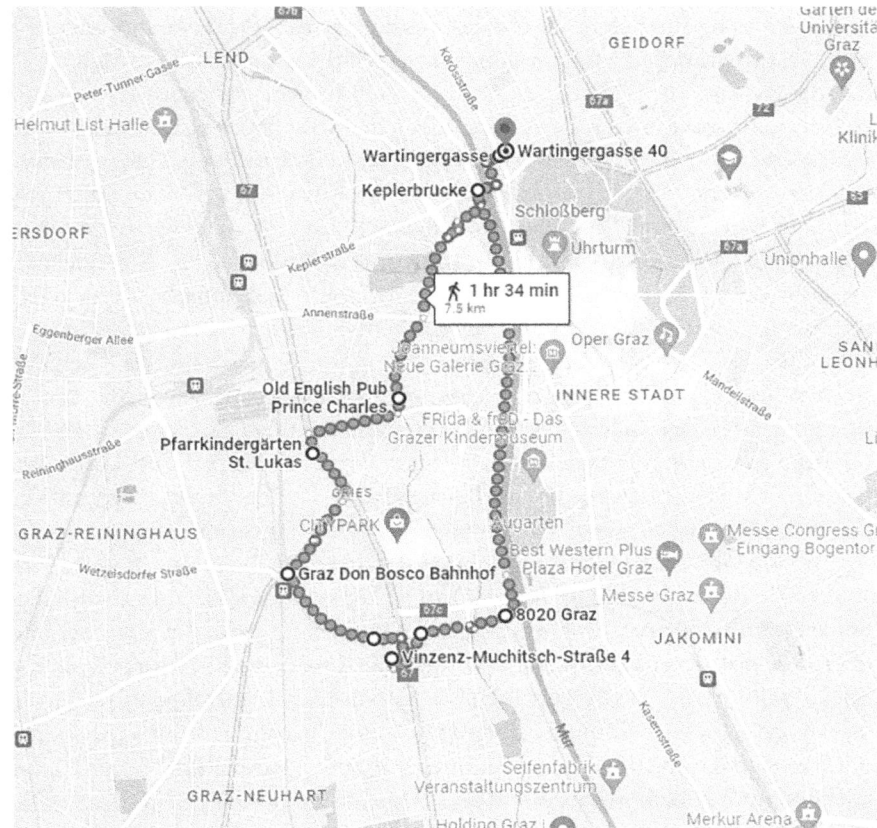

Figure 5.1 https://www.google.de/maps/dir/Wartingergasse,+Graz,+Aust ria/47.0771119,15.4325427/47.0568546,15.4343449/47.056007,15.4285516/ 47.0548591,15.4265562/47.0557947,15.4254189/47.0589377,15.4195824/Pfarrkinde rgarten+St.+Lukas/47.0672488,15.4270679/Wartingergasse+40,+8010+Graz, +Austria/@47.0667097,15.4091504,14z/data=!3m1!4b1!4m27!4m26!1m5!1m1!1s0x4 76e359b2173aad7:0xb201feb1942c676f!2m2!1d15.4339591!2d47.0787491!1m0!1m0! 1m0!1m0!1m0!1m0!1m5!1m1!1s0x0:0x2edd78df59345e66!2m2!1d15.4212525!2d47.0 646132!1m0!1m5!1m1!1s0x476e359b103c4933:0xbee01d5cf73b202a!2m2!1d15.4343 614!2d47.0789989!3e2. © Google 2019

The city in question is in some ways a bifurcated city, divided by the river running through it. The eastern "half" includes the historical center, whose late medieval architecture and roof tops have brought the city UNESCO recognition. In class term, the city's eastern half is considerably more affluent than most of the west; these inequalities are immediately apparent—and most clearly visible from the city's main tourist-attraction, a formerly fortified, steep hill (i.e., the *Schloßberg*) in its center—from the different districts' housing stocks and the relative distribution of green space. Yet, the east-west divide is cut across by further zonal divides, making parts of the north (with some notable exceptions, again west of the river) relatively better off than the city's south. My run through the south-west, marked on the map above, took me through some of the city's least affluent, working-class neighborhoods, which—historically and still today—(have) attract(ed) most inward migration.

Demographic shifts and many family histories (my own included) partly resonate with Burgess' "ecological" model (1928): not entirely dissimilar to Chicago of the interwar period, Graz—Austria's second city—also includes areas with characteristic "zones in transition" (i.e., places of [former] industrial production and points of first settlement for successive "waves of migrants") that are often also residential areas for the working class excluded from upward mobility. Most of the neighborhoods I crossed that day— including the large, now more multicultural apartment blocks in which my paternal grandparents had lived for decades and my parents and I for a few years—fit that particular part of Burgess' model of residential segregation. At the same time, other local empirical realities diverge notably from the model. Graz is, as already hinted, not concentric in its spatial and class-structures; here, inequalities follow local patterns and manifest in the divides between affluent areas in the east, north-east or far north of the city, and those less prosperous districts in the west, north-west and south respectively. Social mobility, when it occurs (like for my parents and me, who moved from one of the addresses marked on the map to a larger apartment on the city's northern edges in 1984), also manifests in suburbanization, but its local patterns reflect local geography: Graz is surrounded by hills on three sides, its hinterlands are nowhere near as expansive as are Chicago's (i.e., with the exception, there, of Lake Michigan to the windy city's east). In Austria's second city, "radial extensions" are only possible up to a point and in some directions, and the areas beyond the city's surrounding hills become quickly culturally homogeneous.

Other urban spaces I crossed on my run that day resonate more clearly, though also only partially, with the later framework provided by the LA model of urban sociology. The latter, as the earlier summary has shown, reveals the historical specificity underpinning Chicago School conceptualizations of urban life; those were arguably "time-bound" to a context of "immigrant acculturation and [...] the end of a serious depression" (Gans 2005: 50) and already out of step with postwar "industrial decentralization," growing affluence, and suburbanization. Michael Dear thus contrasts the Chicago

School's modernist paradigm to the post-modern, Los Angeles school of thought. The former, Dear argues, bore the imprint of Fordist, industrial production, in which city centers were precisely that—central to urban life. Also, modernist urban sociology understood the city as a "unified whole" and assumed a "linear evolutionist" narrative postulating a trajectory "from tradition to modernity" (Dear 2002: 14). By contrast, contemporary cities—as paradigmatically illustrated by Los Angeles—display new defining characteristics that require different conceptual tools. A postmodern "theory of urbanism" captures global, post-Fordist systems of "flexible production" and the information economy; an "acute fragmentation of the urban landscape," cultural diversity and polarization; a culture of consumption uneasily juxtaposed to exclusion and surveillance of the poorest in "carceral" parts of the city; and an acknowledgement of cities as also "chaotic spaces" that include "pathological forms such as transnational criminal organizations" (Dear 2002: 20–24).

Select aspects of Graz today, as the descriptive account above began to sketch, partly resemble the LA model of a patchwork of diverse and sharply differentiated neighborhoods, divided by their class and ethnic make-up and no longer concentrically structured around an inner (administrative) core. The very act of crossing the river, from east to west, entails the crossing of a boundary into districts that are the city's most culturally diverse and more deprived. Although the city retains its innermost (and most historical) first district, consumption patterns have increasingly been "displaced" into suburban shopping malls and other consumption spaces closer to the city's outer districts over recent decades. Sections of postmodern cities, and Graz is no exception, also display elements of "religious polarization" (Dear 2002: 24); urban contradictions and ambivalences manifest in sometimes uneasily coexisting "possibilities for reactionary and progressive politics" (Nicholls 2011: 189). Focused on some of the city's least prosperous parts, my running notes captured traces of each of these characteristics of postmodern urbanism: parts of the districts of *Gries* and *Lend* are commonly derided, on the right of the political spectrum, as dangerous, crime-ridden, and examples of a purportedly failed multiculturalism. Concerns about alleged Islamic radicalization in some local mosques have been articulated over recent years. At the same time, there are well-known examples of local churches working hard and successfully at enabling the development of "bridging capital" (Putnam 2000) across ethnic and religious boundaries, and of creative industries and cultural initiatives in the districts in question. Elsewhere in the area, we saw evidence of the carceral network coexisting with public art and lived multilingualism (i.e., the art project on the outer walls of the city's high-security prison). Meanwhile, yesteryear's already scarce green spaces in this part of the city have been further depleted by car dealerships and the commercial as well as symbolic "work" they accomplish in our postmodern consumer societies.

The dual focus on fragmentation and socioeconomic polarization provided by LA School urban sociology is usefully complemented by literature that looks beyond accounts of today's "superdiversity" (Vertovec 2007; Wessendorf 2013) to examine connections and identifications between specific localities, global flows and various "elsewheres." Levitt and Glick Schiller's "transnational social field" perspective also resonates in Graz, in particular along my running route sketched above. Lend and Gries are the city's districts with the longest histories of inward migration. Relatively affordable housing has long made those parts of the city appealing to newly arriving migrants: during the late Habsburg era from other parts of the multiethnic empire; in the post-war period in the context of "guest-worker schemes" between Austria and former Yugoslavia and Turkey; more recently, the areas have also become home to migrants from sub-Saharan Africa, recent Eastern European EU-accession countries and elsewhere. While inward flows of people, and in Appadurai's (1990) terminology multiple "ethnoscapes," are certainly not new to these areas, a process of further demographic diversification has taken place since my childhood. (I vividly remember my fascination, as a five-year-old, with our "exotic" and kind Syrian neighbor in the aforementioned block of flats, where most other residents were considerably more homogenous then, in ethno-national and religious terms, than they are today.) And, as reflected in urban localities around the world, our era's technological and commercial interconnections across long distances have created more active "diaspora spaces." Internet cafes, money-sending facilities, ethnic associations, non-Austrian newspapers being sold locally, prayer rooms, supermarkets catering to particular ethnic groups have all multiplied in the areas through which I ran that day, powerfully testifying to the local prominence of transnational "ways of being" and "ways of belonging" (Levitt and Glick Schiller 2004).

Sociology should also instill greater reflexivity in ourselves, enabling fuller self-knowledge and a more complete understanding of our own subject-positions, our stories and how they connect to larger structures. Returning that day, to the place I still consider my primary and first "home" (i.e., I scored my first goals on the playground mentioned earlier, cried inconsolably when my mum dropped me off on my first day in the local kindergarten, and learned many priceless life-lessons in my granddad's allotment), one sense dominated all else for me: in the course of three-and-a-half decades my own life had turned from being singularly focused on this particular part of "my" city, to being profoundly transnational. Not only many of the people whose shops, places of work, residence and worship I ran past that day live lives defined by transnational "ways of being and belonging"; so do I. These days, I spend much of my time thinking and writing about "home" from considerable geographical distances. Our family has since both contracted (generationally) and expanded (geographically): my grandparents' generation has passed away; concurrently, while "abroad" as a student in the 1990s, I met who would—years later—become my wife. She is Greek. Incredibly, decades earlier, in the 1960s her Greek dad (from Korinthos and then Athens) had been a pharmacy student in—of all places—Graz (i.e., my Austrian city of birth described in this chapter). The address of one of my father-in-law's student flats at the time was just east of the river, and a mere stone's throw from where my own dad and his parents lived in the 1960s, then also still east of the river, but toward the southern end of the city in another one of its working-class neighborhoods (i.e., *Jakomini*). Our fathers, my own and my wife's, never met as young men in the 1960s, despite unknowingly living so close to one another in the city discussed above. Our dads' first encounter would only take place decades later, just before our wedding in Greece. Life writes strange stories, we all know this. Thinking about those sociologically means recognizing their deeper historical and wider structural particularities and conditions of possibility. In our era, those conditions are in many ways profoundly transnational. This in itself is not a historically novel phenomenon. But the extent of our inter-connectedness, the reach of today's global flows and their impact on ever-growing proportions of the world's population call for sociological attention. In the case of my family's histories, their new transnationalism thus now connects Athens, Graz, and my own and my wife's working-lives "abroad." At the same time, some of those connections have a longer, often largely undiscovered history. In August 2016, on a warm summer evening in Greece, my father and my father-in-law thus reminisced about Graz in the 1960s; about the Austrian city described above which they had both called "home" at the time, before the man who would decades later become the father-in-law to an Austrian sociologist returned to his primary "home" in Athens. Transnational ways of being, of belonging and of remembering all intermesh in our lives.

There is more to be done by the urban sociologist to capture the workings of transnational, global flows in our everyday urban lives. In the next section to this chapter, I turn to some relevant, recent methodological innovations. Cognizant of the multidimensionality and ubiquity of transnational flows in our midst, some sociologists have pioneered novel and exciting ways of fine-tuning our perceptions and of thus refining our ability to record the global in the local.

Capturing Global "Sensescapes" Locally

As the earlier discussion has reminded us, cities and their social particularities have long constituted a core theme for sociologists. Recent research has shown how a focus on particular urban spaces can help illuminate a wide range of important contemporary topics: from chronic social exclusion (e.g., Hall 2017), the nighttime economy and the discourses surrounding it (Hubbard and Colosi 2015), to the everyday, often ambivalent, complexly negotiated (rather than inevitably conflictual) nature of interethnic relations (Lee 2006). In the remainder of this chapter, we turn our attention to another thematic interface, namely between urban sociology and the for our purposes most pertinent literature on glocalization. Defining the latter as the "'local' manifestation[s] of a larger, all-encompassing global modernization" (Robertson 2016: 67), the question as to how "the glocal" can be captured empirically as it manifests in specific urban spaces warrants further discussion. In what follows, we will stay within the "scapes-and-flows" paradigm that provided a conceptual starting point for this book. This calls for a definitional reminder of what flows and scapes are. Building on Appadurai (1990), I have taken *flows* to include all sentient beings, phenomena, substances and entities—from humans, animals, media, information more generally, capital, signs, commodities and other objects, to risks, raw materials, waste, discourse and ideology—that routinely cross-national borders and move or are circulated between distant but structurally interconnected localities. *Scapes*, meanwhile, are "the networks of machines, technologies, organizations, texts and actors that constitute various interconnected nodes along which the flows can be relayed" (Urry 2000: 35). The particular contributions to recent urban sociology that are discussed next focus our attention on a specific subset of such flows and scapes: those involving people (or "ethnoscapes" in Appadurai's original formulation), signs, commodities, foods and foodstuff. In discussing a small selection of relevant studies, I once again foreground the methodological question as to how the flows and scapes in question have been documented.

Empirically, the first example focuses on Los Angeles, the city that has—as we saw earlier—been taken to be *the* paradigmatic example of a postmodern cityscape. To repeat points already made, core-observations associated with the "LA School" center on the local effects of post-Fordist de-industrialization, on social exclusion, and on increased surveillance in deprived neighborhoods. Where the Chicago School, and Burgess (1928) more particularly, postulated a "zonal" model of concentrically organized cities, the LA School observes a very different, contemporary urban geography: deeply affected by postindustrial restructuring, city spaces—in LA and in comparable metropolitan areas elsewhere—are shown to be "radically diverse, radically conflictual, radically open" (Nicholls 2011: 190). Fragmentation has replaced yesteryear's center-to-periphery urban structure. In the LA version of today's cities, at least some of their constitutive spaces are decidedly "chaotic," revealing—among other characteristics—political polarization as well as the workings of "pathological [...] transnational criminal organizations" (Dear 2002: 20–24). So what does this look like in detail? And which strategies have been employed to capture such postmodern urban spaces?

A thematically and methodologically highly pertinent contribution to urban sociology has been made by Lorena Muñoz's research on Latino/a immigrant street vendors in two LA neighborhoods, namely "Garment Town" and MacArthur Park. Located southeast of Downtown LA, "Garment Town" not only constitutes many Mexican immigrants' "first point of entry" to the US, but it is also known for its garment industry and sweat shops as well as for its Latino grocery stores; inadvertently corroborating further urban characteristics highlighted by the "LA School," Muñoz (2012: 7.1, 7.6, 7.9) also reports "ongoing police raids," local business owners' politicization, and gang members' "petty extortion"—collecting "rent" from informal ("unpermitted") street vendors in exchange for information about imminent police raids—as everyday features of life in "Garment Town." At the time of the US census in 2000, some 85 percent of local residents had declared their ethnicity to be "Latino,"[4] nearly 54 percent were "foreign born," and almost 81 percent of people living in the neighborhood spoke a language "other than English" at home. MacArthur Park, meanwhile, houses predominantly Latino residents and Korean businesses. Having previously suffered from a "negative image" associated with high crime rates,[5] the area has more recently seen the use of surveillance cameras, investments by private developers, and some gentrification that has displaced many of the "permitted vendors" the area had previously been known for. Conducting long-term fieldwork (i.e., for a period of three years) across these two neighborhoods, Muñoz's focus lies on the "sensory landscape" in areas where "hundreds of Latino immigrant street vendors" sell—among many other things—Central American and Mexican garments and foods daily, using the trunks of their cars, local sidewalks, parking lots, fences and benches as "retail space" (Muñoz 2012: 5.1, 7.6). In due course, we will turn our attention to what has been described as a "sensory turn" (Rhys-Taylor 2013: 393) in urban sociology, which may be yet more accurately described as a "multi-sensory turn" (Lyon and Back 2012) insofar as it mobilizes all our senses in attempts to grasp aspects of urban life. A first indication of such an endeavor—and of the methodological adjustments it demands— is evident in Muñoz's work, for she combines an interest in the words, stories and "sounds of street vendors" with the use of "visual field methods" to capture her research participants' "moving," semiotic "landscapes" (Muñoz 2012: 7.6, 8.2, 4.3). By drawing together oral histories and forms of "photo documentation," Muñoz captures a part of the informal economy that is both distinctly local *and* transnational—or "glocal" in the truest sense of the word. Further, the visual domain is crucial here: for her research participants depend on being visible for their economic survival; concurrently, however, visibility is unmistakably "double-edged" for Latina/o immigrants, as they are also "targets of enforcement" and surveillance by local authorities and of racialization by many others (Muñoz 2012: 1.1, 1.4, 1.5).

The most relevant question for our purposes is what Muñoz's methodological approach and her use of visual methods, in particular, are able to offer and reveal. Context, as so often, is key here. And the widest relevant context, as Muñoz shows, is that provided by "processes of economic globalization, [including] flexible production, informal service sector work, and subcontracted manufacturing." Against this general backdrop, and in the specific setting provided by Mexican and Central American migratory histories to California, Muñoz illuminates how street vending—as an economic strategy utilized by, according to "conservative estimates," some 10,000 people "on any given day in LA"—constitutes a "sustainable choice of employment [...] that resist[s] institutional regulatory efforts by the local state." More than that, the colors, foods, "textures" and signifiers of identification on offer enable Latino street vendors and (many of) their customers to "foster a sense of place" in an often less than hospitable environment, and a sense of place that "transcends national and international borders" (Muñoz 2012: 3.3, 7.4–7.7). Methodologically, Muñoz's extensive use of still photography is particularly noteworthy: in the course of her three years of ethnographic immersion, she took some 4000 images, thereby capturing Latina/o street vendors' "use of space and how this changed over time"; "rich in detail that may otherwise be overlooked," such visual data also enables—especially when analyzed in tandem with fieldnotes and recorded conversations— the "co-construction of knowledge" by the (visual) ethnographer and her research participants (Muñoz 2012: 4.4–4.6). Concurrently, Muñoz also underlines the need for reflexivity on both the assets and limitations of such "situated" and "co-created" knowledge. First, Muñoz acknowledges the different roles she came to perform in the course of her research, which saw her frequently switch from being a researcher, to being a customer, to assisting street vendors with some of their work. While such "blurring" of the relative emphases on a researcher's diverse actions is not uncommon in participant observation, other reflexive insights Muñoz shares speak to obstacles she also encountered. Muñoz herself is the granddaughter of an ("undocumented") Mexican immigrant who had worked in San Jose's cannery factories and as a "part-time fruit vendor" after crossing the border from Tijuana; her family history fed into the research process. Such biographical "positionality," as Muñoz illustrates, helped her negotiate access, communicate with and understand many of her research participants and their own (hi)stories. At the same time, her ethnic and linguistic background did not open all relevant doors in the field, it also jarred—in a manner of speaking—others. This was due to how family histories are enmeshed with deeper "layers of historical experiences" and collective political struggles. Muñoz thus reports that it took her much longer to "to establish trust" with Central American participants: speaking Spanish with a Mexican accent was enough to create distance in such encounters, to tap into histories of inter-ethnic distrust, and to bring "to light the silent ethnic conflicts and sentiments that some Mexicans and Central Americans have in Los Angeles" (Muñoz 2012: 4.9).

In short, Muñoz's ethnography also entailed some more complex interpersonal negotiations that reflected her own background. This underscores yet again, if any further evidence were needed, that social research is of course always a social process in its own right, which should not be misconstrued as a decontextualized or depersonalized collection of straightforward "facts" in a political vacuum. As all examples of the application of the sociological imagination discussed in this book show, social researchers are also social, historically situated actors who—for all their methodological reflexivity and analytical skills—also carry their own biographical "baggage" and view the social world, at least in some contexts, from the distinctive vantage points of their own subject positions. What is more, social researchers are themselves viewed by others in those subject positions. In Muñoz's case, the complex interplay of biographical circumstances and methodological skill enables her to reveal a "degree of agency" (Muñoz 2012: 3.3)—clearly constrained by multiple, overlapping structures of power—in the (informal) economic lives of Mexican and Central American vendors on the streets of LA. Muñoz demonstrates that to comprehend their lives we need to also extend our gaze to the workings of local authorities (e.g., the police, immigration control), to locally operating gangs, the enduring legacies of migration histories, the everyday experience of racialization, and to the specific urban geographies of the neighborhoods in question. Amid all of this, Muñoz's "visual field methods" and long-term ethnographic immersion constitute her means for capturing Latino immigrants' "spatial claims and settlement practices" underpinned by their entrepreneurial practices and associated "landscape signifiers": sidewalks are thus shown to be partly "claimed" by vendors whose "displays of foods, umbrellas and murals" and repertoire of ethnic symbolism (e.g., "Mexican flags, eagles, and the Lady of Guadalupe") reflect the transnational flow of "culture and custom via Mexican and Central American immigrant influence"; against all external constraints, street vendors thereby "exercise agency in reorganizing public space," as their presence and produce—variously manifestations of "cultural additions [and] resistance"—"weave" themselves into the urban "landscape and ultimately change the space" (Muñoz 2012: 8.1–8.2).

With our second, select illustration we move from one "global city" (Sassen 2001) to another, from LA to London. More accurately, I next return to Dawn Lyon and Les Back's innovative study of Deptford market in South East London that was already mentioned in a previous chapter. Long part of London's "riverside economy," Deptford—as a place of ship building, manufacturing, and a market for fish and other (imported) foods—constituted a significant local node for the British empire. Subsequently bypassed by some economic flows, following the "revolution in containerization" since the 1960s, the area's history has also been shaped by successive global migrations and its market has come to constitute an "agora of multiculture" (Lyon and Back 2012: 4.1–4.3) Against this backdrop, Lyon and Back offer detailed case studies of the two aforementioned local fishmongers, their contrasting life histories and entrepreneurial strategies. Seen in their broader contexts, these fishmongers' everyday lives and work also reflect "how global connections are threaded through the local economy" (Lyon and Back 2012: 1.3). As a necessary precondition for capturing such entanglements of the global with the idiosyncratically local and biographical, Lyon and Back make a compelling epistemological case for the importance of both "the visual" *and* "the aural" that underpins their use of "observations, photography and sound recordings" in Deptford market. Having started their explorations as part of a wider project on the applications of "new media" in social research, Lyon and Back built on their photographic documenting of the market and on a strategy of "hanging around" their main research participants—*Charlie* and *Khalid*—who, we are told, enjoyed, the ethnographic interest invested in them while also showing some reluctance to being formally interviewed. Increasingly aware of the richness of the "background sounds of work in the market," Lyon and Back concluded that their interests required them "to listen as well as to look." Listening offered ways of capturing aspects of everyday local life that the "freeze frame of the photographic image" would have missed. At the same time, Lyon and Back's strategies for tapping into the aural dimensions of Deptford market went far beyond conventional methods of listening (i.e., interviews with select research participants as part of what we may consider to be the standard methods-toolbox in the social sciences). In fact, Lyon and Back echo earlier criticisms of too many social researchers' un-reflexive "over-reliance on the interview," whereby a methodological choice sometimes precedes and can thus be out of step with the actual research questions being posed. Instead, Lyon and Back's broader use of visual and aural methods, which led them to produce "several hundred images and several sound recordings," enabled them to capture something else: "areas of social life that are difficult for people to verbalise [...] that are in one way or another beyond or on the edge of consciousness, or that are part of one's *habitus*"[6] (Lyon and Back 2012: 2.4).

The most relevant characteristics of Lyon and Back's work for our purposes are therefore the following: their interest in how parts of the global economy "touch down," in a manner of speaking, in a local market; their epistemological premise that a capturing of those facets of everyday life that, following Anthony Giddens' (1984) distinction, fall into the domain of "practical" rather than "discursive consciousness" (i.e., essentially the routinely practiced but rarely spoken of) demand novel methodological strategies; and the particular data Lyon and Back's "multi-sensory" ethnography generates. The obvious question arises as to what the weaving together of these three core-features in Lyon and Back's work reveals with regard to glocalization. To answer this, a closer look at their two main research participants is necessary. Charlie, the first of the two fishmongers in question, is described as a "white Londoner" and the "oldest surviving member" of a family of fishmongers going back three generations. Charlie's business is a long-established part of the local economic infrastructure. His ("tacit and embodied") craft reflects an inherited family tradition and involves a "deep sensory connection to the fish as material, object and product of his labour"; at the same time, as Lyon and Back (2012: 5.1, 5.14, 5.8) also record, Charlie is acutely aware of how the fish market has changed "as the local population has become more culturally diverse" and as global fish imports now "serve the local tastes derived from [...] international pathways of migration." This is where Khalid, Lyon and Back's second key research participant, enters the scene, so-to-speak, both as an economic competitor and entrepreneurial innovator. Born in Kashmir, Khalid initially struggled to establish himself in Deptford market, being "frozen out by Charlie's network." Khalid's response involved mobilizing his own (diasporic) network of connections and suppliers, as well as a diversification of products his business now offers (i.e., including fish, Halal meat, a range of other foods and commodities catering to the area's diverse residents): showing a more astute awareness of his customers' culturally heterogeneous tastes and consumption patterns than "any policy-maker or sociologist," Khalid's shop resembles a "map of the local ethnoscape"; he himself, the authors suggest, may be considered a quintessential "craftsman of urban multiculture" (Lyon and Back 2012: 6.1–6.8).

Lyon and Back's account of Deptford market and particularly their depiction of Khalid reflect a "multiculture at work," which they analyze through Paul Gilroy's concept of *conviviality* (Lyon and Back 2012: 7.2). The convivial, according to Gilroy, refers to a spontaneous but widespread "ability to live with alterity" without anxiety, fear or violence but also without "announcing" itself; convivial are those "processes of cohabitation and interaction that have made multiculture an ordinary feature of social life [...] in postcolonial cities"; and while conviviality certainly does not indicate an "absence of racism" in such urban spaces, it "makes a nonsense of closed, fixed, and reified identity" (Gilroy 2004: xi; 161). Given that conviviality thus relates to the domain of largely taken-for-granted everyday practice, rather than to consciously articulated political positions, it is arguably also best captured through research methodologies focused on the mundane and generally overlooked. Thematically and methodologically highly relevant in this context is Alex Rhys-Taylor's study of another London market. More concretely, Rhys-Taylor (2013: 394, 395) offers some remarkable insights into the "olfactory and gustatory exchanges between migrants to cities and the local culture," through which a convivial metropolitanism is—at least in part—achieved and experienced; this in turn, as Rhys-Taylor elaborates, demands a "honing" of our "sociological attention to the mundane, everyday sensory experience of urban space" in which smell and taste play an important role. This is powerfully illustrated in his account of Ridley Road Market in East London, one of several locations the author visited twice weekly for two years, subjecting it to "sensorial attention" and producing "inventories of [...] their sounds, smells, flavors and textures":

> [The] first smell I encounter [...] is that of pungent fruit commingling with the sweetish petrol smell from the nearby road [...] [I] start separating the fragrances of different fruits: the delicate turpentine inflections of mango, melons that smell not entirely unlike overfill bins and the alcohol-tinged scent of ripe bananas. These smells [...] gain strength as I pass more fruit stalls [...] a warm yeasty smell enters my nose, followed by a blend of South Asian spices: coriander, cumin and cardamom [...] [T]he baking smell [...] from the local bagel bakery [is] a residue of the market's early twentieth century Jewish users [...] [T]he smell of the sea [from] a cluster of fishmongers [...] [is] interspersed with relatively odourless, yet visually and aurally aggressive, toy stalls. From these arise the nutty pastry smell of dumplings and patties, mixing the unmistakable smell of bacon being fried on one side, and the sugary burnt smell of caramelized onion [...] [and] accompany the steaming halal hot dogs [...] [T]he muddy scent of potatoes laced

with spiky coriander [...] a distinctive fusion of smells—polythene bags, dusty factory storage and mass transit—all emanating from a luggage stall [...] [M]usical mélange competes with the calls of a nearby fruit vendor: "Bunches of banana, cheaper than in Ghana" [...] [The] walk continues [...] [with a] new set of fragrances [...] "Egyptian musk", "Sandalwood", "Laxmi Pooja" [...] Attention to this smell is, however, diverted by the smell of marijuana [...] a large blue bin labelled "Strictly not for human consumption", a label I do not see until it is too late: [the] powerful but highly localized smell of fish guts and decomposing cardboard. (Rhys-Taylor 2013: 395–397)

It is thus through sustained ethnographic attention to the "sensescape" at a market in East London that Rhys-Taylor captures the tastes, smells and textures of transnational produce as it touches down, in a manner of speaking, locally. Simultaneously beyond many people's conscious awareness and an integral part of lived conviviality, foodstuffs clearly rank prominently among the global flows that shape many of our urban spaces in this epoch of glocalization. Beyond the seemingly banal, there are questions of deep sociological significance that the research discussed in this section helps us name and address. Those are questions about experiences of urban pluralism, as well as about how those may be best documented and made sense of.

We have covered wide-ranging conceptual and geographical terrain in this chapter. Following some reflections on how local knowledge and bodily immersion in a locality can combine in efforts to capture urban spaces over time, I revisited prominent moments and paradigms in the history of urban sociology. Building on this brief history of ideas in this particular sub-disciplinary branch, I then turned to how the urban setting I know best (i.e., Austria's second city of Graz) —and some of the *glocalizing* shifts discernible in it—can be illuminated through a selective and critical synthesis of different strands from within different conceptual frameworks (i.e., those variously associated with classical Chicago School urban sociology, the later "LA School," and yet more recent work on post-secular and diasporic urbanity). This paved the way to a discussion of select, methodologically innovative contributions to urban sociology that have, through various forms of multisensory ethnography, captured local manifestations of some of the global "flows and scapes" that constitute this book's focus. As we discover next, however, the wide-ranging discussion in this chapter does not exhaust the relevance of urban spaces for a sociological understanding of glocalization. In the next chapter, we will therefore continue our engagement with specific urban spaces and phenomena. Our focus thereby shifts toward the semiotic realm—the (public) domain of symbols and signs.

Notes

1 Urban movement, and walking in particular, have long occupied prominent places in social and cultural research. This applies, first, to walking as a topic of discussion or, even, as a unit of analysis: one may cite Michel de Certeau's discussion (1984: 91–110) of *walking in the city* as indicative of some of the "tactics" the powerless employ to temporarily evade the grid or "web" of power and control, in which their (everyday) lives are embedded. Similarly relevant are Georg Simmel's reflections on the historical significance of the "tumultuous" modern city (Lichtblau 2019: 42) or Walter Benjamin's famous observations of the *flaneur* (Lauster 2007). Second, walking has come to be recognized as offering considerable methodological-epistemological promise for the qualitative social sciences: see, for example, Lindner's (2007: 151ff) discussion of *Wanderlust* as a hallmark of Chicago School sociology (also Bulmer [1984: 77] for a discussion of how the practice of "walking around the city" helped shape Robert E. Park's thinking). More recent illustrations of some methodological applications of walking include Peyrefitte's (2012) use of "visual tours" as a means of understanding local actors' perceptions and experiences of inner-cities; and Natali's (2019) discussion of "itinerant soliloquies" as a "multi-sensorial way" of accessing research participants' experiences of environmental harm in some of today's global cities.

2 Tangentially relevant, in this context, are Hockey and Collinson's (2006) reflections on the intersections of autoethnography and the "distance runner's perspective."

3 Given the long-standing prominence of walking as both a thematic issue and a methodological tool in the social sciences, the critical interjection as to what exactly *running* may add is to be expected. Clearly, the case being made here must be for particular methodological gains (i.e., the argument cannot be tantamount to just indulging this sociologist's favorite pastime). In answer to this question, let me emphasize that running is by no means here being advocated as a sociological substitute for, but as an addition to, to walking. This having been said, there are a number of features particular to running that provide unique benefits to field researchers. First, there is the obvious benefit that running enables us to cover and immerse ourselves in larger terrains within shorter stretches of time. Second, there is the curious phenomenon well-known to trained runners that running is often experienced as less tiresome than walking the same distances tends to be. Third, running not only takes us further but it also tends to traverse a wider range of different kinds of spaces (when compared to walking): as a means of moving, running is less tied to activities such as sight-seeing or shopping; running is less likely to engage us, or get us misread, as "tourists." Instead, running tends to be decoded as, and often amounts to, a cultural practice that requires local knowledge and involves largely local residents; as part of an everyday life lived in situ, running puts us into closer or easier proximity to the ethnographic project of immersion in a local lifeworld. Similarly, journalist Tom Rottenberg has recently argued that long runs in cities are ideally suited to getting us to "see" more, to notice the ambivalent characteristics of urban living—such as the "simultaneity of beauty and pain"—that cannot be reduced to an "either-or" logic (Rottenberg 2021).

4 My formulation here is deliberate, for the selection and ticking of a predefined "box" on a census constitutes an example of what Richard Jenkins (1997) calls "social categorization" and describes as a form of (predominantly) external classification.

Put differently, people's actual, lived ethnic self-understandings—or what Jenkins describes as "group identification"—may diverge considerably from the designations "on offer" in official, top-down exercises such as the provision of census information.

5 For a similar, though geographically distant discussion of a locally endured, negative "reputational geography," see Parker and Karner (2010).

6 The conceptualization of the habitus invoked here is that provided by Pierre Bourdieu. Bourdieu (1977: 72–83) famously defined the habitus as a set of "structuring structures" that include "durable, transposable dispositions," a "socially constituted system of cognitive and motivating" patterns (e.g., culturally shared categories and tastes), and "schemes of thought" that enable the "intentionless invention of regulated improvisation" in the face of unforeseen circumstances. In short, this central concept in Bourdieu-ian sociology describes (sub-)culturally shared "perceptions, appreciations, and actions" that tend to aid the reproduction of the social conditions and relations out of which the habitus emerges in the first place.

Chapter 6

GLOCAL PALIMPSESTS

Description → *Analysis* (→ Criticism)

Core parts of this book are about how we may arrive at valid, sociological claims to knowing and understanding our present moment that is widely experienced as novel and qualitatively different from what preceded it. Skeptics may argue that assumptions about the uniqueness of one's times are nothing new, perhaps a historical constant in its own right, perhaps a sign of a recurring historical myopia. After all, have people not always considered their own epoch to be particular, and often particularly challenging? Leaving this question for historians to ponder, there are—as we have seen— compelling reasons to assume that there are indeed structural and cultural particularities that warrant depictions of the "here and now" as distinctive. The concept of *glocalization* provides, arguably, the most apt term for capturing the particularities in question.

In epistemological and methodological terms, previous chapters have gone some way toward developing central arguments offered in this book: namely that the flows, interconnectedness, interdependencies and counterreactions that define our age of glocalization demand novel or refined ways of generating data; this is particularly so for the tradition of empirical, qualitative sociology that Max Weber (1972 [1922]) famously defined through its focus on *understanding* (or more evocatively captured by the German term "verstehende Soziologie"). Previous chapters have conveyed some of the methodological richness of sociology's qualitative toolkit today. Admittedly, relatively few contributions to the discipline have met Weberian standards for illuminating the interplay of meanings, social action, and resulting social relationships and institutions. Yet, we have seen that there is no shortage of methodologically innovative work able to help sharpen social scientists' senses for the many ways in which "the global" and "the local" intersect. In this chapter, I push the argument a step further: I again commence with empirical questions about where (else) to go looking for some of the manifestations of glocalization. Following the structure of previous chapters, the argument will then turn a more distinctly analytical corner to ask how some of the resulting observations may be read and interpreted. This also helps prepare the ground for the subsequent chapter, in which I will argue that updated ways of perceiving, recording and making sense of our lived realities sociologically must be accompanied not only by relevant analytical frames but also by a willingness to engage with the social world critically. I begin this chapter, once again, in a very specific locality.

At the *Donaukanal*

I propose to set the scene for our exploration of another facet of glocalization in a way that is consistent with my previous call for the keeping of research and field diaries for the purposes of recording new observations and the questions, to which they give rise. The following account of a very particular urban site was the result of one of my many stays in Vienna over the last two decades. Contextualizing, "thick description" (Geertz 1973) of the locality in question is then enhanced further, echoing the methodological trajectory of Chapter 1, by paying particular attention to some of the area's prominent visual features.

> 19 April 2019
>
> Today I am in my favorite city, not the one I know best, that would be Graz, but the place where I have spent my happiest and sociologically most perceptive times over recent years. Vienna is a city of tourism, rich in history and what artistic and political elites associate with "high culture" (i.e. classical music, museums housing some of the Western world's most famous paintings, including some that testify to one of the most creative periods of cultural, literary and intellectual production—the fin-de-siècle—on record). There are the famous sites no tourist will miss, most of them historically connected to the former Habsburg Empire or its gradual demise and eventual disintegration.
>
> But Vienna has other sites, ones much more meaningful especially to its young, but often overlooked or missed by those who only briefly visit the city. Amongst those sites are the spaces created, and continuously being added to, along the two banks of the *Donaukanal*. The *Donaukanal* is a 17 kilometers long side-branch of the river Danube that separates Vienna's nineteenth-, ninth-, first-, third-, and eleventh districts on one side, from the city's twentieth- and second districts on the other. Along its busiest and central stretch, which separates the first from the second districts along a distance of nearly 2 kilometers, the banks of the canal have become—in the new millennium—a youthful, eventful and constantly changing area.

Today, the Donaukanal's central section can variously be described as a party mile, as the space from which boats setting off for other places attracting tourism along the Danube (e.g. Bratislava, the Slovak capital located a mere one hour and fifteen minutes by boat, or a nature reserve on the outskirts of Vienna) leave; as a place of leisure and consumption, with walkers, runners, cyclists, artists, bars, cafes and nightclubs all cramming into two narrow bands of concrete between the canal on one side, and Vienna's metro-system and one of her busiest roads on the other. It is also a culturally diverse and decidedly young space: a space of drinking, rich in graffiti, and—as the olfactory layers clouding parts of the canal's banks during the evening hours suggest—of cannabis-smoking for some; but also and much more commonly, of ice creams shared by friends and lovers during Vienna's often hot summers. It is a space of music, laughter, sun-bathing, occasional conflicts; and a space of profound sociability.

It was today, on my most recent trip to the Donaukanal, that an important realization dawned on me. Here, hardly anyone amongst the young has their eyes fixed on their smart phones. Over recent years I have found myself, with growing frequency, worrying about what the digital revolution is perhaps *also* doing to the kinds of simple (or not so simple?) face-to-face interactions that, on a superficial reading, may appear to be squeezed out by social media and otherwise digitally mediated communication among many of us today. In my least charitable moments, these worries can spill over into a deep cultural pessimism. I have even wondered—"hypothesized" would be too strong and scientific a word for what is a more mundane process of me ordering my impressions—whether the communicative revolutions of the last three decades may be (indirectly) related to the worrying increase in mental health concerns reported by growing numbers of (young) people today. If I was to formulate a possible and at first sight perhaps paradoxical proposition, it may be to postulate that the more digitalized communication becomes, the more pronounced experiences of isolation, atomization and loneliness may become, too. The Donaukanal proves this spectacularly wrong. If one wants to see young people communicate face-to-face, with all the skill and enjoyment I sometimes miss in other social settings, a place of "traditional" sociability in a manner of speaking, then this is the place to be. It is not that young people no longer communicate the way I and my generation recognize and grew up with, the young just do it in places where few of the "older ones" seem to go after dark.

In addition to its sociability, the Donaukanal is also a space of constant artistic expression. What were simply kilometers of grey, dull concrete a couple of decades ago, are now multi-colored works of art in a state of constant change and expansion: beautifully crafted, often abstract depictions with no obvious meaning to most passersby; messages seemingly directed at particular individuals (whether friends or lovers); (semi-)humorous, cartoon-like murals; political slogans; national flags; nicknames, references to current affairs, statements about the police; cultural commentaries (e.g. about television or other media); ethnic symbols; sub-cultural allusions and cross references; countless tags; appeals for solidarity with the excluded and discriminated against; but also seemingly random—or sub-culturally, perhaps interpersonally encoded[1]—sequences of letters. Many hundreds of graffiti from across all these categories mingle in close, ever-changing juxtaposition on the banks of both sides of the central stretch of the Donaukanal. Having come here for many years, I know that by the time of my next planned stay in Vienna, a mere three months from now, these walls will again look a little different, just as colorful, just as rich or even fuller, but new names, new intertextual allusions and new cross-references to then current affairs, and many more tags will have been added.

Figure 6.1 Photograph taken by the author (July 2021)

How might we read such spaces sociologically? And what on earth, if anything, might they have to do with globalization and glocalization? Or, more accurately perhaps, what is the relative weight of relevance of "the global" and "the local" here? In order to address these questions, I will shortly (re)turn to a very specific, extremely small subset of what are many hundreds of graffiti along several kilometers of embankments that constitute the *Donaukanal*'s central stretch. My selection of specific graffiti for more sustained attention reflects the very question about the interface of the global with the local that has directed me throughout this book. In order to get beyond mere description of the selected signs and statements discussed below, contextualization, once again, turns out to be key. Further, I will propose that spaces like the banks of the *Donaukanal* require a semiotic sensitivity and novel analytical approaches capable of reading their complex and constantly changing *signscapes* (Nasar and Hong 1999). Such sensitivity and the insights it can help spur in turn require a preliminary theoretical overview, with which I will start the discussion offered in this chapter.

From "Webs of Significance" to Urban *Palimpsests*

Few scholars have shaped our understanding of the symbolic dimensions of social life quite as enduringly as the American anthropologist Clifford Geertz. A seminal part of Geertz's intellectual legacy revolves around his advocacy of "thick description," a term he borrowed from Gilbert Ryle, as the ethnographer's methodological strategy and trajectory. Thick description, according to Geertz, requires detailed contextualization and a willingness to observe and record from different angles and through various means (e.g., interviews, everyday conversation, participant observation, document analyses, a sensitivity—one that ethnographers typically acquire over time—toward vernacular expressions and locally prominent, though widely taken-for-granted meanings). In Geertz's own terminology, thick description aims at capturing "structures of signification" or "codes," in order to then "determine their social ground and import." By way of elaboration, the focus of Geertz's *symbolic anthropology* rested on a "multiplicity of complex conceptual structures, many of them [...] knotted into one another, which are at once strange and [...] inexplicit" and which it was the ethnographer's task "somehow first to grasp and then to render"; this task, Geertz added, could be "like trying to read [...] a manuscript—foreign, faded, full of ellipses, incoherencies [...] and tendentious commentaries" and often not written in "conventionalized graphs of sound" (Geertz 1973: 9, 10).

This offers some initial, useful thoughts on the purpose and challenges of interpreting subcultural meanings like the ones articulated through the street art either side of the *Donaukanal* and described above. However, the relevance of Geertz's approach goes considerably further and extends deep into the conceptual domain. Geertz saw culture in semiotic terms, as a system or wider context of shared signs and meanings. As social beings, humans live their lives "suspended in webs of significance" we ourselves "have spun": Geertz takes culture "to be those webs" and he defines cultural analysis as an "interpretive search" for the meanings that orient the *in situ* production, perception and interpretation of social action. What is more, Geertz also conceded that cultural analysis thus defined remained "intrinsically incomplete" and "essentially contestable": the chief reason for this lies in the fact that the anthropologist (or sociologist) essentially offers "second-order interpretations" of the actor's first-order interpretation or "emic point of view" (Geertz 1973: 5–29). Put differently, such an understanding of ethnography as a way of "penetrat[ing] an unfamiliar universe of symbolic action" (Geertz 1973: 24) approximates Anthony Giddens's (1984) previously mentioned account of qualitative social science as revolving around a "double hermeneutic" whereby the pre-interpreted is subject to further interpretation by the social scientist. Geertz also helps us see the potential divergences between the first-order meanings and second-order readings involved in such a process.

Our later return to the locality described above will need to be informed by an awareness of the premises and promises of Geertzian "thick description" and (sub)cultural/semiotic analysis, as well as of their inherent provisionality and limitations. To add to the challenge, my particular examples of symbolic action and expression in this chapter present us with further difficulties. Those are related to the genre and register of expression at hand, namely graffiti. In an article on "becoming a visual sociologist," John Grady (2001: 95) reminds us of the "three-stage process" at the heart of the sociological method: the definition of "a universe of meaning," followed by a "sampling [of] that universe," and the coding of the resulting data. Familiar and convincingly methodical though this is, what if our chosen "universe of meaning" keeps changing not only over fairly lengthy stretches of time but if, instead, flux and constant amendments are part of its very semiotic and semantic being (i.e., in terms of both the outward signifiers and the transmitted meanings it contains)? How can such a constantly changing universe of meanings *in flux* be sampled and coded? Arguably, street art and locations of the kinds described above epitomize such symbolic actions and meanings in constant (re-)making. Conceptually and methodologically, this calls for more thought and discussion. My suggestion here is that the concept of the *palimpsest* and what we may call a "palimpsestic methodology" (Karner and Kazmierczak 2017) can provide us with the required analytical traction.

Originally associated with classical studies scholarship, the notion of the *palimpsest* describes a multiply rewritten text to which annotations, erasures and substitutions are applied over lengthy periods of time (e.g., Jauss 1993, Assmann 1999: 151–158). More recently, the term has come to be recognized as offering broader heuristic value across a range of disciplines and research settings. Gérard Genette's (1997) theory of "transtextuality" is noteworthy here, as is more recent work on "hypertextuality" in the digital domain (e.g., Kazmierczak 2008). Yet more relevant to our purposes, urban studies and literary scholars writing about cities have appropriated the concept to capture urban spaces and "imaginaries" as *urban palimpsests* (Huyssen 2003: 7, Levey 2014) or have read entire cities as "both a physical space and a site of writing" and as "constantly rewritten or revised text[s] in which history and imagination, memory and forgetting [are] impossible to disentangle" (Thomas 2010: 2, 3; also Battaglia 2014). More recently, the notion of the palimpsest has been extended yet further to trace the *longue durée* roots and ideational strands selectively reappropriated in the ideological service of present-day neo-nationalisms (Karner and Kazmierczak 2017). This chapter, then, builds on such diverse thematic and methodological applications of the concept of the palimpsest and seeks to develop them further.

Before applying a version of a palimpsestic methodology to the locality described above, further preliminary comments are needed. More particularly, the analytical dividends offered by "the palimpsest" as a heuristic device warrant more specification. Claire Launchbury and Cara Levey (2014: 1) offer precisely this when they describe palimpsests as "multi-layered configurations of meaning" defined by, in Max Silverman's terminology, "underlying traces which have never fully disappeared [...] [and] the superimposition and productive interaction of different inscriptions." This complements Anit Bhatti's (2014: 36) account of palimpsests as "negat[ing]" essentializing conceptualizations of "authenticity" and as recognizing that the "multiple layers" of continuously rewritten cultural texts are all significant in their contexts of articulation, circulation, reception and potential further reappropriation. In the particular application offered here, I begin to probe a specific urban palimpsest for its historically and locally specific "configurations of meaning" and for some of its constitutive discursive and semiotic layers. Relating this back to the growing scholarship on palimpsests summarized above, this is underpinned by my premise that not only ancient manuscripts, urban architecture or texts about cities can be read palimpsestically. Instead, I push the concept yet further by illustrating how the banks along Vienna's *Donaukanal* can be read as an urban-cum-ideological palimpsest (Karner and Kazmierczak 2017: 5) in constant (re-)making. "Ideology" is thereby defined as comprising ideas and social practices that play a role in the reproduction or—more relevant to the materials at hand—the contestation of existing power relations (Augoustinos 1998). As we shall see, such (publicly articulated) ideas and social practices are themselves partly constituted by, and reference, various argumentative, semiotic and experiential sources and strands in a manner geared toward present circumstances and political objectives.

Putting the heuristic of a palimpsest to meaningful analytical use in the urban setting at hand requires careful historical contextualization and ethnographically enabled local knowledge. In short, what is needed is thick description. Crucially, such local knowledge, and the analytical insights that build on it, also need to be attuned to global events, frames and influences that local actors reference. With my theoretical apparatus thus outlined, I next (re-) turn to the (sub)cultural, semiotic palimpsest in question.

Reading Vienna's Palimpsests

Interpretations of Vienna's cityscapes as palimpsests, including a focus on politically charged signs within them, are not new. The late Tony Judt (2010: 1), one of the most important historians of the twentieth century, frames his recollections of Vienna in the enormously consequential year of 1989 by suggesting that the city was indeed a "palimpsest of Europe's complicated, overlapping pasts." Judt's observations drew on Vienna's then recent history, the city's architecture, geographical location, as well as on the selectivity of cultural memories still dominant at the end of the Cold War. While "the imposing, confident buildings lining the great Ringstrasse[2] were a reminder of Vienna's one-time imperial vocation," Judt argues that the city's later historical experiences had also left local traces: from the fin-de-siècle when Vienna was the "fertile, edgy, self-deluding hub of a culture and civilization on the threshold of apocalypse"; the interwar experiences that included the traumatic reduction of a formerly "glorious imperial metropole to the impoverished, shrunken capital of a tiny rump-state" as well as the city's then pioneering municipal socialism; to, subsequently, Austria's darkest historical chapter as a "provincial outpost of a Nazi empire to which most of its citizens swore enthusiastic fealty" (Judt 2010: 2). Falling, after the end of World War II, into the "Western camp" and embracing the purported "status of Hitler's 'first victim'," Austrians soon came to reap the benefits of postwar Western Europe: "capitalist prosperity underpinned by a richly endowed welfare-state," social peace, practically full employment, "external security assured by the implicit protection of the Western nuclear umbrella" although the country remained, as constitutionally enshrined since 1955, permanently, or in Judt's formulation, "smugly" neutral. In the process, Vienna had become a "Western city," in very close proximity to the Iron

Curtain: "surrounded by Soviet 'eastern' Europe," and cultivating a "new identity as outrider and exemplar of the free world" (Judt 2010: 2).

Typical of palimpsests, of course, is their selectivity of what is added, retained and partly overwritten or erased. The selectivity of local cultural memories in the postwar era is also captured by Judt: Vienna, he argues, both invoked the city's "older glories" and was noticeable "reticent" with regard to much more difficult facets of the city's past. The latter included many of her residents' Nazi allegiance during World War II; reticence also manifested, at the time, as widespread amnesia concerning Viennese Jews who had contributed majorly to "art, music, theatre, literature, journalism and ideas that were Vienna in its heyday" before their persecution, dispossession, expulsion and mass murder during the Holocaust (Judt 2010: 3). Unlike the contemporary politics typically articulated along the *Donaukanal* (see below), Judt's observations focus on the conservative, in some quarters decidedly reactionary, (neo-)nationalist strands in Viennese and Austrian society that would also come to shape the 1990s and the new millennium in important ways (Karner 2020a: 139–213). Recalling another visit to Vienna 10 years after 1989, Tony Judt also draws attention to how prominent political messages at the time reflected then recent social shifts:

[I]n October 1999 I found the Westbahnhof [western railway station] covered in posters for the Freedom Party of Jörg Haider who, despite his open admiration for the "honourable men" of the Nazi armies who "did their duty" on the eastern front, won 27 percent of the vote that year by mobilizing his fellow Austrians' anxiety and incomprehension at the changes that had taken place in their world over the past decade. After nearly half a century of quiescence Vienna—like the rest of Europe—had re-entered history. (Judt 2010: 3)

In addition to sketching some of the longer histories behind the empirical setting discussed here, these particular observations by Tony Judt also make an implicit methodological case: namely that publicly disseminated signs that communicate political positions (e.g., electoral posters) can offer snapshots of wider sentiments and their mobilization. The street art to be discussed here reveals political messages very different from, and often diametrically opposed to, the nationalism reported by Judt. What such contrasting messages have in common, however, is the fact that their analyses require careful contextualization.

My descriptive account above of the banks of the *Donaukanal* was produced two decades after Judt's second set of impressions of Vienna, three decades after his first. In the period since then, during what Judt describes as Austria's (and much of Europe) "re-entering history," social, demographic, and political changes in (and far beyond) the city have indeed been far-reaching. Throughout the 1990s and into the new millennium, rates of immigration to Austria were considerably above the Western European average (Weigl 2009: 47), leading to a new diversification of Austrian and especially Viennese society as well as to a reactionary neo-nationalism in some quarters (e.g., Karner 2020a: 165–186). Today, thirty years after the disintegration of the Iron Curtain that had previously separated Vienna from its Eastern European neighbors very close by, the city has—of course not for the first time in its history—again become a place of multiple crossroads and highly visible, highly heterogenous *ethnoscapes*. Austrian politics in the early twenty-first century has indeed displayed some of the hallmarks of glocalization discussed throughout this book, namely the complex interplay of global flows and their local (re)appropriation and, at times, localist opposition to them. Concurrently, Vienna in particular has acquired an international reputation as a particularly "livable" city, as offering a high quality of life that is repeatedly acknowledged in the city "rankings" typical of our late modern era (see Reckwitz 2020: 226).

To return from wider historical contexts to the particular locality introduced above, it should be noted that soon after I had written my account of Vienna's Donaukanal, one of the city's best-known museums ran an exhibition (i.e., on *street art and skateboarding*) highly pertinent to the present discussion. Clearly, street art had become a local issue important and noticeable not only to inquisitive sociologists. The museum's press-information at the time is worth quoting at length:

> Vandalism or art? Street art and skateboarding continue to polarize opinion. If the general public viewed these overlapping scenes as a disruptive nuisance during the 1990s and 2000s, today street art and skateboarding are regarded as pop-cultural phenomena. Not only [do] they lend cities an urban flair, they also contribute to tourism and the local economy. Even the art market has begun to take notice [...] Whose city? Graffiti and street artists play with our notions of urban space, characterized as it is by the omnipresence of advertising and established rules. These artists' works surprise, delight, and disturb, all the while interrogating existing power relationships. Vienna is their focus, even if their approaches are as diverse as the scene itself—by turns self-serving, political, feminist, and playful. More than thirty artists who have left their mark on the cityscape over the past twenty-five years have taken over the museum's walls. The result: creations that go beyond the artists' works in the public realm [...] Street art

und graffiti use the city itself as a canvas. The constant transformation of urban space reveals new kinds of lettering, stickers, stencils, and murals to careful observers on a daily basis. Yet these discoveries often disappear just as quickly as they appear—painted or pasted over, or simply scrubbed away. It is precisely because of this ephemerality that documentation plays an important role. Often it's only a photo that remains. (Wien Museum 2019)

There is much in this to guide our discussion. First, the *Wien Museum* notes that public perceptions of street art, though still split, have shifted toward a growing recognition of graffiti as a legitimate pop-cultural practice. Second, the politics of street art take central space here: not only are street artists recognized as "interrogating existing power relations," but their work is seen as feeding into the crucial questions as to "whose city" people inhabit and as to how urban spaces get made and remade. Third, without using the term, the account above captures some quintessential urban palimpsests: after all, we are told that street artists "use the city as a canvas," on which perpetually added-to images and messages are subject to "constant transformation" by being "painted over or simply scrubbed away." And finally, this "ephemerality" again underscores the methodological challenge as to how we might capture, conserve and read a constantly changing semiotic field. With this in mind, let us return to the particular locality described above.

As has already been mentioned, in the new millennium the two banks of the *Donaukanal*—particularly along the stretch that separates the city's first and second districts—have become a popular, youthful and particularly busy area. From spring until autumn, the area's outdoor bars, artistic initiatives, community gardens, daily sociability and spaces for sports and other leisure activities attract locals and visitors alike. As I have discussed elsewhere (Karner 2020c), however, most noticeable are the continuously "re-graffitied" walls either side of the canal: there, artists' tags sit alongside more elaborate depictions that display neighborhood- and football-team allegiances, symbols of ethnic-diasporic identification, and political statements (i.e., generally from the Left). The many examples of the latter include, on the north(-east)ern bank of the canal along its busiest section that also marks parts of the second district's boundaries, a particular, large graffiti mural—against a dark red backdrop—that makes reference to the 2007 album "Zona Antifascista" by German anarcho-punk band Guerilla. In the context of some of the other messages nearby to be discussed shortly, it is both plausible and necessary to read this intertextual allusion to a particular musical subculture as an example of what semiotics defines as *polysemy*, or the "plurality of meanings" (Chandler 2017: 246) of a sign or text. In this particular case, a graffiti mural such as the one in question also participates in space-making that here takes on a partly political tone. Political statements also enable self-identifications that draw boundaries, whether explicitly or inadvertently, between the position being advocated and an ideological "other." In addition to alluding to a particular punk album, the graffiti in question clearly carries such political connotations. More concretely, the ideological "echo" at hand is of *Antifa*, the international, internally heterogenous, far-left, anti-fascist movement. This connotative connection is substantiated by the fact that the very same album (Zona Antifascista) by Guerilla is also discussed and accessible on the website of an "anarcho-punk community," which self-defines as "an international community of punks united against capitalism, racism and authoritarianism" and which displays, among other activists' logos, the Antifa symbol (Anarcho-Punk.Net 2021). To return to the graffiti and its local context, in subtle ways this reference to the title of a punk album arguably also lays claim to its surroundings as—in a manner-of-speaking—an "anti-fascist zone." With the political boundaries and opposition it communicates, the mural arguably reflects a critical awareness of Austria's twentieth-century history (i.e., the country's descent into fascism in the 1930s, followed by Austria's annexation by Hitler's Germany in 1938 and the roles played by Austrians during World War II and the Holocaust) as well as a state of ideological polarization that has come to define Austrian politics in the crisis-prone new millennium (Karner 2020a: 189–213; 2005). Put differently, the process, first observed by Tony Judt more than two decades ago, of Vienna, Austria and Central Europe "re-entering history" includes such politicized, at times polarizing, and historically aware forms of artistic expression.

Other, select contributions to the signscape described above show that and how the walls alongside the *Donaukanal* have become perpetually overwritten canvases for street artists' commentaries on current affairs, both local and transnational or global. On the other side of the canal, almost exactly opposite the mural just mentioned, an equally rich tapestry of graffiti includes a number of national flags, notably those of Egypt, Cuba, Albania, and Bolivia. This can be read as a reflection of some of Vienna's "superdiverse" (Vertovec 2007) *ethnoscapes*. Whether the choice of some of those flags, that is, of Cuba and Bolivia, may also reflect the graffiti artists' political leanings can only be speculatively raised as a potential question for future research into the motivations and histories of production underpinning particular murals. More immediately interpretable is a locally well-known name graffitied in large, bold, white, capitalized letters back on the second district's embankments: Ute Bock, a former youth and social worker in Vienna who became widely known for her work with and for asylum-seekers. Following her retirement, Ute Bock had founded an NGO to provide apartments, postal addresses and advice for (homeless) asylum-seekers (Karner 2007b: 93; Ute Bock Flüchtlingsprojekt 2021). Long before her death in 2018, Ute Bock had become a public figure known for her humanitarian work, supported by civil society initiatives, the subject of documentaries, but also maligned by the nationalist Right. With Ute Bock's legacy and NGO continuing, there have been initiatives by artists to commemorate her in public (e.g., Salzburger Nachrichten 2019), while the nationalist FPÖ continues to publicly slander her by interpreting her past work not as vital humanitarianism but as supporting alleged gangs and their purported drug-dealing (e.g., FPÖ Wien Favoriten 2020). When I recorded my observations in April 2019, the then still recent backdrop included the much-discussed "refugee crisis" of 2015/2016 (see Krzyżanowski, Triandafyllidou, and Wodak 2018). As across Europe, the mass-arrival of (forced) migrants from war-torn Syria and elsewhere had polarized the Austrian public, pitting inclusivist civil society initiatives against an ever-more pronounced, often nationalist anxiety over the refugees' predicted, purportedly unmanageable impact on Austria (Karner 2020a: 199–202; 2020b). It is in this context that other graffiti prominent at the time need to be read: not far from the Ute Bock graffiti just mentioned, right above the waterline of the *Donaukanal* and hence best visible from the opposite embankment, the statement "solidarity knows no boundaries" (*Solidarität kennt keine Grenzen*) makes a powerful point. This declaration has become a guiding motto for international refugee-aid organizations in their pleas to national governments to allow migrants (semi-)permanently stranded in camps on Greek islands and elsewhere to be resettled across Europe and to have their asylum-claims processed under more bearable circumstances (e.g., Schweizerische Flüchtlingshilfe 2020). For our present purposes the appearance of this statement calling for solidarity with (distant) refugees among the graffiti in question shows two, closely interrelated things: first, the political nature of some of the statements on display along the *Donaukanal* corroborate that this is indeed an urban palimpsest that—as pointed out in the above-quoted Wien Museum's press-release—"interrogates" existing power relations. As with the other examples already discussed, the statement in question clearly positions its maker(s) and intended audience in relation to defining political debates of recent years and in unambiguous opposition to the nationalist Right. In Paul Edwards' (2021: 20)[3] suggestive terminology, what the graffiti in question thus also offer is a "vocabulary of protest." Second, graffiti referencing Ute Bock and calling for transnational solidarity are simultaneously local and global in their orientation; while few people outside of Austria are likely to have heard of Ute Bock, locally her name is inexorably associated with global migratory flows and human compassion that transcends national boundaries. What the graffiti discussed here amount to, then, is a form of inclusivist glocalization: local voices here respond to global flows in a spirit that defies nationalist anxieties and calls for boundary-transcending solidarity. It is also worth noting that recent migrations are not the only global flows, traces of which are discernible in the locality in question: towering above the Ute Bock graffiti (and the many other murals surrounding it) is the regional, multistorey headquarters of the international banking group Raiffeisen. Put differently, signs of transnational *financescapes* and of inclusivist, local responses to some of our era's *ethnoscapes* "sit" here in close proximity to one another.

This is an apt point at which to remember a central argument running through this book: namely that a meaningful sociological engagement with globalization must recognize that the latter comprises many types of cross-border flows. In connection to this, we are also able to trace other such transnational interconnections, their histories, and manifestations in places like the one in question here. Local historiography reveals that long-distance flows to the *Donaukanal* are not a recent or new phenomenon. In his detailed historical study, former shipping captain Alfred Karrer includes documentary sources testifying to the transnational flow of goods—particularly coffee, sugar and cotton—from Amsterdam, via the rivers Rhine, Main, a then newly constructed canal traversing parts of Franconia and Bavaria, and the Danube to, eventually after an undertaking that took 53 days at the time, the banks of the Donaukanal as early as 1846 (Karrer 2011: 13). In the course of the nineteenth and twentieth centuries the international shipping of goods along the Danube became very significant for Central Europe's economies. The extent of this was particularly apparent in the summer of 1976, when Vienna's main bridge crossing the Danube collapsed, thereby blocking the actual river to international shipping for nearly two months. During this period, the much smaller side-branch that is the Donaukanal came to play a vital, economic function: involving complex logistical operations, in August and September 1976 some 150 ships, many of them transporting cargo across several European borders (including the Iron Curtain, which cut across the Danube some forty-five kilometers downstream at the time), were able to bypass the site of the collapsed bridge and the blocked section of the main river by being rerouted through the Donaukanal (Karrer 2011: 47ff.).

To return to the transnational flow of signs and ideas or ideologies (or *signscapes* and, in Appadurai's terminology, *ideoscapes*) as the conceptual focus in this chapter, Karrer's local historiography also provides some additional momentum for our discussion of graffiti along the canal's banks. Karrer's research has compiled an impressive range of photographic sources, enabling longitudinal insights into how the Donaukanal has changed over the decades. For our purposes particularly noteworthy is the virtual absence of graffiti, except for only very few isolated examples, until the new millennium. And even photographs of areas that are now entirely covered by street art still show those as largely bare concrete walls as late as 2004, 2005, and 2006 (Karrer 2011: 121f.). Seen in its wider context, this corroborates the rapidly growing popularity of graffiti during our current, late modern moment, and it echoes the historical trajectory traced in the Wien Museum's earlier-quoted press release of the changing perceptions of street art from "disruptive nuisance" to "pop-cultural phenomenon." All this having been said, Karrer's collection of local photography also reveals, when very carefully sifted, one earlier exception. The particular image, which shows a section of the Donaukanal in the early 1950s, is highly pertinent to my earlier focus on politically charged, or at least positioned, graffiti. The photograph in question shows an isolated graffiti on the banks of the canal that read "Hands off Korea!" (Karrer 2011: 42). The immediate context at the time was that provided by Vienna's (as well as Austria's) subdivision into four Allied occupation zones between 1945 and 1955. The Donaukanal itself passes through what were, at the time the picture in question was taken, Vienna's US, Soviet, and British sectors. In other words, this statement against the UN's and principally the USA's involvement in the Korean War (1950–1953) as one of the Cold War's earliest and bloodiest military confrontations possessed an undeniable local resonance. Put differently, the (geopolitically) global here intersected with the local context of the city's (and Austria's) subdivision into Allied occupational zones during the first decade of the post-war era. Thus, resonant both with the geographically distant Korean War and with local circumstances, the "Hands off Korea" graffiti qualified as an early sign of glocalization. Further, not only was its political-ideological character self-evident, but the slogan itself circulated considerably more widely in far-Left circles at the time: this is shown, for instance, by the fact that the very same political slogan had already appeared in the official newspaper of East Germany's Communist Party in July 1950 (*Neues Deutschland* 1950).

There therefore turns out to exist a noteworthy "pre-history" to what started as a carefully contextualized reading of a tiny selection of current murals along the Donaukanal's now tensely graffitied, and continuously re-graffitied, embankments. Each of the graffiti, both historical and contemporary, discussed here also testifies to a semiotic form of glocalization, whereby global events, influences and flows are refracted through local circumstances and points of reference. In a next analytical step, I shall offer further reflections on what such palimpsests may be able to tell us about urban settings more generally.

The (G)local in Urban "Archives"

In a recent plea to "give the local its due," Victor Roudometof (2019: 801) has argued that by paying sociological attention to the "process of place-making" we may also be able to develop an appreciation of types of localization that respond to globalization in ways very different from nationalist "versions of exclusivist localism." The locality discussed in this chapter, Vienna's Donaukanal, provides empirical, semiotic evidence of such an alternative or inclusivist localism. As has already been mentioned, however, a cosmopolitan response to global migratory flows and calls for interethnic solidarity are not the only way, in which this particular locality interfaces with global events and developments. At the time of writing (in the spring of 2021), there are growing concerns, articulated particularly among some of Vienna's left-leaning Green politicians, about the area's growing commercialization; in other words, there are local fears that the youth culture lived on the canal's embankments may be about to be marginalized by the locality's growing commercialization (Wittstock 2021). If we take the "marketization" (Fraser 2014) of the formerly non-commodified, or the "economization of the social" (Reckwitz 2020: 193), as manifestations of neoliberal, global capitalism, then bottom-up "place-making" along the Donaukanal is decidedly discerning in the global flows it welcomes (i.e., migrants') and others it opposes (i.e., financial investments that commodify public space and transform it into mainstream commercial opportunities). Such ambivalences show that glocalization can take different, in some ways, contradictory forms in a single locality. In other words, there is here no such thing as globalization being either endorsed or rejected, but local reactions are considerably more nuanced and specific with regard to different global flows. This, in turn, also corroborates Roudometof's (2019: 812) points that we need to recognize the local as "not imaginary but real to inhabitants," that there are "emotional connections between people and locales," and that places mediate "globalization's impact on our lives."

In terms of the methodological questions as to where and how to look for the complexities of such glocalizing place-making, I have argued for a "palimpsestic approach" in this chapter. As my earlier conceptual outline indicated, this is in line with a growing body of scholarship that recognizes that urban spaces are continuously being *re- and overwritten* in terms of the meanings communicated, shared and contested therein. Whilst one of the roots of such work can be located in Gerald Suttles' (1984: 284) observation that "a fuller account of urban life requires more attention to the cumulative texture of local culture," subsequent elaborations have included definitions of palimpsests as comprising temporally and spatially "condensed traces" of the past (Silverman 2014: 100); and of the "city-palimpsest as layered text" that contains multiple, coexisting "traces of the past" and is tantamount to an "urban memory machine," through which "the city and its [...] places are written, reinterpreted and reframed" (Launchbury and Levey 2014: 1). While graffiti of the type discussed here, including the walls and surroundings they (re-)shape, are arguably quintessential examples of such urban palimpsests, this discussion has shown that interpreting such *signscapes* requires local knowledge and historical contextualization. Other relevant empirical studies have demonstrated as much. Diana Battaglia, for instance, has shown Havana to be "a palimpsestic city where different spatial and temporal strata have been built one on top of the other," and in ways the eschew homogeneity; instead the urban palimpsest of the Cuban capital also includes "counter-spaces and counter-histories" (Battaglia 2014: 54). Sticking closer to the original literary applications of the concept, Alfred Thomas has approached the city of Prague—and writings about Prague—as palimpsest-like: Thomas shows how Prague is akin to a "constantly rewritten or revised text" that is full of "memory, forgetting and effacements"; Prague thereby appears as "analogues to an ancient manuscript" that is "difficult to decipher" and "multilayered," and on which "numerous writers have left their trace without completely effacing the presence of their predecessors" (Thomas 2010: 2–7).

As my earlier discussion, such observations focus predominantly on the production of meanings by specific authors or creators of cultural texts and signs about, or in, particular localities. However, there is of course the similarly important question as to how meanings are received, read and possibly reappropriated. Cara Levey shifts the discussion in precisely this direction with her work on "intentional monuments" in Montevideo and Buenos Aires. Regardless of their officially "intended purpose," memorials are thereby shown to be "subject to different readings, treatments and threats over time" (Levey 2014: 67). Projected back onto the Donaukanal, this raises the question as to what, if anything, local residents or passersby actually make of the "vocabularies of protest" (Edwards 2021) discussed earlier. A similar, conceptually focused discussion of *visual rhetorics* is worth mentioning here. An early, influential contribution to this area of research set out a "three-step process" for the analysis of images: the identification of the "functions" of an image; of how successfully this is articulated; and of its "legitimacy" (Foss 1994). In a critical response, Valeri Peterson subsequently argued that this "evaluation schema" operated with distinctly "modernist assumptions" that are inappropriate for certain types of visuals: particularly images that are "fragmented, multiple [...] polymorphous, or highly stylized," that have no "explicit or identifiable authors or purposes, and visuals with multiple authors," Peterson (2001: 23) argues, challenge the "modernist distinctions between form and content, the separation of art from everyday life [as well as] hierarchical distinctions between elite and popular culture." It is noteworthy, of course, that graffiti fit Peterson's account of this alternative type of visual elements. For those, Peterson advocates a "postmodern sensibility" with its characteristic "shift in emphasis from content to form/style," and to the "fragmentation" and use of "pastiche" in certain visuals. Further, Peterson advocates a "more elemental approach to visuals" that pays attention to the "building blocks" of an image, such as "light, line, color, perspective, shading and volume." Finally, Peterson's postmodern approach "decenters the critic," as well as the creators of images, by interrogating "how visual elements communicate identity, meaning, and culture to the people who see and make sense of them" (Peterson 2001: 23, 26, 27). My discussion above began to pay attention to some of those "building blocks" (e.g., color, size) of the visuals in question; and the discussion shared Peterson's insistence that such visual elements have to be "read" against their local and historical backdrops. Put differently, contextual knowledge and cues are vital for identifying what, following Stuart Hall (2014), we might call "dominant" or intended encodings of often indeterminate or polysemic images and messages. While I have been able to interpret the selected graffiti in their (g)local contexts, Peterson's intervention provides a useful reminder of the fact that the analysis offered above nonetheless remains incomplete. The "decoding" (Hall 2014) side of the equation thus remains the object of important *reception studies* in the future.

Whether a chosen focus lies on the intended or "encoded" messages of specific visuals, as in the discussion above, or on reception studies that can only be anticipated here, a more basic question presents itself: what do images like the ones described and discussed here amount to, when viewed in their wider contexts? If they are, as I have argued, to be read as part and parcel of the wider representational domains that are integral parts of cities, how are we to define their (sub)cultural status? One answer is to read urban palimpsests like the ones found alongside Vienna's Donaukanal as part of the city's lived archives. Recent contributions to urban sociology have broadened our understanding of archives as "active sites" that take many forms and record parts of the past *and* present; encountered in diverse documents as much as in public spaces and, increasingly, in the digital realm, today's diverse and lived archival practices involve a wide range of social actors, they "evoke richly layered temporalities," "provide rhetorical resources for the formation of identities," and illustrate how local "knowledge is created and contested" (see Parker and Karner 2011: 295–304). Simply put: the Donaukanal is part of Vienna's lived and distinctly palimpsestic archive thus defined, in which signs and ideas pertaining to the local and global interface.

Reflecting on the (micro)politics surrounding public spaces in Ottawa, Deborah Landry has made an argument that is conceptually and thematically highly relevant to this chapter. To understand graffiti murals, Landry argues, we need to "read the symbols in relation to th[eir] culture, time, location [and] [...] other symbols, [as] signs only make sense in relation to the context in which they are embedded"; further, and in inadvertent corroboration of the argument made earlier, many such morals "provide a window of what is sayable" in public spaces where "moral orders" are "played out" and fought over (Landry 2019: 690–692).[4]

Empirically, the discussion developed in this chapter constitutes but a possible starting point for what could become a highly fruitful way of capturing—metaphorically speaking—the full kaleidoscope of an urban culture that is not only at once profoundly local *and* global, but also much else besides; not least, the urban (sub)culture that this discussion has begun to reveal is in parts deeply political, if by "political" we understand any engagement with existing relations of power. What has been offered here is best read as an invitation for further, more wide-ranging semiotic analyses of these or other urban palimpsests and as an outline of what such analyses require. After all, my own contextualization and discussion of a tiny subsection of what are many hundreds of graffiti along several kilometers of the Donaukanal's banks was by definition extremely selective. My intention and focus, however, have of course been deliberate and guided by my thematic and conceptual focus on "glocalization." What this discussion certainly reveals is the potential for signscapes to reveal much about local history and about a locality's many entanglements and interconnections with distant places, geographically remote cultural influences, and global migratory flows. The discussion has also shown that the ensuing analysis benefits from a conceptual vocabulary suited to how "in-flux" some such signscapes are.

Attentive readers will have noticed that my descriptive account of the Donaukanal at the start of the chapter also introduced another key-theme, to which the discussion above never returned: that of digital communication and digital technologies, as well as of some of their unintended consequences. This omission will be rectified in our next and penultimate chapter.

Notes

1 Read through the semiotic terms first coined by Swiss linguist Ferdinand de Saussure, in the case of such encoded signs the *signified* (or meaning) communicated by the sign's outward form (i.e., the *signifier*) is known and shared only among the members of an exclusive in-group.

2 The *Ringstraße* is Vienna's best-known boulevard, along which many of the Austrian capital's most impressive buildings (e.g., the state opera, the imperial palace,

the parliament, the city hall, the university, the *Burgtheater*, some of the city's most frequented museums, the stock exchange) are located. The Ring encircles—in roughly u-shaped fashion—the city's first district on three sides, whilst its two end points both connect with the *Donaukanal*.

3 In an analysis of German satirical magazines in the early twentieth century, Edwards (2021) sketches an approach to politically charged visual representations relevant to this discussion. Edwards shows how visual illustrations were used to criticize German colonialism from different ideological positions and through different visual registers, some of which nonetheless remained locked in stereotypical ways of constructing the German "self," the African "other," and Europe's other colonial powers. What matters for our purposes is twofold. First, Edwards' analysis involves detailed contextualization, whereby images are carefully related to domestic politics and to German colonialism in South-West Africa at the time. Second, Edwards (2021: 4, 5) recognizes the political work accomplished through satire, which requires "a knowing audience invested in the critique of the familiar." Edwards (2021: 20) thus captures a "vocabulary of protest" among Germans critical of colonialism in the early 1900s. While street art along the Donaukanal can only in isolated cases be read as satire, it also provides much evidence of contemporary vocabularies of protest that need to be read in current contexts, both local and global. However, such vocabularies of protest are not necessarily ideologically coherent or unified. Politically charged street art spotted during a visit in July 2021 therefore targeted and criticized phenomena as varied as toxic masculinity, Europe's fortification, and Covid vaccinations.

4 Also relevant here are Rolf Lindner's (2007: 323) conceptualizations of cities as "symbolic spaces filled with meanings" and as "complex systems of symbols and emotions."

Chapter 7

NEW TECHNOLOGIES EVERYWHERE?

Logging the *Digital Revolution* in Everyday Life

Although "globalized technologies" constitute only one aspect of globalization, they are arguably the dimension that brings global flows "closest to home" (Lemert 2015: 14). How, then, might one capture, self-reflexively and hence critically, one's own everyday reliance on our era's information and communication technologies? One possible starting point for such an undertaking is a simple recording exercise: in a randomly chosen week, how many hours do we spend doing particular things, communicating digitally, consuming information and entertainment via channels and through means that simply did not exist until not very long ago? Here is my own, in many ways atypical "technology and communication log" compiled during a week in early September 2020 (Table 7.1).

This is idiosyncratic. Timing and immediate context must be borne in mind: early September constitutes an unusual point in the annual cycle of academic work, when "we" still get to spend proportionally more of our time doing research, writing publications, and preparing our teaching rather than engaged in administrative matters and the delivery of teaching. What is more, the point in time captured here was still profoundly shaped by the Covid-19 pandemic: with more of our lives spent at home, our reliance on digital means of communication was clearly pronounced. Concurrently, especially for those of us with families in different countries, and whatever our general attitude toward our technological age, the personal importance of video calls across long geographical distances cannot be overstated. At the same time, my nonexistent use of social media (neither as an active contributor nor as a consumer thereof) arguably shows me to be old-fashioned and anachronistic. Other people's categories of activity will undoubtedly be far more numerous and, in light of their "fuller" digital lives, considerably more nuanced and multifaceted. Yet, this tentative table says something profound, particularly as it captures one week's activities in the life of a digital skeptic.

Table 7.1 Technology and communication log, one week in early September 2020.

Activity	Total hours per activity
Work-related emails	8
Work-related virtual meetings	4
Other work time in front of laptop	32
Skype conversations, private	4
Skype, leisure sessions (exercise, language lessons)	3
Internet browsing	3
Internet media consumption (e.g., newspapers)	4
Online shopping	1.5
Digital communication (text messaging, private emails, etc.)	2.5
Cable television, news	5
Internet radio	10
Social media	0
Films/TV series consumed via Netflix, Amazon	14

The picture becomes even more revealing when Table 7.1 is read alongside Table 7.2, which summarizes my non-digitally-mediated activities in the same week in question.

Further explanation is needed at this point. The proportion of digitally mediated to non-digital activities is noteworthy: the sum total of the first log amounts to ninety-one hours across seven days, compared to a sum total of ninety-nine hours of non-digital activities (including six hours of sleep per

Table 7.2 Log of non-digital activities, one week in early September 2020.

Activity	Total hours per activity
Sleep	42
Face-to-face communication at home	24
Face-to-face communication outside the home (neighbors, acquaintances)	0.5
Cooking, eating	17.5
Traditional shopping	1
"Analog" media consumption (e.g., newspapers), reading	4
Running/exercise	6
Domestic chores	2.5
Other time spent outside the home	1.5

night, which for non-Fitbit-wearers are by definition non-digitalized). Clearly, the overall total (= 190 hours) is more than the 168 hours contained in a seven-day week. The reason for this is obvious: several of the categories included above allow for parallel activities (e.g., I routinely have my internet radio playing whilst working; many face-to-face conversations in the household occur in parallel to cooking, eating). At the same time, the categories included across the two logs do not exhaust all my activities (e.g., I did not measure or include time spent in the bathroom in the week in question). With these caveats added, and having acknowledged the contemporary anomaly of social media not featuring in my week's activities, there is nonetheless a basic and remarkable sociological and historical insight the above logs enable: a generation ago, when my parents were my current age, their working lives and more general weekly routines would not have contained or even known *any* of the activities, at least not in the particular technological format they now take, to which I dedicate ninety-one hours a week. Put differently, even a relative technological skeptic spends more than half of a week's total hours (i.e., even when we include the hours spent sleeping in our count) in digital mode. As an illustration of the fundamental shifts we have experienced in the course of the transition into our digitally powered *network society* and *information age* (Castells 1996), this is powerful and poses further sociological questions. In this final chapter, I thus turn to interrogating some of the wider and unintended consequences that go hand in glove with our world's digitalization. As in previous chapters, I begin by providing conceptual grounding for the subsequent exploration of a small selection of examples, through which broader and critical questions can be gleaned and addressed.

Context, Concepts, Criticism

In his historical reflections on "sociology's moments," John Holmwood (2013) offers a meta-disciplinary account that identifies three particularly significant contexts, in which sociologists have occupied different structural positions vis-à-vis wider publics. The three moments Holmwood distinguishes were, first, the period of the late nineteenth and early twentieth centuries, during which the general discovery of the "social self" underpinned reforms of capitalist production and enabled sociology to claim a specific intellectual and political space (i.e., as a discipline dedicated to enquiring into the "social self"). During the second "moment," broadly in the era of mid-twentieth century welfare-state capitalisms, sociology began to fluctuate between its professionalization and, subsequently, its sub-disciplinary fragmentation into critical sociologies responding to the new social movements of the 1960s and 1970s. Since then, Holmwood suggests, neoliberal *marketization*, and more specifically its colonization of universities, have come to undermine sociology's public role and the discipline's critical potentialities. Taking this as a point of departure, I would like to develop Holmwood's idea of the present as constituting a very particular historical moment, with specific structural and ideological arrangements that impact sociology as much as the world at large, further. More narrowly, we need to ask ourselves the question as to what critical sociology can—or, normatively speaking, *should*—offer our age. While Holmwood's unsettling assessment of sociology's marginalization in the neoliberal academy needs to be taken seriously, I will argue that there are also grounds for hope: more specifically, sociology is capable, and it is already doing this in some quarters, of helping to chart new paths for critical knowledge of, and public engagement with, our "glocalizing" and digital world. If, and this is an assumption I share, sociology can be "an expression of democratic citizenship [that is] centrally concerned with facilitating public debate over pressing social issues" (Holmwood 2015: 50), then our digital, information age provides no shortage of opportunities for critically minded sociologists.[1]

Technology, viewed sociologically, cannot be made sense of in isolation. Technology is never used, and innovation never occurs, in a social vacuum. The sociological imagination, famously defined by C. Wright Mills (2000 [1959]) as the ability to see the structural and historical in which our purportedly private experiences are embedded and through which our life-worlds are simultaneously enabled and constrained (Eriksen 2016a), needs to be applied to the technological dimensions of our lives as much as to any other. More concretely, today's communication and information technologies are part of the wider social shifts and transnational interconnections that form the focus of this book. It follows that simplistic, though commonplace judgements of digitally enabled social changes as either positive and inevitable or, in their equally distorting technophobic counterarguments, as unambiguously negative, do not stand up to scrutiny. Technology "is" neither just good, nor just bad; instead, technologies have good and bad uses. And, importantly, the multiple changes technologies can help bring about are not always or entirely planned or plannable. Instead, technology—its development, production, use, consumption and wider societal ramifications—entails unanticipated consequences. Much of this was already summarized by John Urry at the turn of the millennium when he pointed out that the internet, originally a technology invented for military purposes, had "developed into a system enabling horizontal communication which cannot be controlled or effectively censored by national societies" (Urry 2000: 40). Both the unintended consequences and the expressive, democratizing potential of (digital) technology are contained in these observations. My intention in this chapter is to take the (critical) contextualizing of the digital revolution underpinning our era further.

Such an undertaking is helped by some of Charles Lemert's observations of globalization. The latter, Lemert (2015: 95) argues, is "both a process and a[n emerging] structure." More accurately, to comprehend globalization we need to understand the changing "dynamics" between "*speed, technologies*, and the *relations* we have with our fellow beings and material things" as well as with "fixed *spaces*" (Lemert 2015: 18, 29; *original italics*). This profound change involving several dimensions of social life, each with much longer histories, began to crystallize into new structures in the 1970s and 1980s. Few sociologists have done as much to illuminate this transformation as Manuel Castells in his trilogy on *the information age*. According to Castells (1996: 13), the information technology revolution since the 1970s (i.e., epoch-defining changes to information and communication technologies) has been integral to a "restructuring of the capitalist system." Yet, for all the interconnections between technology and the economy, we need to differentiate their respective, recent transformations, which Castells separates through a conceptual distinction between *modes of development* and the (Marxist) notion of *modes of production*:

> Capitalist restructuring [and] the rise of informationalism are distinct and their interaction can only be understood if we separate them analytically [...] to place the distinction between pre-industrialism, industrialism and informationalism (or post-industrialism) on a different axis from the one opposing capitalism and statism [...] [It is] essential [...] to maintain the analytical distance and empirical interrelation between modes of production (capitalism, statism) and modes of development (industrialism, informationalism). (Castells 1996: 14)

At its simplest, a mode of production relates to questions of ownership (i.e., of the means of production), the organization of work and, crucially, the relations of power implicated therein. Conversely, modes of development are "technological arrangements through which labor works to generate" products; and in our era's "informational mode of development, the source of productivity lies in the technology of knowledge generation, information processing, and symbol communication" (Castells 1996: 16, 17). The recent and continuing interplay of technological and economic transformations is further illuminated by David Harvey's (1989) analysis of how the capitalist tendency to overcome periodic crises through a "reorganization of time-space" leads to novel forms of capital accumulation: this, according to John Urry (2000: 124, 125), helps account for the shift into post-Fordist, "flexible" production and the "hugely magnified speed of monetary and other transactions" enabled by new information and communication technologies since the latter decades of the twentieth century. The manifestations of such "flexible accumulation" have been far-reaching. They have included the "emergence of entirely new sectors of production, new ways of providing financial services, new markets," often widening inequalities, and "a vast surge in 'service sector' employment as well as to industrial ensembles in hitherto underdeveloped regions" (Harvey quoted in Lemert 2015: 116). Informationalism, then, comprises a "new technological paradigm" and has seen the "emergence of a new social structure" that implicates the domains of production, human experience, and power (Castells 1996: 14, 15). It is these wider, societal dimensions of our digital age that are at stake in this chapter.

Synthesizing different contextual and conceptual strands, the question arises as to what a critically minded social science is able to offer at the current historical "moment" (Holmwood 2013) dominated by digital capitalism. I have emphasized throughout this book that interdisciplinarity is essential for sociological engagement with our glocalizing world. This also applies, arguably particularly so, to a critical interrogation of our informational mode of development. Further, my repeated use of the attribute "critical" for the type of sociological approach advocated here is deliberate. Written into the social sciences, and particularly the Marxist, feminist, and other traditions furnishing "conflict theories" (Ferraro 1995: 279), is a long-standing commitment to not only capturing the social world but to subjecting it to critical scrutiny. Without suggesting that the step from analysis to criticism and from there to the design of purportedly better alternatives is straightforward or should define all sociologies, the *critical* element is undoubtedly part of what makes the social sciences relevant and important in a period of multiple crises and widening inequalities. Such a critical component, in turn, can take different forms. One form of criticism is epitomized in Theodor Adorno's (1984) questioning of cultural categories, and his revelation of how widely taken-for-granted building blocks of thought and speech can be profoundly *ideological*; by this he means that common categories of thought reflect, and work in the interest of, existing institutions and asymmetrical power relations. Adorno's critical reflections on the idea of "progress" is a case in point. Once subjected to Adorno's scrutiny, the concept of "progress" can no longer be seen as a self-evident description of the purported, general direction of human development. Instead, it reappears as only a very specific, though arguably also necessary trope, one that is accurate only as a highly circumscribed descriptor of particular aspects of our lives, such as the technological domain. The critical element here goes hand in hand with a feature of the kind of sociological work that I have emphasized throughout: that of careful and detailed contextualization of our objects of analysis. It is by contextualizing talk about progress, by contextualizing our digital technologies, and by contextualizing the widely assumed link between the two (i.e., the widely unquestioned presumption that digitalization paves the way into a better future), that a general tendency of "fetishizing progress" (Adorno 1984: 118) can be resisted and rethought. Let me clear: none of this denies the many advantages digitalization brings; none of this should be misread as a technophobic, reactionary counter-position to today's *Zeitgeist*. What the following amounts to, however, is an insistence on questioning totalizing statements about where "we are allegedly going" and what "the future is all about." Technological progress throughout recent years and decades has often been awe-inspiring, life-changing, and world-transforming. However, "technological progress" must indeed not be confused for a utopian blueprint. When viewed from an alternative angle, that is, namely those of the environmental consequences of human action or of our technological might being put to military purposes, the history of modernity appears in a very different light; its balance sheet is at best mixed and, seen critically, extremely disconcerting, for it is modernity—the purported and self-defining epoch of progress and reason—that has created the capacity to destroy all human and other life on our planet many times over. Technology needs to be placed in its wider contexts, for it never dwells in a social or political vacuum. Its (unintended) consequences are many and far-reaching. It is also for an understanding of the latter—that is of the unanticipated, inadvertent *other* outcomes, implications and by-products of our digital age—that our (glocalizing) era needs critical sociologies.

The strands of sociological research and theorizing explored throughout this book are intrinsically interdisciplinary. Conceptually, thematically and methodologically, they interface with other forms of critical social science. In the remainder of this chapter, the two key themes explored through recent contributions to such a critical social science are what I will describe as technology's *seductive* power and, with recourse to long-established sociological thought (Merton 1936), the "unintended consequences" of human action.

Criticism in the *Age of Surveillance Capitalism*

Critical observations of the potential for darker, possibly rather sinister by-products of our digital age are not new. Here again, John Urry was among the first to spot some novelties of the digitally enabled "postmodern life." This began with the now commonplace observation that "cyberspace is a globally networked, computer-sustained, computer-accessed and computer-generated […] set of overlapping, virtual 'communities'" that are seeing a blurring of the "boundaries of the human body as machines and humans interact far more intimately" than in previous eras; the potential consequences include the "death of the human subject" as humans are being "reconfigure[d] as bits of information [...] subject to computerized monitoring and control through various systems" (Urry 2000: 71, 76, 77).

More recently, arguably the most searching critique of our still relatively new, digital mode of development has been formulated by Shoshana Zuboff. In *The Age of Surveillance Capitalism*, Zuboff paints a deeply troubling picture of the turns our digital world has taken since Urry's earlier observations at the turn of the millennium. Emerita Professor at Harvard Business School, Zuboff draws on a range of sociological "classics," from Marx, Weber and Durkheim to Adorno, Arendt and Polanyi. Although none of these greats of social and political theorizing can be singularly claimed by any one scientific discipline, the sociological tenor of Zuboff's creative reapplication (or re-tailoring) of their respective bodies of work to present circumstances is undeniable. At the heart of Zuboff's powerful critique of surveillance capitalism is what C. Wright Mills would have recognized as fitting his definition of the *sociological imagination*: the ability to see the structural and hence always wider and historically specific circumstances, out of which "our personal troubles" emerge, to which they are connected, and only through which they can be made sense of. To think sociologically, as I have emphasized repeatedly, therefore means to resist individualizing accounts and to insist on thorough contextualization.

Shoshana Zuboff's work fits the bill perfectly. Where others continue to celebrate the allegedly democratizing and empowering effects of all things digital, she unearths something altogether different: the dystopian specter of a new system of "extracting" surplus value, in Marxist language, and the emergence of a new "division of learning" in late modern society (i.e., a reappropriation of sociological terms most widely associated with Emile Durkheim and Anthony Giddens, respectively). What is more, Zuboff's analysis has Foucauldian echoes, as she depicts the political asymmetries of our times, a system of one-way surveillance, in which every aspect of our lives and behavior, indeed our very being, is being turned into commodified information for the extraction of surplus value, and for the purposes of both "predicting" and indeed "manipulating" our future actions and decisions, most of all those pertaining to our consumption choices. The digital surveillance system is decidedly one-way, comparable to Michel Foucault's (1991) seminal account of the panoptical structures and logic of the (early) modern era. This system is written, enabled and controlled by the new "priesthood" of AI and computer specialists, by Internet giants (i.e., Google and Facebook in particular);

the "Internet of Things"—or the "ubiquitous computing" that has begun to infiltrate our most intimate of actions, behaviors and relationships—is revealed to threaten our "elemental right to the future tense" (Zuboff 2019: 194). Put more concretely, Zuboff defines *surveillance capitalism* as follows:

A new economic order that claims human experience as free raw material for hidden commercial practices of extraction, prediction, and sales; a[n] [...] economic logic in which the production of goods and services is subordinated to a new global architecture of behavioral modification; a rogue mutation of capitalism marked by concentrations of wealth, knowledge and power unprecedented in human history; [...] as significant a threat to human nature [...] as industrial capitalism was to the natural world in the nineteenth and twentieth [centuries]; [...] a new instrumentarian power that [...] aims to impose a new collective order based on total certainty; [...] a coup from above: an overthrow of the people's sovereignty. (Zuboff 2019: v)

Heralded by some as one of the most significant books of the early twenty-first century, Zuboff's analysis of this new technological-economic power juggernaut avoids technological reductionism or simplistic blaming of the dangers she highlights onto our digital-scientific capabilities or particular corporations' entrepreneurial motivations. Instead, Zuboff attributes the dangers of surveillance capitalism to the historically contingent and hence also reversible co-occurrence of a number of developments: the digital revolution; a lack of regulatory policy (or what she describes as a state of relative "lawlessness" that has long been a condition of possibility for ruthless forms of capitalist expansion); and an economic and political climate dominated by neoliberal marketization and post-9/11 security concerns that have been addressed through investment in surveillance mechanisms and technologies.

Zuboff also depicts an unequivocally globalized world. None of the factors and phenomena at the heart of her analysis are confined—and can therefore be made sense of—within any of one locality or within older paradigms wedged to the "nation-state container" (Beck 2000: 23). Instead, the digital "architectures of ubiquitous monitoring, analysis and control" that Zuboff (2019: 466) alerts us to reveal "a behavioral engineering project of planetary scope." However, the importance of global connections does not translate into global "sameness" (Appadurai 1990: 308). Digital surveillance works very differently or, more accurately, is put to very different uses in different (national) contexts. This is most clearly shown by Zuboff's contrasting accounts of Western-style surveillance capitalism—essentially a "market-driven coup from above" that commodifies and "modif[ies] human behavior as a condition for commercial success" for some of our era's leading companies—and of the Chinese government's digital "tuning, herding, and conditioning [of] people to produce preselected behaviors judged as desirable by the state" (Zuboff 2019: 513, 514; 388, 389), respectively. All this having been said, it is crucial *not* to misrepresent Zuboff's analysis as offering a scholarly version of a conspiracy theory. The emerging picture is far more complex and not mono-causal. The surveillance capitalism Zuboff depicts cannot simply be seen as the teleological endpoint of a process straightforwardly designed and single-handedly imposed by the few (i.e., multinational corporations or powerful state bureaucracies, or their small occupational stratum of scientists and IT experts, although they all play important roles). A more accurate account needs to recognize the more subtle role played by the *behaviorist* ideology underpinning today's "instrumentarian power" and its aims and "means of behavioral modification" (Zuboff 2019: 360). Zuboff illustrates this, in part, through the enduring legacy of Burrhus Frederic Skinner's "radical behaviorism": boldly projecting animals' behavioral patterns onto humans' social behavior and assumed evolution, Skinner's focus was squarely on "action devoid of subjective attribution" and on "measurable behavioral facts that lead to [...] the documentation of causal relationships between environment and behavior" (Zuboff 2019: 366, 367). Parts of this radical behaviorist paradigm reappear in surveillance capitalism's (and its leading internet giants') preoccupation with "big data," "machine intelligence" and "prediction products" that aim to measure, know, predict and shape consumption behaviors. As Zuboff demonstrates, implicit in all of this is a very particular view of human sociability and action: one premised on the "hive mind," in which conformity, calculability and predictability sideline human agency and freedom and which, paradoxically, thereby also departs from the values (e.g., individualism) that have historically underpinned "market capitalism and market democracy" (Zuboff 2019: 8, 409, 504).

Yet, it seems highly unlikely that the rising specter of the "death of individuality" (Zuboff 2019: 438) is what any of the computer scientists and entrepreneurs driving surveillance capitalism *consciously* want to bring about. Their (primary) motivations are surely much more immediate, about driving further technological development and maximizing profits. It seems even more unlikely that any of us participants in the global, digital economy, the "Internet of Things," the continuous monitoring of our current behavior, and prediction of future consumption choices, frame our digital practices in terms of our growing subsumption in a "hive collective" or "termite state" (Zuboff 2019: 504). There is, in other words, a glaring discrepancy between the outwardly professed ethos of individualism, on which (digital) consumerism thrives, and the actual, collectivizing and arguably dehumanizing tendencies of our times that Zuboff reveals. In uncovering the implicit, rarely noticed worldview underpinning recent developments in our digital age, Zuboff also moves us into the domain of the unacknowledged conditions of possibility, and the unintended consequences, of social action. As we see in the following section, this is well-trodden sociological terrain that acquires renewed relevance in the context of the present discussion. More immediately, Zuboff's account of today's surveillance capitalism returns us to the question as to what a critical social science can offer in these particular circumstances. Zuboff's own answer, perhaps best described as a historically self-aware attempt to counter the "death of the human subject" (Urry 2000: 77), is worth quoting at length:

> When I speak to my children [...] I alert them to the historically contingent nature of "the thing that has us" by calling attention to ordinary values [...] before surveillance capitalism began its campaign of psychic numbing [...] I tell them that the word "search" has meant a daring existential journey, not a finger tap to already existing answers; that a "friend" is an embodied mystery that can be forged only face-to-face and heart-to-heart; that "recognition" is a glimmer of homecoming we experience in our beloved's face, not "face recognition" [...] It is not OK for every move, emotion, utterance, and desire to be catalogued, manipulated, and then used to [...] herd us through the future tense for the sake of someone else's profit [...] I tell them, "these things are unprecedented." [...] If democracy is to be replenished [...], it is up to us to rekindle [...] outrage and loss over what is being taken from us [...] What is at stake is the human expectation of sovereignty over one's own life [...] the inward experience from which we form the will to will and the public spaces to act on that will. (Zuboff 2019: 521)

The question, if we accept Zuboff's assessment, is how we could allow all this to happen. Translated into social scientific terms, this becomes a question of power, which—following Max Weber's (1972 [1922]): 531) seminal conceptualization—comprises "relationship[s] between human subjects which [...] impose the will of some [...] on others by the potential or actual use of violence, physical or symbolic" (Castells 1996: 15). Such asymmetrical relationships usually implicate enduring, structural configurations and closer analysis reveals that what is needed is an understanding of the workings of power; or, in quasi-Weberian terms, of *how* exactly the imposition of someone's will on others becomes possible and unfolds in a given context. For this purpose, in turn, it is worth remembering how the workings and dynamics of power have been conceptualized in prominent literary and social theoretical contributions. This has included, perhaps most famously, George

Orwell's account in *1984* of total, or more accurately, totalitarian surveillance. Translated from literary into sociological terms, Orwell's is an account of highly oppressive, deindividualizing power exercised by a dystopian state. In the realm of cultural theory, meanwhile, we associate the (historically contextualized) analysis of power most closely with Michel Foucault's oeuvre. Foucault's account of power centers, particularly in his earlier works (e.g., Foucault 1991), on the workings and effects of modernity's core institutions. Foucault argues that common to many of them—such as prisons, asylums, hospitals, armies, or factories—are panoptical surveillance and the centralized keeping of information (i.e., files) about the individuals subject to institutional power. Yet, Foucault's account is more subtle than Orwell's: Foucault conceives of power as a ubiquitous, multidirectional social force, which seeps through all crevices of the social body and which is *productive* insofar as it creates very particular human beings at particular moments in history. While Foucault's "microphysics of power" offer more nuance than Orwell's trope of "big brother," the consequences of the workings of power as depicted by Foucault are at least as far-reaching: modernity is shown to be a period of "one-way surveillance," in which humans are turned into "docile" individuals through the workings of institutions and the modern individual's internalization of the logic of power at work around them.

Arguably, once we fast-forward to the present, different "diagnostics" of power are needed. What "we," more accurately those of us who live the relatively privileged lives of Western consumers, experience in the digital age appears to require another understanding of power: building on Zuboff's analysis, we might describe this as technology's *seductive* power. This is not to deny the continuing relevance of Orwell's insights into oppressive power, nor of Foucault's understanding of power's productive capacities, but seductive power captures how and why digital technologies appeal to us; they are undeniably individually empowering insofar as they offer novel realms of self-expression, new forms of sociability, and hitherto unknown forms of convenience. However, as Zuboff illustrates, they also create much else that is too rarely noticed yet requires our urgent attention. This takes us within the much larger domain of the *unintended consequences* of social change and action.

The Unintended Consequences of "Rare Earth" Extraction

In unmasking some of the wider economic, political and existential consequences of the technological developments of our age, Shoshana Zuboff illustrates one particular example of a long-established sociological motif: the recognition that initially localized events or discoveries tend to have unplanned and often global ripple effects. Such acknowledgement of the "unanticipated consequences of purposive social action" can be traced to the ground-breaking work by Robert Merton (1936). Thematically most relevant to this book, however, was Ulrich Beck's era-defining *Risk Society* (1992). There, Beck traced what events such as the nuclear disaster in Chernobyl, in the spring of 1986, revealed about the then current phase in the history of modernity. Beck's groundbreaking discussion revealed several novel phenomena: first, risks were no longer localized, they operated on a much larger, transnational, in some cases positively global scale. And, second, scientists' ability to calculate, predict and hence help manage the "fallout"—in the case of Chernobyl quite literally—of our now locally produced but globally shared risks had undeniable limitations. Chernobyl, and a wide array of events and developments since, have demonstrated this beyond all doubt. Radiation was not and could not be confined to the area around the power station, nor to the Ukraine; within days of finding out about an accident the Soviet authorities had initially attempted to keep a lid on, people across Europe were watching their weather forecasts with growing concern, attempting to gage which way the wind would blow the nuclear fallout, and where it might no longer be safe to allow children to play outside. Could nuclear scientists be believed in their predictions of how serious the risk was, or of how long it would persist? Furthermore, as impossible as it was to geographically delimit or localize the fallout, as elusive have attempts to define its temporal persistence turned out to be. Decades on, news continue to break fairly regularly of still heightened radiation levels in wild mushrooms in various parts of Europe.

Since Ulrich Beck's tracing of the contours of a new, increasingly global(izing) risk society, his account has turned out to be paradigmatic of the insecurities, uncertainties and imponderables of our current era in human history. From the ozone layer, desertification and deforestation, subsequent nuclear accidents such as in the Japanese precinct of Fukushima in 2011, to the climate and plastic crises, Beck's account[2] resonates. In each of these cases, local actions and events have much wider, sometimes positively global, in all cases decidedly unintended consequences; after all, none of the discoveries that have reshaped—and in the short run often improved—our lives over the last 200 years set out to also result in any of the crises humanity now faces. Ours is a world of the most complex entanglements, of unplannable chain reactions operating on multiple levels and in different directions, and of entirely unforeseen contingencies. What is more, the environmental (and of course also inevitably political) crises just alluded to also entail an epistemological crisis: (How) do we, or can we, know what exactly we are up against? Do scientists know? And if not, what then?

Acknowledging the multiple, unintended consequences of human action and the limits to our ability to plan for our global risks does not turn sociology into a conservative, nostalgic force. Instead, what this makes a case for is the contemporary need for critical voices. Combining contextualization with epistemological reflexivity, our strength lies in never seeing things in isolation. In C. Wright Mills' spirit, we know that "things," "events," and "people" need to be understood in relation to their surrounding conditions of possibility and structural entanglements. In a world of global interconnections, this makes naïve, celebratory declarations of "simple facts" unconvincing. This is not, however, a recipe for nihilistic relativism, but for modest claims to what we know. Sociology in our global age should, we might conclude, be guided by a form Socratic modesty: not quite by "I know that I know nothing," but by "I know that there are limits to what any of us know, perhaps we know more than we did yesterday, but we can do better, we must do better, and ultimately the world's complexity is likely to elude any definitive, absolute or final statements."

This is not, to be clear, a plea for a return to the postmodern "incredulity" (Lyotard 1984) of any "metanarrative" or definitive truth claim. Instead, it is a plea for modesty, caution, and criticism; a plea to resist simplicity, however much we ourselves may crave it. Whatever else we take globalization to entail, it describes a complex and complicatedly interconnected world. More than twenty years ago, John Urry (2000: 19) demonstrated why "chaotic, unintended and non-linear social consequences" made a case for the social scientific use of *chaos and complexity theories*:

> The classic example is the famous butterfly effect, where miniscule changes at one location produce, in very particular circumstances, massive weather effects elsewhere. Such complex systems are characterized by counter-intuitive outcomes that occur temporally and spatially distant from where they appear to have originated. Complexity theory emphasizes how complex feedback loops exacerbate initial stresses in the system [...] There are very strong interactions [...] between the parts of a system and [...] a lack of a central hierarchical structure. (Urry 2000: 121)

In such circumstances, social scientists' first principle may just be an act of courage: to face complexities and contradictions without pretensions of omniscience but with every intention to improve, in piecemeal fashion, our understanding of them.

This is the right point at which to return from the theoretical realm to concrete examples, so that we might work toward an understanding of just "how actions have consequences in the lives of other people [...] remote from us" (Holmwood 2007: 81). There are myriad such examples in our world today. The one to be discussed here relates closely back to our digital infrastructures or, more accurately, to some of the raw materials they require. The raw materials in question are the so-called rare earths, without which twenty-first century life as we know it would be impossible and the extraction of which has—at present—extremely far-reaching and damaging "side effects." In chemical terms, the group of elements known as the "rare earth family" comprises seventeen elements—though precise inclusions in this category have changed over time—with "exceptional magnetic and conductive properties"; contrary to their common labelling as "rare," these elements are in fact "relatively abundant" and "dispersed throughout Earth's crust" (Klinger 2017: 42–44). Yet, the relative abundance of these particular elements essential to twenty-first century technologies sits in noteworthy juxtaposition to the fact that the mining of rare earths is geographically concentrated in specific locations: most importantly, in Inner Mongolia, but increasingly also in a number of ecologically and geopolitically "sensitive" areas (e.g., parts of the Brazilian border regions in the Amazon, Afghanistan, Greenland, the world's oceans) and, in due course conceivably on the Moon. Julie Michelle Klinger's recent study of rare earth mining—along shifting "frontiers" of these elements' extraction—is remarkable both for its illumination of how our digital lives entail precisely the complex entanglements of global connections and unintended, local consequences discussed above; and for the methodological arsenal Klinger brings to bear on the subject. Truly "global in scope," Klinger's multisited fieldwork (2017: 36) in parts resembles Caroline Knowles' "traveling methods," discussed in a previous chapter, and the transnational following of a particular object and the people and social relationships that go into its making (Knowles 2014: 14). To capture rare earth extraction across multiple geographical sites and institutional levels, Klinger combines archival with ethnographic research in China, Brazil, Germany, Australia, and the US. Through long-term immersion and her competence in the required languages, Klinger is able to document the "multiple forms of knowledge," the "actor networks," and the experiences of local populations involved in, or affected by, rare earth mining. Building on archival research on the histories of geological exploration in the areas in question, Klinger's fieldwork immerses her in wide range of relevant social settings and institutional domains: from "offices in state and national capitals," the "cars of powerful officials [and] penthouse bars," to the "heady gatherings of aspiring space miners," the "homes of laborers [...] [and the] settlements and shanties of displaced people and clandestine miners" (Klinger 2017: 38). The methodological rationale for such an approach is clear: a social scientific understanding of one of our era's core industries necessitates an approach that is both transnational and sensitive to the profound power asymmetries involved, for rare earth mining involves global economic and geopolitical actors, national governments, as well as some of the world's most marginalized populations. Before turning to the "spatial politics" Klinger unmasks, the centrality of rare earths to twenty-first century life requires further clarification:

> Because of their exceptional magnetic and conductive properties, this family of soft, ductile metals is essential for a diverse and expanding array of high-technology applications fundamental to globalized modernity as we know it. Global finance, the Internet, satellite surveillance, oil transport, jet engines, televisions, GPS, and emergency rooms could not function without rare earth elements. They are necessary to produce the navigation components of the most advanced remote warfare technologies, such as drones and smart bombs [...] They are critical components of green technologies, such as wind turbines, solar panels, and hybrid fuel-cell batteries [...] essential in the development of nanotechnologies and [they] are used in the production of consumer electronics such as smartphones, hard drives, and flat screen monitors [...] So thoroughly embedded are rare earths that an analysis of their role in modern life precludes a straightforward commodity chain or sector-specific analysis [...] There is no singular "rare earth market" [...] but rather multiple markets for the seventeen elements (and combinations thereof) with widely divergent availabilities and applications. (Klinger 2017: 45)

Put simply, our contemporary lives, individual and collective, would be unthinkable—in their current, digitalized forms—without rare earths. But what does this have to do with the unintended consequences of social action?

To understand what we might describe as a rare earth nexus of global connections and local "by-products," we need to follow Klinger on her multisited, ethnographic and archival research journey, particularly into the family homes and local communities of some of the miners of rare earths. In keeping with the social scientific imperative for contextualization, Klinger (2017: 135ff., 104) demonstrates that the "changing geographies of the global rare earth frontier" (i.e., the fact that elements that are not as uncommon as the attribute "rare" would suggest are mined in particular places at particular times) are neither accidental nor down to singular, causal forces (e.g., such as the widely circulating, though misleading notion of a "Chinese monolith" monopolizing all rare earth production, or the equally inaccurate suggestion that the "invisible hand of laissez-faire capitalism" single-handedly explains the status quo). Instead, and this inadvertently echoes some of the tenets of complexity theory mentioned earlier, Klinger reveals how the "spatial politics" of rare earth extraction implicate a range of complicatedly entangled historical legacies, geopolitical and domestic power struggles, and transnational economic interests. Thus, the continuing importance of the Bayan Obo mine in Inner Mongolia, which at the time of publication of Klinger's book provided about half of the global rare earth supply, reflects the convergence of several factors: the area's historical status as a contested region whose geological riches were variously coveted and claimed—between the late nineteenth and the middle of the twentieth centuries—by European (i.e., German, British, French) powers, by Japan, by Chinese nationalists and communists alike, and by the Soviets[3]; subsequently, China's infrastructural and ideological investments in the area as a "border region" deemed to be both in need of "taming" and crucial to China's economic development; and powerful extralocal actors who—playing the "economic globalization game" in their "search for new frontiers" and the "fastest rate of accumulation"— have been attracted by Inner Mongolia's "ideal combination" of "cheap labour, lax environmental regulations" and "business-friendly practices" (Klinger 2017: 56, 71–73, 111). As Klinger goes on to show (2017: 167–197), the more recently emerging (/ prospective) rare earth frontier in a remote, far northwestern part of the Amazon, which contains far from the only deposit in Brazil (albeit perhaps the country's least accessible one), reveals a similar interplay of geopolitical and mining interests, along with the Brazilian government's "resource nationalism" and its attempt to assert control over "a historically contested border region" at the expense of Indigenous rights.

It is, then, by "thinking" and researching "globally" that Klinger is able to document the complexities and interconnections of a truly transnational system with far-reaching, but widely unknown local consequences. Rare earth elements constitute an essential part of the "material basis for the hardware of global technological modernity: from the darkest and most dystopic to the greenest and greatest" (Klinger 2017: 49). This refers to the demand or consumption part of the system. On the supply and extraction side, meanwhile, transnational economic interests in profit maximization play an important part, alongside governments' similarly consequential geopolitical and domestic interests. At present, it is particularly in areas that have "historically eluded the reach of centralized power" that rare earths are mined; in what Klinger (2017: 11) describes as "sacrifice zones" the "negative externalities" of rare earth extraction are concentrated, and a sinister, "utilitarian principle" defines "local landscapes and lives" as expendable in the purported interests of a greater good. What this means becomes apparent once we enquire into the by-products of rare earth extraction. The mining of each ton of rare earth produces roughly another ton of "radioactive wastewater; seventy-five cubic meters of acid wastewater; 9,600–12,000 cubic meters of waste gas containing hydrofluoric acid, sulfur dioxide, and sulfuric acid; and approximately 8.5 kilograms of fluorine"; the release of "arsenic, heavy metals, and radioactive materials," compounded by miners' exposure to acids and toxic chemicals used in the production process, explains the extremely serious environmental and health-related "costs" carried by local populations; from cancer to organ damage, from "radioactive rivers" to livestock no longer able to graze due to the effects of skeletal fluorosis, it is through such "molecular, unintended, and poorly controlled processes that the rare earth frontier [...] cuts through the human [and animal] body at the cellular and atomic level" (Klinger 2017: 55, 117, 119, 120).

In China, meanwhile, with contamination long reaching the Yellow River and hence affecting a much larger proportion of the country's population, the severity of the crisis is being recognized and attempts are afoot to shift the problems associated with mining "elsewhere" by moving into a different segment of the global rare earth markets, namely the "rare earths high-technology development" area (Klinger 2017: 59, 136, 133). Concurrently, the emerging and anticipated, new "frontiers" of rare earth mining still reveal, when viewed in their global contexts, similar patterns of environmental outsourcing typical of the "contemporary global division of toxic labor" (Klinger 2017: 56). The (new) "sacrificable" generally remain unseen and unnoticed by, and hence ultimately unknown to, consumers of the many commodities that would not work without rare earths. Our lives are, as Klinger (2017: 59) compellingly demonstrates, closely "entangled" in rare earth markets that do not allow for "unidirectional" analyses.

What started with a seemingly innocuous digital log of my everyday practices has brought us to parts of Inner Mongolia and the Amazon. What connects such disparate contexts are rare earths: chemicals known to few of us, without which none of our daily lives would assume the forms they currently take, and the production of which has local consequences unknown to almost all of us. At stake here is not a false attribution of singular "causes," nor a moralizing about individual or collective guilt. Instead, a first but urgently needed step is a recognition of such global connections, of the extreme asymmetries of power and privilege (and their lack) that both connect and divide human beings from each other across vast distances, and, closely associated with this, an acknowledgement of some of the unintended, but undeniably negative consequences of our digital lives.

A Planet on the Brink of "Overheating"?

The argument that globalization today presents the social sciences with significantly altered parameters and challenges is certainly not new. With narrower regard to sociology, Jean-Christophe Le Coze (2017: 63–65), for example, has argued that a discipline previously grounded in a methodologically nationalist "vision of society from the perspective of national boundaries" now finds itself having to respond to a very different context: one dominated by key developments of the last two decades, including "profound transformations in communication exchanges, cultural-national identities, migration flows, economic dynamics, political institutions [...] [and] 'systemic risks'" (Le Coze 2017: 62). Further reflections on the implications of such transformations for sociology, and the social sciences at large, lead to the recognition that there are two sets of challenges to be differentiated: one conceptual, the second existential (and hence political).

To elaborate on a point made in the introduction, John Urry was among the first to argue for some necessary sociological adjustments to shifting social realities. Urry's (2000: 1, 12) case for the "new rules of sociological method" to reflect the twenty-first century's "diverse mobilities" and multiple "scapes and flows" (see Appadurai 1990) reserved central space for new technologies. While his list of such technologies is in need of being updated, the trajectory of his argument has retained its timeliness:

[G]lobalisation involves replacing the metaphor of society as region with the metaphor of the global conceived of as network and as fluid [...] [N]ew objects, new machines and technologies [...] dramatically compress or shrink time-space. Globalisation entails infrastructural developments routed [...] across societal borders. Such technologies include fibre-optic cables, jet planes, audiovisual transmissions, digital television, computer networks [...] [the] Internet, satellites, credit cards, faxes, electronic point-of-sale terminals, portable phones, electronic stock exchanges, high speed trains and virtual reality. There are also large increases in [...] military technologies [...] as well as new waste products and health risks [...] not simply caused and treated within [...] "regions." These technologies carry people, information, money, images, and risks [...] across national societies in increasingly brief moments of time [...] [Such] technologies do not derive directly [...] from human intentions and actions. They are intricately interconnected with machines, texts, objects and other technologies. (Urry 2000: 33)

Conceptually and methodologically, previous chapters have traced some of the subsequently most successful social scientific responses to these rapidly and continually transforming social realities: from work on "world-objects" in our era of "containerization" (Martin 2016), the development of "traveling methods" particularly along some of globalization's "backroads" (Knowles 2014), to the multisensory sensibilities cultivated and applied in research on the local manifestations of global migratory flows (Lyon and Back 2012; Rhys-Taylor 2013). It is some of the existential and political implications of the world today, as depicted by Urry and others since, that warrant further reflection.

Particularly relevant here is an argumentative thread developed by Norwegian anthropologist Thomas Hylland Eriksen (2016a, b). Eriksen's first observation pertinent to our discussion concerns what may appear, to some, as a profound paradox: the fact that in our age of "high speed modernity [...] belief in progress has been dampened," thus challenging three centuries of Enlightenment thinking and its association of modernity and change with "progress" (Eriksen 2016a: 469). Today's political-cum-epistemic fragmentations, as illustrated by the current popularity of conspiracy theories and the "echo-chambers" enabled by social media, illustrate this powerfully and disconcertingly.[4] Second, Eriksen returns us once again to one of this chapter's central themes, namely that of the unplanned consequences of social action. In an epoch of "complex systems," Eriksen points out, such unintended consequences can in fact often be "more conspicuous than the planned outcomes"; and their range can be staggering: the "car [thus] led to pollution and accidents, the information revolution to the pollution of brains" (Eriksen 2016a: 470, 481). This is made even more pernicious by frequent temporal lags between our actions and their unplanned consequences. Some of the long-term consequences of industrial modernity, including climate change, have not only been unplanned and undeniably negative. Some such consequences indeed take decades and generations to manifest; or as Eriksen (2016a: 470) puts it, "what seemed to have been the salvation of humanity for 200 years, namely inexpensive and accessible energy based on fossil fuels, [has arguably] become its damnation." Third, and of most immediate relevance to the phenomenon of *glocalization*, Eriksen (2016a: 470, 482–485) points at frequent incongruences or conflicts between the "social" and the "cultural scales" of people's life-worlds[5]: although "embedded in global networks of production and consumption" (i.e., this is the "social scale"), growing numbers of people are also (culturally/politically) investing in localist counterreactions against global modernity, such as nostalgic identity politics that aim to "slow" or "cool down" the forces of globalization.

At the heart of Eriksen's discussion lies a powerful metaphor: in the early twenty-first century and following many decades in which the pace of change has kept increasing, so Eriksen's central proposition, we are in danger of "overheating." The planetary scale of our era-defining threats, along with the clear "tension between economic development and environmental sustainability" (Eriksen 2016a: 471), illustrates this. The possibility of our collective *overheating* becomes yet more plausible when placed in historical context: "we are now seven times as many as we were at the end of the Napoleonic wars," Eriksen records, while "energy use has grown [yet] much faster than the world population"; and while consumption levels are extremely uneven, our overall "energy use [has] grown by a factor of twenty-eight," with the side effects of "pollution and environmental degradation [...] climate change and depletion of non-renewable energy resources" (Eriksen 2016a: 476). Continuing growth of this kind, Eriksen concludes, may indeed be "impossible."

In terms of its overall analytical trajectory, this chapter has expanded very considerably. What started as a discussion of our daily reliance on digital technologies, has ended up touching on some of the profound environmental risks and crises of our times. To be clear: in keeping with my overall argument, I am certainly *not* now pushing for simplistic, purportedly mono-causal, quasi-explanations. The suggestion being made is most certainly not that somehow our digital infrastructures or their entanglements with contemporary capitalism are to be singularly "blamed" for what Eriksen describes as a world in danger of overheating. However, and in keeping with my emphasis on complex systems and the unintended consequences of social action within them, digital technologies play multiple roles, some of them designed, others not, in the structures, entanglements and interdependencies of our era. Can technology help solve the climate crisis? Only time will tell, but we must certainly hope so. Are digital technologies currently contributing to our unsustainable levels of energy use and resource depletion? Most certainly, though of course in—unplanned—tandem with many other factors. Do our digital lives have far-reaching, albeit unintended and enormously damaging consequences in the lives of distant others? Yes, as the realities of rare earth mining, for instance, demonstrate.

One conclusion to draw at this point is that acute crises within complex systems require multi- and interdisciplinary answers and research programs, within which the social sciences—and more narrowly sociology—have important contributions to make. The wider scientific response to climate change—as one of the core indicators, according to Eriksen, of modernity's *overheating*—is beginning to reflect this. A recent summary (Koehrsen et al. 2020) of the expanding, transdisciplinary field of climate change research confirms that sociologists' contributions have become more prominent over the last decade, reflecting a growing recognition of sociology's "critical potential" to the study of one of our century's most pressing issues. Needless to stress that sociology's contributions here feature merely alongside other disciplines', in a context that requires a pooling of heterogeneous scientific questions, approaches and methodologies. But it is similarly obvious that a discipline dedicated to illuminating different patterns of the relations and interdependencies between human beings, as well as their effects (see Simmel 1992 [1908]), has much to contribute to our understanding of how human behavior is impacting the planet's climate. At the same time, participation in this perhaps most timely of interdisciplinary endeavors provides sociology with opportunities to "critically reflect upon and [...] reinvent its [own] perspectives" and to "expand our sociological imagination": this is beginning to happen through the formulation of an "environmental sociology" that subjects the discipline's historical anthropocentrism—that is its "neglect of non-human aspects of society"—to critical scrutiny and that creates sociological ways of "perceiving humans as part of the natural environment" (Koehrsen et al. 2020: 740, 754). All of this should be seen as part of a wider and distinctly *critical* social science. As formulated by Lövbrand et al., we now live in "the Anthropocene," an unprecedented "geological era fully dominated by human activity" whose "great acceleration in social and economic development" has also spurred dramatic, albeit unintended environmental change that "threatens the planetary support-system upon which human civilization depends"; for a full account and adequate response to our era's complex environmental challenges "no single discipline" will suffice on its own (Lövbrand et al. 2015: 211, 214, 215).

To return to the narrower topic of digital technology, there is a distinctly sociological contribution with which to bring this chapter to a conclusion. This involves asking questions about our relationship with digital technology, and about our motivations for utilizing it. To do so, we might reapply a distinction John Holmwood has made in relation to education, in order to then, in a second step, invert this distinction when projected onto technology. Education, Holmwood (2007: 88) asks us to remember, is—or rather should be—an "end rather than a means." So how about digital technologies: do we consider them to be ends, or means? For sociologists, this will echo Max Weber's seminal distinction between "value-rational" and "instrumentally rational" motivations underpinning human behavior. Weber defined as "value-rational" (*wertrational*) social actions that are motivated by "conscious belief in the unconditional value—ethical, aesthetic, religious or otherwise—of a behavior, irrespective of its results or success." Such actions constitute ends in themselves. "Instrumentally rational" (*zweckrational*), by contrast, are actions expected to lead to particular results, from the "outside world and other people"; here, the behavior in question is seen to constitute a necessary "condition" or "means" for successfully accomplishing other, "purposeful, rational goals" (Weber (1972 [1922]: 12, *my translations*). When we approach our digital lives (and "logs") with this distinction in mind, interesting questions open up: do we—individually and collectively—think of technology instrumentally, as a necessary means for achieving something else? If so, what is this "something else"? Self-expression? Democratic participation? Economic advantage? New forms of sociability? Practical ways of solving specific problems or confronting large, structural issues? Clearly, the answers will vary with, and depend on, circumstances. Undoubtedly, each of these answers—and others—will apply to some contexts. But are there also grounds for concluding that in some cases digital technology is treated as an end in its itself? And if the use of digital technologies is seen—in "value-rational" fashion—as an end irrespective of outcomes and applications, does this call for the kind of criticism of cultural categories, practices and ideological assumptions that I mentioned earlier? Put differently, might we need to suspect that where Adorno identified a "fetishization" of the idea of progress, we now see the "fetishization" of digital technologies, irrespective of contexts and their unintended consequences?

So if, following Holmwood, education ought to be seen as an end (i.e., value-rationally) as opposed to being instrumentalized into a means, might a normative response to technology be the inverse? Should we, in other words, only condone instrumental uses of digital technologies (i.e., when they enable us to accomplish goals external to the application of technology) but be concerned about the cultural elevation of digital technology into an end in its own right? This may seem plausible at first sight, yet also falls short. After all, it is not at all clear that social action always only falls into one category of motivation; the value-rational and the instrumental can certainly blur into each other. Further, not all instrumentally rational applications of digital technology are unproblematic or desirable. This is shown most powerfully by Shoshana Zuboff's work discussed earlier: Zuboff's criticism of surveillance capitalism rests precisely on its *instrumentarianism*, on the fact that digitally enabled knowledge about human behavior becomes "a means to others' commercial ends" (Zuboff 2019: 9). In Weberian terms, this is clearly instrumentally rational social (/economic) action; at the same time, it raises profound political and ethical questions.

This critical engagement with our digital era has involved key sociological themes, including the context-specific workings of power, as well as the unintended consequences of, and motivations underpinning, social action. With regard to the historical and structural circumstances we find ourselves in, this discussion has also touched on seminal analyses of "informationalism" (Castells 1996), on the contemporary relevance of "complexity theory" to the social domain, and on arguments about modernity's "overheating"

(Eriksen 2016a). Starting with a seemingly banal exercise of recording daily routines, the sociological imagination has taken us in diverse directions. The grounds we have thereby covered have been extensive. The tone of some of my conclusions has been noticeably cautious, tentative and questioning, rather than categorical and assertive. This is no coincidence: our era is defined by enormously complex questions, some of them distinctly sociological, some transdisciplinary, others political, some ethical, yet others all at once. It is not our role as social scientists to generate misleadingly simplistic, quasi-answers to such complexity. Instead, a crucial step involves an acknowledgment and mapping of complexity. The kind of critical sociology needed today is arguably at its most effective when it interjects difficult, challenging questions into public debate and into the flow of everyday life that all too often remains uninterrogated. We will return to this spirit—one of criticism, challenge, and contextualization—in my conclusion to this book.

Notes

1 Other prominent examples include Hartmut Rosa's (2019) critical sociology of late modern attempts to establish "resonant" relationships in the face of our era's multiple crises (i.e., crises of the environment, of democracy, and of mental health).
2 Subsequently, in his last book, Ulrich Beck (2017: 35, 47) described ours as an "epoch of side effects" and "chain reactions."
3 Echoing the discussion in Chapter 4, we here encounter another example of what Gurminder Bhambra (2007) describes as our widely unacknowledged but consequential, and distinctly transnational, "connected histories."
4 Arguing along similar lines, German media scholar Bernhard Pörksen has observed that we are beginning to witness growing disillusionment with social media: their dystopian potential for driving political polarization and a disregard for reasoned, inclusive public debate is increasingly being recognized (Klenk 2021).
5 This distinction resembles Ulrich Beck's (2017: 25, 42) observation of the discrepancies between many people's irrevocably transnational-cosmopolitan "frames of action" on one hand, and their often inward-looking, at times positively exclusivist beliefs, on the other.

CONCLUSION

Attentive readers will have noticed an intertextual allusion in the title of this book to Gabriel García Márquez's novel *Love in the Time of Cholera*. Where the latter's title centers on love, this book focuses on sociology; and the syntactical place of "time of cholera" is here taken by "times of glocalization." The allusion is not accidental. Its intention is easiest to read with regard to the historical moments invoked by Gabriel García Márquez and this book, respectively. The former depicts an earlier historical moment, which—like present circumstances—was also characterized by far-reaching social shifts, experienced as deeply unsettling by some of the novel's protagonists; by environmental degradation, particularly the problem of waste and the depletion of natural resources; and, as the novel's title makes clear, an epidemic constitutes the backdrop to García Márquez' story of entwined biographies and loves. Set in a very specific geographical location and in a different time (i.e., in Colombia from the late nineteenth to the early decades of the twentieth centuries), the historical circumstances that frame *Love in the Time of Cholera* offer intriguing points of similarity, difference and comparison for the here and now.

The allusion is more subtle when it comes to love and sociology. What, if anything, might love and sociology have in common? Without wanting to stretch the analogy too far, sociology—like love—demands commitment, care, and passion. Like love, sociology requires focused and personal investment, namely in the "social." Whatever else love is, and I certainly will not attempt a comprehensive definition of love (if such a definition was even possible), it needs a purpose, an "object" or a "recipient," it is directed at something or, more often, at someone. Like those in love, sociologists need to be invested in that which constitutes the focus of their attention. We need to be invested in the social; the social—which by definition implicates others and transcends any individual—has to intrigue and pull us in. It needs to matter to us. Without a fascination with what happens in the spaces and relations between people, between individuals and their wider worlds, it would seem impossible to do sociology. To be fascinated by something means that we pay sustained attention to "it." Quick, purportedly easy answers will not do for those who are fascinated. Our era's obsession with asking individuals for quick soundbites of "what they think" is not sociology. Tweets and memes may become sociological data, but they can only do so when placed into, and read in relation to, their generative contexts. To love someone or something usually means that we also care deeply about the wider worlds in which "they" or "it" are embedded. Similarly, to do sociology requires careful and deep contextualization—the ability and willingness to view our objects of enquiry in their much wider settings, to trace their complex histories, and to contemplate their possible futures.

Anyone who has loved and particularly those whose love has resulted in heartbreak and loss, will know that love is not always easy, it is certainly not always happy or satisfying. It can hurt as much as it can enrich us. It can leave us empty as well as fulfilled. Not dissimilarly, the sociological fascination with the social is certainly not always motivated by, or a conduit for, pleasant insights: far from it, our focus may well be on phenomena that are ugly, unjust, violent, and painful. Sociology can take us to dangerous places and expose us to deeply unsettling realizations. Arguably, this is what a critical sociology, in particular, needs to do. Yet, my intertextual allusion should not be pushed too far. When I first suggested the title, my intention was certainly not to liken glocalization to a deadly illness. In light of the Covid-19 pandemic, which "overtook" my writing of this book, a straightforward parallel between the two titles runs the risk of appearing even more inappropriate now than it did at the inception of this project. Still, with this disclaimer having been made, Gabriel García Márquez' formulation invites intertextual reappropriation because it delineates a *temporal location and framing* for its narrative. This is what this book's title takes the liberty to import from Márquez. My temporal claim has been that sociology needs a reorientation in our current historical moment, which the concept of "glocalization" captures arguably more accurately than any other. The preceding chapters have demonstrated that this disciplinary reorientation is well underway. My focus has been on forms of qualitative sociology—and the wider, often interdisciplinary spaces they share with a number of cognate social science disciplines—that have responded to our era's global flows, and to the varied local responses to such flows, with methodological innovation, conceptual nuance, and epistemological reflexivity. By way of a two-step conclusion to this book, I will redistill some its central insights and briefly reflect on how those insights fit into the history of sociological thought.

I

It has been a recurring, presentational feature of the preceding chapters that I have interwoven personal experiences and reflections with wider sociological discussion. The intention has not been to indulge in autobiographical navel-gazing, but to extrapolate what is sociologically relevant from such experiences to our understanding of glocalization. Readers will judge for themselves how successful these interweavings of the personal and the structural—as applications of the sociological imagination— have been. In any case, my intention has not been to talk about my life for the sake of it—our social media age is already saturated enough with such personal, quasi-confessional narratives—but to focus on how the personal interfaces with others'. This becomes sociology, à la Georg Simmel, once the focus shifts from the purportedly idiosyncratic and decontextualized to the *Wechselwirkungen* (imperfectly translated as "mutual connections and impacts") connecting us to each other and many others. In our globalizing or—more accurately—glocalizing age, such *Wechselwirkungen* span very significant geographical distances and routinely cross borders.

Honest and convincing conclusions to scientific writing need to be self-reflexive, in order to take stock both of what has been achieved and of what has been left unanswered or even unaddressed. Admittedly and clearly, there are some gaping, thematic absences in this book, which some readers will think should have received more, or more systematic, coverage. Issues of class, gender and sexuality, for instance, have received little explicit or sustained attention in the preceding chapters. To state the obvious, each of these central sociological topics matters in, and intersects with, the discussions offered in this book. Given constraints of space and my delineation of a manageable focus for present purposes, a systematic exploration of those intersections can here only be anticipated as an important object of future research and discussions.

In a closely related vein, more could have been made of global capitalism as the necessary, structural precondition for practically everything that has been shown and discussed. However, there is no shortage of excellent, truly groundbreaking analyses of global, post-Fordist, capitalist production and its new, transnational class structure (see, in particular, Piketty 2014; Milanovic 2016; Reckwitz 2020). My intention has been different and distinctive: it has been to explore what a methodologically and conceptually reshaped sociological imagination is enabling social scientists to show about where and how the global and the local intersect. As we have seen, glocalization calls for interdisciplinary borrowings and approaches. Qualitative sociologists find themselves sharing thematic and methodological spaces with other social science disciplines. Anthropology has long recognized the embodied dimensions of ethnographic fieldwork and the understandings it generates (e.g., Okely 2012). A similar process is also afoot in (qualitative/interpretative) sociologists' attempts to capture the systemic, long-distance interconnectedness and its entanglements with the local that define our times (e.g., Knowles 2014): full "immersion" and a "multi-sensory" turn (e.g., Lindner 2007: 320, 321; Lyon and Back 2012) offer, as has been shown, new insights pertinent to the global and local conditions shaping the early decades of the twenty-first century. What we have discovered in this book, then, involves not only "the art of listening" (Back 2007) but also an olfactory sensitivity (Rhys-Taylor 2013), practices of seeking out generally overlooked locales that illuminate and condense significant aspects of our "local-global nexi" (Beck 2000). The emerging sociologies of glocalization discussed in this book thus involve finding new ways of travelling, of moving through places, of looking for underexplored vantage points and "backroads" (Knowles 2014); of listening to the commonly silenced or unnoticed. A sociological imagination fit for this moment or era of glocalization requires an ability to sense in multiple ways and to always contextualize data carefully. Contextualization, in turn, benefits from new additions to our discipline's tried and tested methodological and conceptual "tool-kits": one of the examples of such additions outlined above involved the tracing of some of the continually rewritten urban *palimpsests* of our twenty-first century cityscapes. Other parts of our discussions have returned to long-established sociological concepts, such as the *unintended consequences of social action*, as well as to some of the discipline's analytical principles including the *double hermeneutic*. We have seen that while such concepts and principles are highly relevant to our glocalizing era, they also require further recalibration in light of long-distance, systemic interconnections and varied, local responses to cross-border flows.

Other dimensions of sociological practice that have accompanied us pertain to the domains of social theory and the wider (or potential) societal roles and impact of sociological thinking. Put differently, we have also encountered questions about sociology's politics that warrant further reflection.

II

Predating Gurminder Bhambra's calls for recognition of our "connected histories" (Bhambra 2007) as well as current attempts to decolonize university curricula, David Parker ruffled some feathers some 25 years ago by asking whether sociology departments would "always be teaching Marx, Weber and Durkheim." More accurately, Parker differentiated the sociological canon, which he accused of "marginaliz[ing] other voices and other places," from sociological thinking; the latter, Parker insisted, was "much broader" and could not be "confined to the discursive horizon of Western modernity" (Parker 1997: 123, 132, 136, 137). Parker's charges were quickly countered by Nicos Mouzelis. Mouzelis agreed that the sociological canon—itself, though, the outcome of "long debates and theoretical confrontations" and not a "dictatorial edict"—should indeed be expanded, but that such enlargement should be subject to the quality criteria set by the discipline's founders; for Mouzelis (1997: 245, 246), those are standards of "cognitive potency, analytical acuity, power of synthesis, imaginative reach and originality." While Mouzelis' riposte was in my view very convincing, it left an important part of Parker's argument largely unaddressed. Parker had not only queried the continuing centrality of the "founding fathers," he had also problematized a "myopic focus on modernity" that could stand in the way of a "more enriching sociological vision." Interestingly, and this is the argument I propose to pick up here, Parker also found fault in the longer genealogy of sociological thinking that was on offer: according to Parker, when sociology's more distant historical roots are discussed, a purportedly unhelpful "orthodox narrative" traces those roots from industrializing France and Germany to classical Greece, with Plato's *Republic* being seen as the "absolute starting point" (Parker 1997: 124). Put simply, Parker criticized a narrowness of vision—both historical and intellectual— that he claimed to detect in much academic sociology. The charge deserves to be taken seriously, as indeed it has been. Concurrently, however, Parker's argument stopped prematurely, just where he could have pushed beyond his own charges. Plato is certainly not the only place to look for sociology's *longue durée* roots, but it is a legitimate place to do so. And by reflecting on the central figure in some of Plato's writings, namely on Socrates, we may be looking at an early example of precisely the kind of sociological thinking that Parker calls for.

What do I mean by this? In order to illustrate the critical, though also humble and self-reflexive spirit that sociology can (and arguably should) instill, there may be few more illustrative historical exemplars to turn to than Plato's teacher. At first sight, it may seem unusual to interpret Socrates, one of the founding fathers of philosophy who left no written traces himself and whose thoughts and ways we can only access through what others have remembered and said about him, as a proto-sociological figure. At closer inspection, however, the comparison of what we know about Socrates with the trajectory of parts of the earlier discussion is less outlandish.[1] Two partly shared facets, in particular, stand out and arguably justify thinking of parts of this book, and hence of sections of contemporary social science, as being underpinned by a "Socratic spirit." First, there is the much-repeated starting point of non-knowledge (i.e., "I know that I know nothing") and the questioning attitude widely attributed to Socrates (Kniest 2003: 37, 38) to be remembered. Such epistemological caution and modesty are in my view the best possible starting points to sociological enquiry, for they mitigate against the dangers of circular thinking (i.e., whereby conclusions are predetermined at the outset of an argument and immune to counterevidence). Put differently, in accounts of Socrates we see an epistemological humility at work, a reflexive engagement with arguments, both our own and others', that should matter to anyone engaging with pronouncements about our shared lives. Second, we are told (Martin 2009) that Socrates combined such epistemological modesty with an astutely critical approach to the things his contemporaries believed and did: a questioning attitude that refused to be blindly complicit with political and cultural consensus; Socrates' was a mind willing and brave enough— in his case truly irrespective of the costs and risks involved—to point out contradictions and dangers in the things people claimed and thought. In short, in Socrates we encounter a socially critical attitude, versions of which resurface in some—and arguably some of the best—contemporary sociology. Put differently, when social scientists call widely taken-for-granted assumptions, practices and structures into question, we see a quasi-Socratic, often badly needed critical spirit at work.

This "Socratic spirit", alluded to in parts of the earlier chapters, thus combines reflexivity and critical, public engagement with widely held beliefs, "commonsensical" ideas, and ways of life practiced or aspired to by an epoch's majority. To be clear: more than twenty-four centuries on, certainly not all types of sociology are defined by such a questioning, (quasi-)Socratic trajectory. But the latter appears—in modified and methodologically heterogeneous forms—in genres of sociological writing that Michael Burawoy describes as "critical" and "public sociology." According to Burawoy (2005: 5, 7, 8), public sociologies revive "sociology's moral fiber" by "taking knowledge back to those from whom it came"; public sociologies, which assume diverse forms depending on the publics engaged with and the "value commitments" of the sociologists involved, thereby create "double conversations"[2] with "people who are themselves involved in conversations." What is more, Burawoy's case for public sociologies takes its particular shape against the backdrop of our historical moment. Inadvertently corroborating this book's premises, Burawoy (2005: 6, 19) confirms that while globalization is "wreaking havoc" with the nation-state as sociology's previously taken-for-granted "unit of analysis," the "global only manifests itself through […] local processes." This is a concise formulation of glocalization. Our discussions have sketched some such local manifestations of the global; in doing so, they have in turn reaffirmed Burawoy's (2005: 20) expectation that a present-day sociology requires "global dimensions." These dimensions are given further specificity in John Holmwood's outline of the "challenges" globalization poses for a "new public sociology": Holmwood calls for a social science "of connections" that departs from "universalizing tendencies" and recognizes the "local character of social thought"; the desired result is a "series of local social sciences in dialogue [...] and open to transformation [through] other perspectives and locations of knowledge" (Holmwood 2007: 79). This may be thought of as a glocalization of social research and social theorizing. Translated into the terms of the present discussion, a sociology "of connections" also demands more (quasi-Socratic) humility, as we seek to transcend the trappings of ethnocentrism and to "provincialize social science" by "think[ing] beyond boundaries," both disciplinary and national (Holmwood 2007: 86).

Michael Burawoy's 2004 presidential address to the American Sociological Association, in some ways indeed a reflection of the "state of the discipline" at the time, also made reference to an earlier argument that I mentioned in the introduction to the present book. The argument in question is the thesis of *The Decomposition of Sociology* formulated by Irving Horowitz in the early 1990s. Taking its cue, in part, from Max Weber (including Weber's essay on "objectivity in social science"),[3] Horowitz's assessment was that sociology was in danger of becoming guided by "ideological thinking," "special agendas" and "political loyalties rather than scientific canons" (Horowitz 1994: 10, 12, 15). For Horowitz, an unfolding "politicization of social research" had reached crisis dimensions and purportedly reflected a state of disciplinary decline, in which "social advocacy [...] [i]nstead of being a possible consequence of decent social research [...] ha[d] become the very cause of social research" (Horowitz 1994: 37, 183). Ideological circularity, whenever and wherever it happens, is an undeniable problem for any scientific discipline.[4] However, nearly thirty years on, my assessment of how sociology and other critical social sciences are responding to the global flows, disparities, political reactions and tensions of our time is considerably more positive than Horowitz's in the 1990s. The methodological inventiveness, epistemological reflexivity, conceptual innovations, and critical interventions shown by social scientists on the basis of—rather than as a precondition for—their work all paint an encouraging picture of our discipline(s): the (critical) social sciences, including sociology, are meeting the challenges of capturing a transnationally interconnected social world in flux and of interjecting political questions when research insights call for them. In contrast to Horowitz, the alternative judgement that "sociology has never been in better shape" and that the wider "climate" (i.e., one of deep inequalities, widening marketization, and political polarization) "is drawing people to the critical and public moments of sociology" (Burawoy 2005: 18) makes sense precisely against the backdrop of a glocalizing world of multiple crises depicted throughout this book.

None of this diminishes the challenges and difficulties involved. As a science of the social, sociology is itself of course also part of the social.[5]

Good sociology is bound by standards of rigor, transparency and systematicity. Good sociology should aim never to be circular, thereby heeding Horowitz's argument as a warning rather than as a depiction of scholarly practice, but to be guided by carefully and reflexively collected data. Concurrently, a commitment to capturing and understanding the social world does not preclude attempts to critique and help reshape existing structural configurations, where valid data—rather than preformed, uninterrogated positions—underpins such attempts. Put differently, social science can and arguably should entail political engagement; where it does, such political engagement should be underpinned by empirical expertise and knowledge of methods and contexts, rather than by polemics. As Burawoy emphasizes, public sociology can take a number of different forms. A public sociology that is systematic, carefully contextualized, rigorous, self-reflexive—and hence everything every scientific discipline and practice needs to be— does not fit a binary, reductionist schema that simplistically juxtaposes the purportedly "objective" to its alleged opposite, the often pejoratively labelled "subjective." The best of qualitative sociology, select examples of which were discussed in the earlier chapters, can be profoundly political in its research-based pronouncements and their relevance to public discussions that far transcend sociological circles. Such sociologies cannot be dogmatic. They are based on systematically and transparently conducted research, which they combine with a (quasi-Socratic) modesty in the claims being made. Such sociologies know that the most methodical of approaches to the social will leave many questions as yet unanswered; that science includes doubt, that scientific insights are incremental and always subject to being challenged and revised. "Opinions" and "dogmas" are important parts of what we study, they are some of the "raw materials" we focus on and are thus included in the range of phenomena that sociologists examine. But the secondary, interpretative step constitutive of the *double hermeneutic* must go further: it must offer much more by way of context, much greater systematicity and reflexivity than the positions being recorded. Concurrently, our scholarly craft stands and falls by a non-negotiable willingness to question and potentially reject our preexisting assumptions, if the evidence calls for it.

In our era of pronounced individualization and similarly prominent counterreactions against social atomization, scholarly disciplines that look beyond the individual—as sciences of the social—are arguably more urgently needed than ever before. This book has explored how select strands of sociological and other social science research have begun to transcend the trappings of "methodological nationalism" and to capture a "variety of different, autonomous [yet] interlinked modernities" (Beck and Grande 2010: 413, 426). The emerging and rich tapestry of contemporary qualitative social science indicates that much has been done to adjust, methodologically and conceptually, to a world "beyond societies" (Urry 2000). Concurrently, the challenges we face—as disciplines and, yet more fundamentally, as human beings negotiating the crises of the present—are as diverse as they are formidable. Such crises include political polarization and fragmentation as well as environmental degradation that threatens our collective future; other crises manifest in the spatial and infrastructural impoverishment of local life-worlds that are crucial to, yet disadvantaged by, today's global capitalism, in ever-widening disparities of wealth, in the perpetuation of social exclusions and in the frustrations those breed. While some crises, such as the ongoing pandemic, are easily recognizable as such, others manifest more subtly: as the unintended and widely unrecognized consequences of generally valued facets of our times. Some of the political, social and environmental "by-products" of our digital technologies and consumption practices fall into this latter category. Yet other issues are turned into purported crises by some of the most divisive and antagonistic political voices: the nationalist vilification of migration and lived pluralism is a case in point. Clearly, and recent methodological and conceptual refinements in the critical social sciences notwithstanding, much remains to be researched and discussed, as a matter of urgency.

Notes

1 Comparisons of the Socratic method of questioning with contemporary, intellectual contributions to public debate are not new. See, for instance, James McGilvray's (1999) discussion of similarities and differences between Socrates and Noam Chomsky.

2 There is a similarity, in conceptualization and terminology, to be noted here: namely with the notion of the *double hermeneutic* discussed earlier and its understanding of (qualitative) sociology as involving the (meta)interpretation of pre-interpreted social meanings and experiences.

3 For a discussion of competing receptions (and arguably some partial distortions) of Max Weber's work, see Neun (2015). Neun shows that one interpretative school of thought, pertinent to the present book, connects Weber via C. Wright Mills to Burawoy's concept of *public sociology*.

4 In their reflections on the twentieth century, Tony Judt and Timothy Snyder (2015: 266) make a similar and very relevant point in relation to historiography.

5 For a discussion of the distinctiveness of sociology, when compared to natural sciences that are able to claim a monopoly of knowledge over "their" respective domains of enquiry, see, for example, Bauman (1991).

BIBLIOGRAPHY

Adorno, Theodor. *Philosophie und Gesellschaft.* Stuttgart: Reclam, 1984.

Althusser, Louis. *On the Reproduction of Capitalism.* London: Verso, 2014 [1970].

Anarcho.Punk.Net (2021). Accessed 31 March 2021. https://www.anarcho-punk.net/threads/guerilla-zona-antifascista.3309/.

Anderson, Ruben. "Hunter and prey: patrolling clandestine migration in the Euro-African borderlands", *Anthropological Quarterly* 87, no. 1 (2014): 119–149.

Appadurai, Arjun. "Introduction: commodities and the politics of value." In Arjun Appadurai (ed.) *The Social Life of Things*, 3–62. Cambridge: Cambridge University Press, 1988.

Appadurai, Arjun. "Disjuncture and difference in the global cultural economy." In *Global Culture: Nationalism, Globalization and Modernity*, edited by Mike Featherstone, 295–310. London: Sage, 1990.

Assmann, Aleida. *Erinnerungsräume.* München: C. H. Beck, 1999.

Augé, Marc. *Non-Places: An Introduction to Supermodernity.* London/ New York: Verso, 2008 [1995].

Augoustinos, Martha. "Social representations and ideology." In *The Psychology of the Social*, edited by Uwe Flick, 156–169. Cambridge: Cambridge University Press, 1998.

Back, Les. "Dancing and wrestling with scholarship." Sociological Research Online 7 (4), http://www.socresonline.org.uk/7/4/back.html. 2002.

Back, Les. *The Art of Listening*, Oxford: Berg, 2007.

Barthes, Roland. *Mythologies*, London: Vintage, 2000 [1957].

Battaglia, Diana. "The 'other' Havana of Leonardo Padura Fuentes." *Journal of Romance Studies* 14, no. 3 (2014): 54–66.

Baudrillard, Jean. *Symbolic Exchange and Death*, London: Sage, 1993.

Bauman, Zygmunt. *Intimations of Postmodernity*, London: Routledge, 1991.

———. *Globalization: The Human Consequences*, Cambridge: Polity, 1998.

———. *Liquid Modernity*, Cambridge: Polity, 2000.

———. *Community*, Cambridge: Polity, 2001.

———. *Liquid Love*, Oxford: Blackwell, 2003.

———. *Work, Consumerism and the New Poor*, Maidenhead: Open University Press, 2005.

Beaumont, Justin and Baker, Christopher (eds.) *Postsecular Cities: Religious Space, Theory and Practice.* London: Continuum, 2011.

Beck, Ulrich. *Risk Society*, London: Sage, 1992.

———. *What Is Globalization?*, Cambridge: Polity, 2000.

———. *Die Metamorphose der Welt*, Berlin: Suhrkamp, 2017.

Beck, Ulrich and Grande, Edgar. "Varieties of Second Modernity: The Cosmopolitan Turn in Social and Political Theory and Research." *The British Journal of Sociology* 61, no. 3 (2010): 409–443.

Becker, Jochen, Klingan, Katrin, Lanz, Stephan and Wildner, Kathrin (eds.) *Global Prayers: Contemporary Manifestations of the Religious in the City.* Zürich: Lars Müller, 2014.

Benzecry, Claudio E. "Azul y Oro: The Many Social Lives of a Football Jersey." *Theory, Culture & Society* 25, no. 1 (2008): 49–76.

Bhambra, Gurminder K. *Rethinking Modernity: Postcolonialism and the Sociological Imagination.* Basingstoke: Palgrave Macmillan, 2007.

Bhatti, Anil. "Heterogeneities and Homogeneities." In *Understanding Multiculturalism,* edited by Johannes Feichtinger and Gary B. Cohen, 17–46. New York: Berghahn, 2014.

Blackshaw, Tony. *Zygmunt Bauman,* London and New York: Routledge, 2005.

Billig, Michael. *Banal Nationalism,* London: Sage, 1995.

Block, Fred. "Introduction." In *Karl Polanyi, The Great Transformation,* xviii–xxxviii. Boston: Beacon Press, 2001.

Bocock, Robert. *Consumption.* London/New York: Routledge, 1993.

Bohannan, Paul. "The Impact of Money on an African Subsistence Economy." In *Conformity & Conflict,* edited by James Spradley and David McCurdy, 261–272. New York: Harper Collins, 1990.

Booth, William. "On the Idea of the Moral Economy." *The American Political Science Review* 88, no. 3 (1994): 653–667.

Bott, Esther. "Tourism." In *The Sociology of Globalization,* edited by Christian Karner and Dirk Hofäcker, London: Edward Elgar, forthcoming.

Bourdieu, Pierre. *Outline of a Theory of Practice.* Cambridge: Cambridge University Press, 1977.

―――. *Sociology in Question,* London: Sage, 1993.

Boutros, Alexandra. "The Spirit of Traffic: Navigating Faith in the City." In *Circulation and the City,* edited by Alexandra Boutros and Will Straw, 118–137. Montreal: McGll-Queen's University Press, 2010.

Brah, Avtar. *Cartographies of Diaspora.* London: Routledge, 1996.

Braude, Lee. "Louis Wirth and the locus of sociological commitment." *The American Sociologist* 5, 233–235. 1970.

Brown, Callum G. "Religion in the City." *Urban History* 23, no. 3 (1996): 372–379.

Brubaker, Roger, Loveman, Mara and Stamatov, Peter. "Ethnicity as Cognition." *Theory and Society* 33 no. 1 (2004): 31–64.

Bryman, Alan. *The Disneyization of Society,* London: Sage, 2004.

Bulmer, Martin. *The Chicago School of Sociology: Institutionalization, Diversity, and the Rise of Sociological Research.* Chicago: The University of Chicago Press, 1984.

Burawoy, Michael. "For Public Sociology." *American Sociological Review* 70 (1) (2005): 4–28.

Burgess, Ernest W. "Residential segregation in American cities." *Annals of the American Academy of Political and Social Science* 140, no. 1 (1928): 105–115.

Burstein, Ariel and Vogel, Jonathan. "Globalization, Technology and the Skill Premium: A Quantitative Analysis." *National Bureau of Economic Research,* working paper 16459, 2010. Accessed 19 August 2021. https://www.nber.org/papers/w16459.

Castells, Manuel. *The Rise of the Network Society,* Oxford: Blackwell, 1996.

Castells, Manuel, Caraça, João and Cardoso, Gustavo. "The Cultures of the Economic Crisis: An Introduction." In *Aftermath: The Cultures of the Economic Crisis,* edited by Manuel Castells, João Caraça, and Gustavo Cardoso, 1–14. Oxford: Oxford University Press, 2012.

Chandler, Daniel. *Semiotics – The Basics.* London/New York: Routledge, 2017.

Chu, Julie Y. "Boxed in: Human Cargo and the Technics of Comfort." *International Journal of Politics, Culture and Society* 29, no. 4 (2016): 403–21.

Coe, Neil, Dicken, Peter and Hess, Martin. "Global Production Networks: Realizing the Potential." *Journal of Economic Geography* 8, no. 3 (2008), 271–295.

Cohen, Stanley. *Folk Devils and Moral Panics*, London: Routledge, 2011.

Coleman, John. "Religious Social Capital: Its Nature, Social Location, and Limits." In *Religion as Social Capital*, edited by Corwin Smidt, 33–48. Waco: Baylor University Press, 2003.

Collins, Patricia Hill. *Black Feminist Thought*, London: Harper Collins, 1990.

Dahrendorf, Ralf. *Homo Sociologicus*, Opladen: Westdeutscher Verlag, 1973.

Dale, Gareth. *Karl Polanyi*, Cambridge: Polity, 2010.

Dear, Michael "Los Angeles and the Chicago School: Invitation to a Debate." *City & Community* 1, no. 1 (2002): 5–32.

Dear, Michael and Dahmann, Nicholas. "Urban Politics and the Los Angeles School of Urbanism." *Urban Affairs Review* 44, no. 2 (2008): 266–279.

De Certeau, Michel. *The Practice of Everyday Life, vol. 1.* Berkeley: University of California Press, 1984.

Easthope, Hazel. "Fixed identities in a mobile world? The relationship between mobility, place, and identity." *Identities* 16, no. 1 (2009): 61–82.

Edwards, Paul. "'Bury the Gold Again before the Europeans Bring Us Their Culture': Witzblätter and the Paradox of German Anticolonialism." *German Studies Review* 44, no. 1 (2021): 1–26.

Euronews. "News of the Day." 25 October (television), 2018.

Eriksen,Thomas Hylland. *Small Places, Large Issues*, London: Pluto, 2015.

Eriksen, Thomas Hylland. "Overheating: The World Since 1991." *History and Anthropology* 27, no. 5 (2016a): 469–487.

———. *Overheating: An Anthropology of Accelerated Change.* London: Pluto, 2016b.

Ferraro, Gary. *Cultural Anthropology.* Minneapolis: West Publishing, 1995.

Fiske, John. *Reading the Popular.* Boston: Unwin Hyman, 1989.

Foss, Sonja. "A Rhetorical Scheme for the Evaluation of Visual Imagery." *Communication Studies* 45, no. 3-4 (1994): 213–224.

Foucault, Michel. *Discipline and Punish.* London: Penguin, 1991 [1975].

FPÖ Wien Favoriten, "FPÖ-Favoriten hält dagegen: Vereinigte Linke Will Ute-Bock-Verkehrsfläche," 2020. Accessed 4 April 2021. https://favoriten.fpoe-wien.at/en/news-detail/artikel/fpoe-favoriten-haelt-dagegen-vereinigte-linke-will-ute-bock-verkehrsflaeche/.

Fraser, Nancy. "Marketization, Social Protection, Emancipation: Toward a Neo-Polanyian Conception of Capitalist Crisis." In *Business as Usual: The Roots of the Global Financial Meltdown*, edited by Craig Calhoun and Georgi Derluguian, 137–158. New York: New York University Press, 2011.

Fraser, Nancy. "Can Society Be Commodities All the Way Down? Post-Polanyian Reflections on Capitalist Crisis", *Economy and Society* 43, no. 3 (2014): 541–558.

Fuller, Steve. *The New Sociological Imagination*, London: Sage, 2006.

Gans, Herbert. "Urbanism and Suburbanism as Ways of Life." Reprinted in *The Urban Sociology Reader*, edited by Jan Lin and Christopher Mele, 42–50. London/New York: Routledge, 2005 [1968].

Garfinkel, Harold. *Studies in Ethnomethodology.* Cambridge: Polity, 2004 [1967].

Geertz, Clifford. *The Interpretation of Cultures.* New York: Basic Books, 1973.

Gellner, Ernest. *Nations and Nationalism.* Oxford: Blackwell, 1983.

Genette, Gérard. *Palimpsests: Literature in the Second Degree*. Lincoln: University of Nebraska Press, 1997.

Giddens, Anthony. *The Constitution of Society*. Cambridge: Polity, 1984.

Giddens, Anthony. *Modernity and Self-Identity: Self and Society in the Late Modern Age*. Oxford: Blackwell, 1991.

Gidley, Ben. "Landscapes of Belonging, Portraits of Life: Researching Everyday Multiculture in an Inner City Estate." *Identities* 20, no. 4 (2013): 361–376.

Gille, Zsuzsa. "From Risk to Waste: Global Food Waste Regimes." *The Sociological Review* 60, no. 2 (2013): 27–46.

Gilroy, Paul. *After Empire*. Abingdon: Routledge, 2004.

Ginev, Dimitri. "Rhetoric and Double Hermeneutics in the Human Sciences." *Human Studies* 21 (1998): 259–271.

Gingrich, André. "Nation, Status and Gender in Trouble?" In *Neo-Nationalism in Europe and Beyond*, edited by André Gingrich and Marcus Banks, 29–49. New York: Berghahn, 2006.

Gingrich, André and Banks, Marcus (eds.) *Neo-Nationalism in Europe and Beyond*. New York: Berghahn, 2006.

Girtler, Roland. *10 Gebote der Feldforschung*. Münster: Lit Verlag, 2004.

Glick Schiller, Nina. "Transnational Urbanism as a Way of Life: A Research Topic Not a Metaphor." *City & Society* 17, no. 1 (2005): 49–64.

Goffman, Erving. *The Presentation of Self in Everyday Life*. Harmondsworth: Penguin, 1990 [1959].

Graeber, David. *Debt: The First 5000 Years*. Brooklyn: Melville House, 2012.

Grady, John. "Becoming a Visual Sociologist." *Sociological Imagination* 38, no. 1/2 (2001): 83–119.

Granovetter, Mark. "Economic Action and Social Structure: The Problem of Embeddedness." *American Journal of Sociology* 91, no. 3 (1985): 481–510.

Gudeman, Stephen. *Economy's Tension: The Dialectics of Community and Market*, New York: Berghahn, 2012.

Hall, Stuart. "Encoding and Decoding the Message." In *The Discourse Studies Reader*, edited by Johannes Angermuller, Dominique Maingueneau, and Ruth Wodak, 111–121. Amsterdam: John Benjamins, 2014.

Hall, Tom. *Footwork: Urban Outreach and Hidden Lives*. London: Pluto, 2017.

Harvey, David. *The Condition of Postmodernity*. Oxford: Blackwell, 1989.

Hobsbawm, Eric and Ranger, Terence. *The Invention of Tradition*. Cambridge: Cambridge University Press, 1992.

Hockey, John and Collinson, Jacquelyn Allen. "Seeing the Way: Visual Sociology and the Distance Runner's Perspective." *Visual Studies* 21, no. 1 (2006): 70–81.

Holmwood, John. "'Only Connect': The Challenge of Globalization for the Social Sciences." *Twenty-First Century Society* 2, no. 1 (2007): 79–94.

Holmwood, John. "Sociology's Moments: Democracy, Expertise and Markets." Paper Presented at the *American Sociological Association*, 108th Annual Meeting, New York, 2013.

Holmwood, John. "Sociology as Democratic Knowledge." In *Sociologists' Tales*, edited by Katherine Twamley, Mark Doidge and Andrea Scott, 49–54. Bristol: Bristol University Press, 2015.

Horowitz, Irving. *The Decomposition of Sociology*. Oxford: Oxford University Press, 1994.

Horvath, Agnes, Thomassen, Bjørn and Wydra, Harald. "Liminality and the Search for Boundaries." In *Breaking Boundaries*, edited by Agnes Horvath, Bjørn Thomassen, and Harald Wydra, 1–8. New York/Oxford: Berghahn, 2015. Accessed 2 June 2020. http://www.flipfloptrail.com/. Accessed 22 May 2020.

http://www.logisticsmatter.com/2016/02/09/boeing-just-patented-an-aircraft-that-picks-up-and-carries-regular-containers/. Accessed 11 May 2020.

https://www.meridioband.com/what-is-italian-leather-10-things-you-should-know/.

Hubbard, Phil and Colosi, Rachela. "Respectability, Morality and Disgust in the Night-Time Economy: Exploring Reactions to 'Lap Dance' Clubs in England and Wales." *Sociological Review* 63, no. 4 (2015): 782–800.

Hutchinson, John. *The Dynamics of Cultural Nationalism*. London: Allen and Unwin, 1987.

Huyssen, Andreas. *Present Pasts: Urban Palimpsests and the Politics of Memory*. Stanford, CA: Stanford University Press, 2003.

Jameson, Fredric. *Postmodernism, or, The Cultural Logic of Late Capitalism*. London/New York: Verso, 1991.

Jauss, Hans. "Ein Abschied von der Poesie der Erinnerung – Yves Bonnefoys 'Ce qui fut sans lumiere'." In *Vergessen und Erinnern*, edited by Anselm Haverkamp and Renate Lachmann, 456–491. München: Wilhelm Fink.

Jenkins, Richard. *Rethinking Ethnicity*, London: Sage, 1997.

Judt, Tony. *Postwar: History of Europe since 1945*. London: Vintage, 2010.

Judt, Tony and Snyder, Timothy. *Nachdenken über das 20. Jahrhundert*. Frankfurt a.M.: Fischer, 2015.

Karner, Christian. "National Doxa, Crises and Ideological Contestation in Contemporary Austria." *Nationalism and Ethnic Politics* 11, no. 2 (2005): 221–263.

———. *Ethnicity and Everyday Life*. London: Routledge, 2007a.

———. "Austrian Counter-Hegemony: Critiquing Ethnic Exclusion and Globalization." *Ethnicities* 7, no. 1 (2007b): 82–115.

———. *Negotiating National Identities: Between Globalization, the Past and "the Other."* Farnham: Ashgate, 2011.

———. *Nationalism Revisited: Austrian Social Closure from Romanticism to the Digital Age*. New York: Berghahn, 2020a.

———. "'Der Balkan' in der *Krone*: Austria between 'Frontier Orientalism' and amnesiac nationalism." *Interventions: International Journal of Postcolonial Studies* 22, no. 6 (2020b): 783–801.

———. "The competing politics of Austrian glocalization: Covid-19, crime and (anti-) racism." *Glocalism: Journal of Culture, Politics and Innovation* 3, no. 2 (2020c): 1–33, https://glocalismjournal.org/wp-content/uploads/2021/03/Karner_gjcpi_2020_3.pdf.

———. "Constructions and (attempted) deconstructions of 'memory nationalism': Central European Lessons", *Journal of Contemporary European Studies*, online first: https://doi.org/10.1080/14782804.2020.1862072. 2021a

———. "The Styrian *Megaphon*: Bridging Representations and Uneasy 'Conviviality' in a Regional Counter-Public." *Journal of Austrian Studies* 54, no. 1 (2021b): 103–124.

Karner, Christian and Parker, David. "Conviviality and Conflict: Pluralism, Resilience and Hope in Inner-City Birmingham." *Journal of Ethnic and Migration Studies* 37, no. 3 (2011): 355–372.

Karner, Christian and Kaźmierczak, Marek. "Palimpsests of the Romantic." *Journal of Contemporary Central and Eastern Europe* 25, no. 1 (2017): 3–22.

Karner, Christian and Weicht, Bernhard. "Markets, 'communities' and nostalgia." In *The Commonalities of Global Crises*, edited by Christian Karner and Bernhard Weicht, 1–33. London: Palgrave Macmillan, 2016.

Karrer, Alfred. *Der Wiener Donaukanal: Vom Treidelschiff zum Katamaran*. Erfurt: Sutton Verlag, 2011.

Kaźmierczak, Marek. *Literatura w sieci tekstów*. Gniezno: Kropka, 2008.

Kellner, Douglas. *Jean Baudrillard: From Marxism to Postmodernism and Beyond*, Cambridge: Polity, 1989.

Kim, Kyohee and Smets, Peer. "Home Experiences and Homemaking Practices of Single Syrian Refugees in an Innovative Housing Project in Amsterdam." *Current Sociology* 68, no. 5 (2020): 607–627.

Klenk, Florian. "Wieso glauben so viele Leute so viel Quatsch, Herr Pörksen?" *Falter* 3 (2021): 23–25.

Klinger, Julie Michelle. *Rare Earth Frontiers: From Terrestrial Subsoils to Lunar Landscapes*. Ithaca: Cornell University Press, 2017.

Kniest, Christoph. *Sokrates zur Einführung*, Hamburg: Junius, 2003.

Knowles, Caroline. *Flip-Flop: A Journey through Globalisation's Backroads*. London: Pluto, 2014.

Koehrsen, Jens, Dickel, Sascha, Pfister, Thomas, Rödder, Simone, Böschen, Stefan, Wendt, Björn, Block, Katharina and Henkel, Anna. "Climate Change in Sociology: Still Silent or Resonating?" *Current Sociology Review* 68, no. 6 (2020): 738–760.

Kong, Lily. "Global Shifts, Theoretical Shifts: Changing Geographies of Religion." *Progress in Human Geography* 34, no. 6 (2010): 755–776.

Kopytoff, Igor. "The Cultural Biography of Things: Commoditization as Process." In *The Social Life of Things*, edited by Arjun Appadurai, 64–91. Cambridge University Press, 1988.

Krzyżanowski, Michał, Triandafyllidou and Wodak, Ruth. "The Mediatization and the Politicization of the 'Refugee Crisis' in Europe." *Journal of Immigrant & Refugee Studies* 16, no. 1-2 (2018): 1–14.

Lane, Jeremy. *Pierre Bourdieu: A Critical Introduction*. London: Pluto, 1993.

Law, John. *After Method: Mess in Social Science Research*. London: Routledge. 2004.

Lal, Barbara Ballis. *The Romance of Culture in an Urban Civilization*. London: Routledge, 1990.

Landry, Deborah. "'Stop Calling it Graffiti': The Visual Rhetoric of Contamination, Consumption and Colonization." *Current Sociology* 67, no. 5 (2019): 686–704.

Lanz, Stephan. "Assembling Global Prayers in the City: An Attempt to Repopulate Urban Theory with Religion." In *Global Prayers*, edited by Jochen Becker et al, 17–46. Zürich: Lars Müller, 2014.

Launchbury, Claire and Levey, Cara. "Introduction – Mutating Cities: Palimpsestic Traces in the Urban Context." *Journal of Romance Studies* 14, no. 3 (2014): 1–4.

Lauster, Martina. "Walter Benjamin's Myth of the 'Flâneur'." *The Modern Language Review* 102, no. 1 (2007): 139–156.

Le Coze, Jean-Christophe. "Globalization and High-Risk Systems." *Policy and Practice in Health and Safety* 15, no. 1 (2017): 57–81.

Lee, Jennifer. "Constructing Race and Civility in Urban America." *Urban Studies* 43, no. 5/6 (2006): 903–917.

Lee, Joonkoo. "Global Commodity Chains and Global Value Chains." *Oxford Research Encyclopedia: International Studies*, 2017. DOI: 10.1093/acrefore/9780190846626.013.201. Accessed 10 September 2019. http://oxfordre.com/internationalstudies.

Lemert, Charles. *Social Things*. Lanham: Rowman & Littlefield, 2005.

Lemert, Charles. *Globalization: An Introduction to the End of the Known World*. London/ New York: Routledge, 2015.

Levey, Cara. "Between Marginalization and Decentralization of Memory." *Journal of Romance Studies* 14, no. 3 (2014): 67–85.

Levitt, Peggy and Glick Schiller, Nina. "Conceptualizing Simultaneity: A Transnational Social Field Perspective on Society." *International Migration Review* 38, no. 3 (2004): 1002–1039.

Lichtblau, Klaus. *Zur Aktualität von Georg Simmel*, Wiesbaden: Springer VS, 2019.

Lindner, Rolf. *Die Entdeckung der Stadtkultur*. Frankfurt/Main: Campus, 2007.

Livezey, Lowell W. "The New Context of Urban Religion." In *Public Religion and Urban Transformation*, edited by Lowell W. Livezey, 3–25. New York: New York University Press, 2000.

Lövbrand, Eva, Beck, Silke, Chilvers, Jason, Forsyth, Tim, Hedrén, Johan, Hulme, Mike,

Lidskog, Rolf, and Vasileiadou, Eleftheria. "Who Speaks for the Future of Earth? How Critical Social Science Can Extend the Conversation on the Anthropocene." *Global Environmental Change* 32 (2015): 211–218.

Lyon, Dawn and Back, Les. "Fishmongers in a Global Economy: Craft and Social Relations on a London Market." Sociological Research Online 17, no. 2 (2012), http://www.socresonline.org.uk/17/2/23.html.

Lyotard, Jean-François. *The Postmodern Condition*. Manchester: Manchester University Press, 1984.

Martell, Luke. *The Sociology of Globalization*. Cambridge: Polity, 2017.

Martin, Craig. *Shipping Container*. New York: Bloomsbury, 2016.

Martin, Gottfried. *Sokrates*. Reinbek: Rowohlt, 2009.

Martin, Dominique, Metzger, Jean-Luc and Pierre, Philippe. "The Sociology of Globalization: Theoretical and Methodological Reflections." *International Sociology* 21, no. 4 (2006): 499–521.

McGilvray, James. *Chomsky: Language, Mind, and Politics*. Cambridge: Polity, 1999.

Merton, Robert. "The Unanticipated Consequences of Purposive Social Action", *American Sociological Review* 1, no. 6 (1936): 894–904.

Milanovic, Branko. *Global Inequality: A New Approach for the Age of Globalization*. Cambridge. MA: Belknap/ Harvard University Press, 2016.

Mills, C. Wright. *The Sociological Imagination*. Oxford: Oxford University Press, 2000 [1959].

Mondon, Aurelien and Winter, Aaron. "Whiteness, Populism and the Racialization of the Working Class in the United Kingdom and the United States." *Identities* 26, no. 5 (2019): 510–528.

Muñoz, Lorena. "Latino/a Immigrant Street Vendors in Los Angeles: Photo-Documenting Sidewalks from 'Back-Home'." *Sociological Research Online* 17, no. 2 (2012): http://www.socresonline.org.uk/17/2/21.html.

Mouzelis, Nicos. "In Defense of the Sociological Canon: A Reply to David Parker." *The Sociological Review* 45, no. 2 (1997): 244–253.

Nasar, Jack and Hong, Xiaodong. "Visual Preferences in Urban Signscapes." *Environment and Behavior* 31, no. 5 (1999): 671–691.

Natali, Lorenzo. "Visually Exploring Social Perceptions of Environmental Harm in Global Urban Contexts." *Current Sociology* 67, no. 5 (2019): 650–668.

Neues Deutschland. "Hände weg von Korea!" 15 July, 1950. Accessed 4 April 2021. https://www.nd-archiv.de/artikel/164753.haende-weg-von-korea.html.

Neun, Oliver. "Der andere 'amerikanische' Max Weber: Hans H. Gerths und C. Wright Mills' Max Weber, dessen deutsche Rezeption und das Konzept der 'public sociology'." *Berliner Journal für Soziologie* 25, no. 3 (2015), 333–357.

Nicholls, Walter. "The Los Angeles School: Difference, Politics, City." *International Journal of Urban and Regional Research* 35, no. 1 (2011): 189–206.

Numrich, Paul D. "Recent Immigrant Religions and the Restructuring of Metropolitan Chicago." In *Public Religion and Urban Transformation*, edited by Lowell W. Livezey, 239–267. New York: New York University Press, 2000.

O'Connell Davidson, Julia and Layder, Derek. *Methods, Sex and Madness.* London/ New York: Routledge, 1994.

Okely, Judith. *Anthropological Practice: Fieldwork and the Ethnographic Method.* London: Berg, 2012.

O'Rourke, Kevin and Williamson, Jeffrey. "When Did Globalisation Begin?" *European Review of Economic History* 6, no. 1 (2002): 23–50.

Orsi, Robert A. (ed.) *Gods of the City.* Bloomington: Indiana University Press, 1999.

Orwell, George. *1984.* London: Penguin Classics, 2000 [1949].

Papadopoulos, Dimitris and Tsianos, Vassilis. "After Citizenship: Autonomy of Migration, Organisational Ontology and Mobile Commons." *Citizenship Studies* 17, no. 2 (2013): 178–196.

Park, Robert E. "Human Migration and the Marginal Man." *American Journal of Sociology* 33, no. 6 (1928): 881–893.

Parker, David. "Why Bother with Durkheim? Teaching Sociology in the 1990s." *The Sociological Review* 45, no. 1 (1997): 122–146.

Parker, David and Karner, Christian. "Reputational Geographies and Urban Social Cohesion." *Ethnic and Racial Studies* 33, no. 8 (2010): 1451–1470.

Parker, David and Karner, Christian. "Remembering the Alum Rock Road: Reputational Geographies and Spatial Biographies." *Midland History* 36, no. 2 (2011): 292–309.

Pechurina, Anna. "Researching Identities through Material Possessions: The Case of Diasporic Objects." *Current Sociology* 68, no. 5 (2020): 669–683.

Peterson, Valerie "The Rhetorical Criticism of Visual Elements: An Alternative to Foss's Schema." *Southern Journal of Communication* 67, no. 1 (2001): 19–32.

Peyrefitte, Magali. "Ways of Seeing, Ways of Being and Ways of Knowing in the Inner City: Exploring Sense of Place through Visual Tours." *Sociological Research Online* 17, no. 4 (2012): 1–17.

Pick, David. "Work and employment in a globalizing age." In *The Sociology of Globalization*, edited by Dirk Hofäcker and Christian Karner. London: Edward Elgar, forthcoming.

Piketty, Thomas. *Capital in the Twenty-first Century.* Cambridge, MA: Belknap, 2014.

Polanyi, Karl. *The Great Transformation.* Boston: Beacon Press, 2001 [1944].

Preda, Alex. "The sociological approach to financial markets." *Journal of Economic Surveys* 21, no. 3 (2007): 506–533.

Pries, Ludger. "Configurations of Geographic and Societal Spaces: A Sociological Proposal between 'Methodological Nationalism' and the 'Spaces of Flows'." *Global Networks* 5, no. 2 (2005): 167–190.

Putnam, Robert. *Bowling Alone*, New York: Simon and Schuster, 2000.

Reckwitz, Andreas. *Das Ende der Illusionen: Politik, Ökonomie und Kultur in der Spätmoderne.* Berlin: Suhrkamp, 2020.

Rhys-Taylor, Alex. "The Essence of Multiculture: A Sensory Exploration of an Inner-City Street Market." *Identities: Global Studies in Culture and Power* 20, no. 4 (2013): 393–406.

Ritzer, George. *The McDonaldization of Society*. London: Sage, 1993.

Robertson, Roland. "Glocalization: Time-Space and Homogeneity-Heterogeneity." In *Global Modernities*, edited by Featherstone, Mike, Lash, Scott and Robertson, Roland, 25–44. London: Sage Publications, 1995.

Robertson, Roland. "Multiple Modernities and Globalization/ Glocalization: A Comment on Eisenstadt." In *Varieties of Multiple Modernities*, edited by Gerhard Preyer and Michael Sussman, 65–70. Leiden: Brill, 2016.

Rosa, Hartmut. *Resonanz: Eine Soziologie der Weltbeziehung*. Berlin: Suhrkamp, 2019.

Rottenberg, Tom (2021) "Wien entdecken beim Longrun: Ich seh, ich seh, was du nicht siehst." *Der Standard*, 10 February. Accessed 12 February 2021. https://www.derstandard.at/story/2000124005580/wien-entdecken-beim-longrun-ich-seh-ich-seh-was-du.

Roudometof, Victor. "Recovering the Local: From Glocalization and Localization." *Current Sociology* 67, no. 6 (2019): 801–817.

Sahlins, Marshall. *Stone Age Economics*. New Brunswick: Transaction, 1974.

Salzburger Nachrichten, 26 April 2019, "Künstler errichten ‚Denkmal' für Ute Bock." Accessed 2 April 2020. https://www.sn.at/kultur/allgemein/kuenstler-errichten-denkmal-fuer-ute-bock-in-wien-69363448.

Sanderson, Stephen. *Macrosociology*. New York: HarperCollins, 1991.

Sassen, Saskia. *The Global City: New York, London, Tokyo*. Princeton: Princeton University Press, 2001.

Schweizerische Flüchtlingshilfe. "Solidarität kennt keine Grenzen," 2020. Accessed 2 April 2021. https://www.fluechtlingshilfe.ch/medienmitteilungen/solidarität-kennt-keine-grenzen.

Silverman, Max. "Afterword: The Palimpsestic Imagination." *Journal of Romance Studies* 14, no. 3 (2014): 100–102.

Simmel, Georg. *Soziologie: Untersuchungen über die Formen der Vergesellschaftung*. Frankfurt a.M: Suhrkamp, 1992 [1908].

Smidt, Corwin. "Introduction." In *Religion as Social Capital*, edited by Corwin Smidt, 1–18. Waco: Baylor University Press, 2003.

Sperber, Dan. *Rethinking Symbolism*. Cambridge: Cambridge University Press, 1975.

Stavrakakis, Yannis. "Discourse Theory in Populism Research: Three Challenges and a Dilemma." *Journal of Language and Politics* 16, no. 4 (2017): 523–534.

Steigemann, Anna Marie and Misselwitz, Philipp. "Architectures of Asylum: Making Home in a State of Permanent Temporariness." *Current Sociology* 68, no. 5 (2020): 628–650.

Stiglitz, Joseph E. "Foreword." In *Karl Polanyi, The Great Transformation*, vii-xvii. Boston: Beacon Press, 2001.

Stock, Inka. *Time, Migration and Forced Immobility: Sub-Saharan African Migrants in Morocco*, Bristol: Bristol University Press, 2019.

Stürner, Janina and Bendel, Petra. "The Two-Way 'Glocalization' of Human Rights or: How Cities Become International Agents in Migration Governance." *Peace Human Rights Governance* 3, no. 2 (2019): 215–240.

Suttles, Gerald. "The Cumulative Texture of Local Urban Culture." *American Journal of Sociology* 90, no. 2 (1984): 283–304.

Sweetman, Paul. "Revealing Habitus, Illuminating Practice: Bourdieu, Photography and Visual Methods." *The Sociological Review* 57, no. 3 (2009): 491–511.

Szakolczai, Arpad. "Liminality and Experience: Structuring Transitory Situations and Transformative Events." In *Breaking Boundaries*, edited by Agnes Horvath, Bjørn Thomassen, and Harald Wydra, 11–38. New York/ Oxford: Berghahn, 2015.

Tausch, Arno. *From the "Washington" towards a "Vienna Consensus."* New York: Nova Science, 2007.

Thill, Brian. *Waste*. New York: Bloomsbury, 2015.

Thomas, Alfred. *Prague Palimpsest*. Chicago: The University of Chicago Press, 2010.

Thomassen, Bjørn. "Thinking with Liminality: To the Boundaries of an Anthropological Concept." In *Breaking Boundaries*, edited by Agnes Horvath, Bjørn Thomassen, and Harald Wydra, 39–58. New York/ Oxford: Berghahn, 2015.

Thorleifsson, Cathrine. "In Pursuit of Purity: Populist Nationalism and the Racialization of Difference." *Identities: Global Studies in Culture and Power* 28, no. 2 (2021): 186–202.

Tsing, Anna. "Supply chains and the human condition." *Rethinking Marxism* 21, no. 2 (2009): 148–176.

Turner, Victor. *The Ritual Process*. London: Routledge, 1996

Urry, John. *Sociology Beyond Societies*. London: Routledge, 2000.

Ute Bock Flüchtlingsprojekt. Accessed 2 April 2021. https://www.fraubock.at/de/.

Valluvan, Sivamohan and Kalra, Virinder. "Racial Nationalisms: Brexit, Borders and Little Englander Contradictions." *Ethnic and Racial Studies* 42, no. 14 (2019): 2393–2412.

Vertovec, S. "Super-Diversity and its Implications." *Ethnic and Racial Studies* 30, no. 6 (2007): 1024–1054.

Walters, William. "Migration, Vehicles, and Politics: Three Theses on Viapolititcs." *European Journal of Social Theory* 18, no. 4 (2015): 469–488.

Warren, Mark. "Faith and Leadership in the Inner City." In *Religion as Social Capital*, edited by Corwin Smidt, 49–68. Waco: Baylor University Press, 2003.

Weber, Max. *Wirtschaft und Gesellschaft (5. Auflage)*. Tübingen: Mohr Siebeck, 1972 [1922].

Weber, Max. "Die 'Objektivität' sozialwissenschaftlicher und sozialpolitischer Erkenntnis." In *Max Weber, Gesammelte Aufsätze zur Wissenschaftslehre*, edited by Johannes Winkelmann, 146–214. Tübingen: Mohr Siebeck, 1988 [1904].

Weigl, Andreas. *Migration und Integration: Eine widersprüchliche Geschichte*. Innsbruck: Studienverlag, 2009.

Wessendorf, Susanne. "Commonplace Diversity and the Ethos of Mixing." *Identities* 20, no. 4 (2013): 407–422.

Wien Museum. "Takeover: Street Art & Skateboarding", 2019. Accessed 29 March 2021. https://www.wienmuseum.at/fileadmin/user_upload/Presse_Neu/Ausstellungen/2019/Takeover/Pressinformation_Takeover_Street_Art.PDF.

Wimmer, Andreas and Glick-Schiller, Nina. "Methodological Nationalism and Beyond." *Global Networks* 2, no. 4 (2002): 301–334.

Wirth, Louis. "Urbanism as a Way of Life." *American Journal of Sociology* 44, no. 1 (1938): 1–24.

Wittstock, Birgit. (2021) "Cannale Commerciale", *Falter* 24 March, 42.

Zuboff, Shoshana. *The Age of Surveillance Capitalism*. London: Profile Books, 2019.

INDEX

'n' refers to end notes number

Adorno, Theodor 160
  idea of "progress" 158–159
affordable housing 120
Agamben, Giorgio 100
age of global interconnectedness 3
air pollution 27
Allied occupational zones 147
Althusser, Louis 65n2
Anderson, Ruben 98
anthropological places 24, 35, 28, 34
anti-immigration politics 93, 103
Appadurai, Arjun 5–6, 120, 146
  commodities, conceptualization of 73
  globalization, conceptualization of
    5–6, 71
asylum-seekers 96, 106
  everyday bureaucracies and 106
  exclusionary forms of populism 107
  homemaking practices 103–108
Athens 121
Augé, Marc 12, 27–28, 34–35, 97
Austria 121, 129, 140–142, 144

Back, Les 17, 22, 81–82, 89
Balkan route 110n3
Battaglia, Diana 149
Baudrillard, Jean 79
Bauman, Zygmunt 36, 39–40, 49, 97
  account of globalization and its human
    consequences 29
  consumerism 30
  ideas about liquid modernity 29–30
  sociological and everyday
    interpretations of social world 49
  sociological commentary 49

Beck, Ulrich 6, 102, 176n5
  Risk Society 165
Bendel, Petra 104
Benzecry, Claudio 79–81
Bhambra, Gurminder 108–109, 180
Billig, Michael
  Banal Nationalism 43, 45
  day survey 45–46
Block, Fred 56
blockage 94, 100
Boca Juniors jersey 80
Bock, Ute 144–146
border patrolling 98
Bourdieu, Pierre 10, 22–23, 48, 131n6
  The Craft of Sociology 48
  everyday classifications and sociological
    classifications, relationship 49
  habitus 10, 22, 41, 48, 131n6
  Outline of a Theory of Practice 10
  principle of non-consciousness 48–49
  socioanalysis 23
Brexit 21, 37, 90, 93
Brown, Callum 115
Burawoy, Michael 182–184
  definition of public sociology 36–37
  four sociologies 37–38
Burgess, Ernest W. 113–114, 122
  model of residential segregation 118

Camus, Albert 100
capitalism 60
  consumer 24
  digital 158
  supply chain 61–62, 65n6
  surveillance 159–164, 175

INDEX

201

refugees' "homemaking practices"
103–108, 110n6
sociological discussions of 94
sub-Saharan migrants 99
transmigrants 103
Mills, C. Wright 11, 36, 89, 156, 160, 166
Misselwitz, Philipp 106
modernist urban sociology 119
modes of development and production 157
money 46, 56–58, 65n1. *See also* financial
actors and markets, sociology of
Mongolia, Inner 167
Moroccan police and military 100
motorways 27
Mouzelis, Nicos 180–181
multinational corporations (MNCs) 59
Muñoz, Lorena 123

nationalism 2, 37, 42n4
nationalist populisms 107
national revival 2
national societies 13
nation-states 13, 15, 37, 116
neo-institutionalism 54
neoliberal marketization 156
neo-nationalism 107–108, 142
Nike International 80–81
nomadic capital 36, 75
non-places 27–33
as means of transport 29
as non-symbolized space 28
proliferation 28
non-symbolized space 28

oil prices 63
opportunity costs 84
Orwell, George 163–164
1984 164
Outer Hebrides 68
outsourcing 18, 29, 61, 85
overheating 173–176

palimpsestic methodology 137–140, 180
selectivity of local cultural memories
141
urban palimpsests 150
Vienna's cityscapes as palimpsests
140–147
Papadopoulos, Dimitris 101–103

Park, Robert E. 113–114
Parker, David 180–181
patriots 1–2
Peterson, Valeri 149–150
photography 22, 33–34, 38, 41n2, 105,
124, 147
benefits of 23
of a locality 23–24, 134–137
plastic city 76
Plato's *Republic* 181
Polanyi, Karl 56–57, 160
core factors of production 31
disembedded economy 30
double movement 32
The Great Transformation 30, 32–33, 55
market economy 30
self-regulating markets 31
policy sociology 37
polysemy 143
postmodern sensibility 150
postmodern urbanism 119
power 54
Prague 149
Preda, Alex 55
Pries, Ludger 15
privatization 18
professional sociology 37–38
proximity 35–36, 64, 130n3, 140, 146
public sociology 37–39, 182
Burawoy's definition 36–37
element of defamiliarization 38
task of 41
public spaces 150–151, 163

qualitative sociology 9, 16, 50, 116,
178–179
quantitative sociology 2–3

radical behaviorism 162
rare earth mining 164–170
rare earths 167
receiving societies 94, 102–103
reflexivity 33–41, 87, 120, 178
refugee crisis 110n3, 145
refugees 90
refugees' "homemaking practices"
103–108, 110n6
religious polarization 119
religious urbanity 115

Lightning Source UK Ltd.
Milton Keynes UK
UKHW010057301122
413082UK00003B/70

9 781785 274121